Mafia, peasants and great estates
Society in traditional Calabria

to Lida

Mafia, peasants and great estates
Society in traditional Calabria

PINO ARLACCHI
*Associate Professor of Sociology
University of Calabria*

Translated by
JONATHAN STEINBERG

CAMBRIDGE UNIVERSITY PRESS
Cambridge
London   New York   New Rochelle
Melbourne   Sydney

Published by the Press Syndicate of the University of Cambridge
The Pitt Building, Trumpington Street, Cambridge CB2 1RP
32 East 57th Street, New York, NY 10022, USA
296 Beaconsfield Parade, Middle Park, Melbourne 3206, Australia

Originally published in Italian as *Mafia, contadini e latifondo nella Calabria tradizionale* by Società editrice il Mulino, Bologna, and © Società editrice il Mulino 1980

First published in English by the Cambridge University Press, 1983 as *Mafia, peasants and great estates: Society in traditional Calabria*
English translation © Cambridge University Press 1983

Printed in Great Britain at
the University Press, Cambridge

Library of Congress catalogue card number: 82-19929

British Library Cataloguing in Publication Data

Arlacchi, Pino
Mafia, peasants and great estates.
1. Mafia – Calabria (Italy)
I. Title
II. Mafia, contadini e latifondo nella Calabria tradizionale. *English*
364.1'06   HV6453.I83

ISBN 0 521 25136 2

Contents

	List of illustrations	vi
	Note to the English edition	vii
	Translator's preface	ix
	Introduction	1
1	The Cosentino	9
2	The society of permanent transition of the Plain of Gioia Tauro	67
3	The system of *latifondo* of the Crotonese	123
	Conclusions	199
	Index	206

Illustrations

Fig. 1	Map of Calabria showing the three area-types studied	3
Fig. 2	Population growth in percentages by year for the Plain of Gioia Tauro, the Cosentino and Calabria	69
Fig. 3	Distribution of agricultural zones in Calabria by taxable yield per hectare cultivated measured in lire per hectare	71
Fig. 4	Underemployed labour expressed as a percentage of the total number of employed persons in each zone of the Italian south	165
Fig. 5	Fertility and mortality in the *comune* of Melissa from 1851 to 1955	180
Fig. 6	Average life expectancy in the *comune* of Melissa from 1861 to 1955	183

Note to the English edition

The publication of this book in English just over two years after its appearance in Italian is the work of two people. Suzanne Berger of the Massachusetts Institute of Technology first read the manuscript and went to a great deal of trouble in her efforts to arrange an English edition. I owe her a debt of gratitude which is specially associated with the beginnings of my professional work and which I cannot forget.

My friend and colleague, Jonathan Steinberg, of the University of Cambridge, took on the burden of translation and the associated editorial tasks. He has dedicated to the enterprise so much intelligence and hard work that the final product can be considered the work of two authors, not one. It is difficult for me to find the right words to express my gratitude and affection for this extraordinary intellectual personality. I consider my meeting with Jonathan Steinberg one of the great good fortunes of my life.

THE AUTHOR

Translator's preface

This book has been written by a sociologist but translated by a historian. The difference between our two disciplines turned out to be more important than either of us imagined when we began. If the historian seeks to find many verifiable causes for particular events, the sociologist tries to see in the particular event those general aspects which may yield, if not laws, at least rigorous models.

The two disciplines use different languages. As a historian I have always observed Orwell's second law of writing: 'never use a long word where a short one will do' but, as I discovered, certain terms, long and abstract though they may be, were essential to the model Professor Arlacchi wanted to build.

The attempt to build three precise and internally coherent models of three different sorts of traditional society is the core of the book. Its success is for the reader to decide. He may be assured that there is nothing in this translation which has not been seen and approved by the author.

Trinity Hall, Cambridge JONATHAN STEINBERG
March 1982

Introduction

This book contains the result of my research on the economic and social structures of the traditional Mezzogiorno, that is, the southern region of Italy, as it was until the 'great transformation' after the Second World War. The decision to begin the research which eventually led to this volume[1] grew out of my dissatisfaction with two views widely held among students of southern-Italian problems, experts on the Mediterranean region and, more generally, by sociologists, economists and anthropologists.

The first consists in the idea that the models of socio-economic organisation of the traditional Mediterranean society of the Mezzogiorno are characterised by a marked uniformity. The second is the belief that there exist two fundamental types of society, 'the traditional' and 'the modern', corresponding to two diverse situations or stages of economic development.

Emphasising uniformities and concentrating on the dichotomy 'traditional/modern' seemed to me to be harmful in an empirical enquiry. It prevented a clear view of one of the most relevant aspects of the Mediterranean world and the Italian south: the synchronic presence in its interior of profound structural differentiation, of qualitative breaks covered by a thin veneer of common culture.

The richness and variety of the comparisons and contrasts to be

[1] The research work lasted from 1974 to 1978 and took place within the ambit of an enquiry into the regional market for labour carried out during the same period at the University of Calabria. The enquiry was coordinated by Giovanni Arrighi and financed through a grant from the Cassa per il Mezzogiorno to the Istituto per lo Sviluppo delle Attività e delle Ricerche Scientifiche in Calabria.

met in the various different regions and sub-regions of the Mezzogiorno seemed to me from the outset to be too great to be adequately synthesised under one concept such as, for example, 'traditional society on the road to modernisation', or 'systems of rural underdevelopment'. The great estate, the *latifondo* or the small peasant holding, heavy industry and family workshops, kinship and market, 'amoral familism' and the *Gemeinschaft* of the village, modern commercial systems and primitive systems of reciprocity, mafia and statism of the Prussian type, coexisted here side by side or at a few kilometres of distance without apparently disturbing each other.

So it was, when I began the research proper on the 'elementary structures' of the Mezzogiorno, I found myself confronting a problem of definition: what should be the units of analysis? Which of the many Mezzogiornos identified by historians, economists and geographers should I choose as the reference point of my study? The Mezzogiorno of the Ionian coastal region with its great estates or the mercantile Mezzogiorno of the 'Greek' coast? The peasant version of the interior valleys or the 'Roman' northern regions and western Sicily? The list is merely the beginning of the types available.

Gradually, as the work proceeded, it became more and more clear that the whole idea of a 'traditional' Mezzogiorno was no more nor less than a 'geographical expression'. Its internal diversity could not be explained by using the classical instruments of the sociology of modernisation or of the economics of underdevelopment. Any attempt to analyse it as a whole ran the risk of ending up with indeterminate abstractions. The very fact that southern Italy presented itself as an imposing deposit of discordant social structures led me to the decision to reduce the territorial dimensions of the unit of analysis and to concentrate my efforts on one only of the seven administrative regions which make up the Mezzogiorno: Calabria. It had the great advantage that it displayed in a relatively limited geographical area practically all the main socio-economic institutions to be found on a much vaster scale within the south as a whole and in many other areas of the Mediterranean.

In a later and more intensive phase of the research, armed with a more adequate understanding of the methodologies and

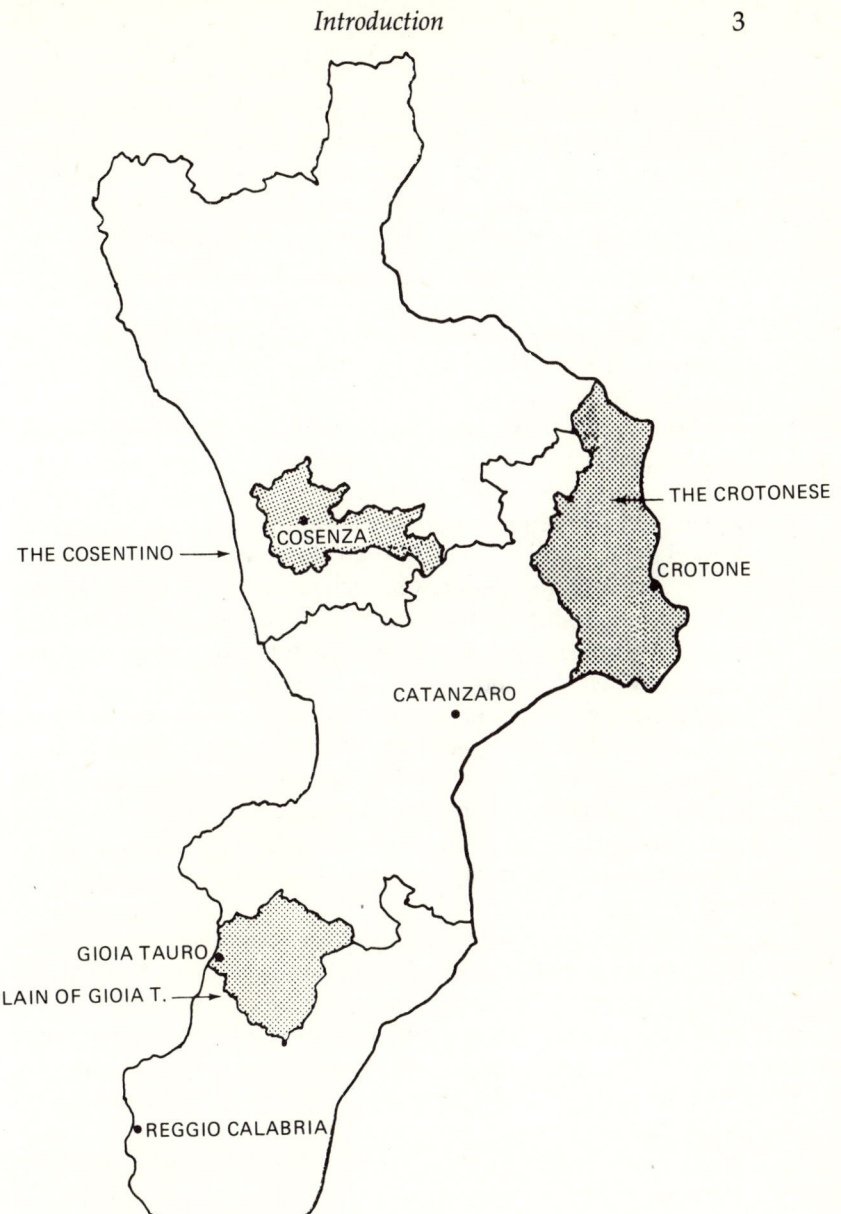

Fig. 1 Map of Calabria showing the three area-types studied: the Cosentino, the Plain of Gioia Tauro and the Crotonese

techniques of anthropology, I came to the conclusion that I should limit the work to a few restricted sub-regional realities which could be considered representative of wholes much more extensive. After several field investigations in a reasonable number of zones and after studying the data about the socio-economic indicators basic to the various zones under consideration, I selected three 'area-types': the Plain of Gioia Tauro on the Tyrrhenian coast in the southern part of the Province of Reggio Calabria; the Marchesato of Crotone on the Ionian coast in the Province of Catanzaro; and the hilly zone around the city of Cosenza in the northern part of Calabria (see Figure 1).

In the course of the following years while the study gradually took shape, I began to realise that the three area-types I had chosen possessed an internal organisation which was more articulated than I had originally assumed. The relations which united the constituent parts of each of the area-types displayed a recurrence and interdependence which seemed to have a necessary character and which could be explained by something very close to an interior principle of organisation. These were not three structures which could be synthesised in some way as parts of one system or three modes of production whose combination gave rise to vaster social formation; these were three distinct, autonomous and notably complex socio-economic systems. Each of them, besides, tended to exclude and fortify the others. Each seemed to be endowed with its own peculiar phenomenology and its own particular mechanism of equilibrium and change.

The individuation of these systems gave me further confirmation of my initial hypothesis that the customary typology of traditional versus modern society was of little explanatory use. Within the universe of traditional types of society the differences between the different forms of social and economic organisation were so great as to be probably larger than those between a traditional society and a modern one.

The examination of the three area-types eventually took the whole of my time. It led to the further conclusions that (1) each of the area-types selected exemplified, in an amplified and abstract way, one of the elementary forms of underdevelopment in the Italian south manifested in the late 1940s, and that (2) the other social and territorial units in Calabria might be regarded as the product of the 'combination' of these fundamental types.

The life of these socio-economic systems of the traditional Mezzogiorno did not unfold in a vacuum. Great general forces repeatedly put their structures and capacity for self-regulation into crisis. Among these forces a primary role was played after 1860 by the competition from a newly unified national market. Each of the three types reacted to the menace in its own peculiar way by developing new institutions and new phenomenologies.

The elementary structures of the first of these types of society, the peasant society encountered in a relatively pure form in the area around the city of Cosenza called the 'Cosentino', were so constituted that it could 'do without' the market for the regulation of its economic relations and tended to discourage forms of permanent antagonistic conflict between individuals and groups. Two potent institutions governed the stability and orderly reproduction of the system, allowing it to withdraw from the market, from the state and from internal conflict: the institution of the family-undertaking and the principle of economic and exogamic reciprocity. The traditional Cosentino was distinguished by the dominion of relations of reproduction over those of production and exchange.

In the clash with the forces of the market for goods, with monetisation and with wage labour opened up by the creation of a unified national market after 1861, the Cosentino succeeded in safeguarding its own equilibrium, above all by means of emigration. The great transoceanic exodus of the early years of this century had as an effect not the disintegration but the return to equilibrium of the economic and social bases of the threatened system. Emigration permitted the reconstitution not only of the family-undertaking but also of non-market exchanges on which the principle of reciprocity rested.

By contrast, a profound integration within the market for goods characterised the second type of society identified, the 'society of permanent transition' of the Plain of Gioia Tauro. Its economic bone-structure was constituted by a broad unstable band of medium-sized agricultural and commercial undertakings in perpetual conflict with each other. Relations of exchange apparently dominated those of production or reproduction.

Given the very high instability of the economic course, subject to unforeseen and unforeseeable fluctuations, the flows of upward and downward social mobility in such a society assumed proportions so massive as to impede the fixing of a stable framework for social classes.

The generalised mobility produced by the chronic instability of market forces was, however, a closed circuit. It was not, that is, inserted in any movement of a more general kind toward the constitution of a new system of social relations. There was no tendency in the short or long run towards *Gesellschaft*. In the Plain of Gioia Tauro no new social roles were created. Society restructured itself from time to time but remained unaltered. It rewound itself about its own central axes. This fluctuation of *corsi e ricorsi*, to use Vico's famous expression, gave rise to a situation which was neither community (*Gemeinschaft*) nor society (*Gesellschaft*). In short, it was a society in permanent transition.

The society of the Plain of Gioia Tauro tended to develop its own original mechanism for reintegrating social cohesion undermined by market forces: the behaviour and power of the mafia-type. The essential characteristic of the mafia was that it was not an organisation or a movement with precise ends and specific programmes but the point of confluence of several conflicting tendencies: the defence of the whole society against the threat to its traditional way of life; the aspirations of the various component groups to 'freeze' the undulating movement of social mobility which ultimately destroyed every institution and all security; personal ambitions and the aspirations of active and ruthless individuals.

Practically all the fundamental structures of the third society I have specified – the system of the *latifondo*, or great estate, with its landless labour force, the *braccianti* – showed an opposite content to that of the peasant society of the Cosentino and a radical dishomogeneity compared with that of the permanent transition of the Plain of Gioia Tauro.

By contrast with the Cosentino, the Crotonese was marked by the presence of great land-holdings and of great economic units in place of the little family farm producing for its own consumption. In the Crotonese in contrast to the tightly knit familial-farming units of the Cosentino, the nuclear family was disintegrated. It had distinct social classes and a labour market instead of a stratification by generations and of the allocation of the factors of production by means of circuits among family and kinship networks. Furthermore, the Crotonese was marked by a sharp separation of economic from social relations as opposed to the indivisible submergence of the one in the other of the Cosentino. In the Crotonese, relations of production dominated those of exchange and reproduction.

By contrast with the permanent transition of the Plain of Gioia Tauro, the qualitative diversity most relevant was the presence in the Crotonese of a principle of centralised regulation of the economic and social movements. In place of a congeries of social and productive monads in conflict, here we find the work of a precise rationality, whose roots were constituted in the relations of production of the *latifondo*. The Crotonese was characterised at every level by the autocracy of the owner of the *latifondo*. The great landed proprietor had monopolistic powers over men and things. The origins of that power in turn can be found in the particular character of lordship and servitude typical of the latifondist enterprise and the society it created. Such a relationship depended on a disequilibrium artificially maintained in the market for agricultural labour which contributed to the maintenance and consolidation of the essentially class-based structure of the entire system.

The great majority of the population of the *latifondo* was composed of persons forced to sell their labour in the market for money wages. They assumed those features of homogeneity, interchangeability and standardisation which are the typical signs of modern social classes. The reaction to market forces on the part of the landless labourers took the form of periodic explosions of fierce class war until in the end a series of circumstances, tied both to the development of the *latifondo* itself and to the course of the Second World War and Italy's defeat, led to a conflict between *latifondisti* and *braccianti* during the 1940s so intense and prolonged that the entire system was destroyed.

These, then, are the three models of underdevelopment which I examine in the following pages. They are unashamedly abstract, general models based on what I see as the internal organising principles of each area-type. I hope, as a sociologist, that they may make a contribution to the refinement of our understanding of the variety and complexity of types of peasant society. I offer them, in addition, for consideration by fellow social scientists interested in the problem of method which the application of theory to reality may pose.

Real people lived their lives in each of the three communities I have studied, and I have never forgotten that the human suffering and struggle which made up the day-to-day existence of many of the peasants studied form part of the larger tragedy of the Mezzogiorno. From Argentina to Canada, from Australia to Scotland, in Germany and Switzerland those peasants, their children and children's children have had to seek an alternative and better way of life than that offered them in the societies of the traditional Mezzogiorno. To those who went away and those who stayed behind, this study is indirectly dedicated.

1

The Cosentino

At the beginning of this century, the novelist George Gissing decided, on a whim, to explore Calabria, an area, as he put it, where 'foreigners are rare; one may count upon new impressions, and the journey over the hills will be delightful'.[1] He landed at Paola, half way down the long western coast of Calabria, and laboriously made his way up the steep coastal mountains which divide the narrow littoral from the interior valleys. It took him three hours, a journey which today on the *superstrada* takes twenty minutes:

At an unexpected turn of the road there spread before me a vast prospect; I looked down upon inland Calabria. It was a valley broad enough to be called a plain, dotted with white villages, and backed by a mass of mountains which now, as in old time, bear the name Great Sila. Through this landscape flowed the river Crati – the ancient Crathis; northward it curved, and eastward, to fall at length into the Ionian Sea, far beyond my vision.[2]

The locals call the 'valley broad enough to be called a plain' the *Conca Cosentina*, 'cosentine shell', or, more generally, the Cosentino. This huge valley, rounded by mountains to east and west, and the 'white villages' which Gissing saw from the height of the pass make up the subject of this chapter. In particular I have chosen twenty-four villages from the 'hilly zones' of the Cosentino, through several of which Gissing would have

---

[1] George Gissing, *By the Ionian Sea. Notes of a Ramble in Southern Italy* (London, 1901), p. 1.
[2] *Ibid.*, p. 15.

passed on his way to the capital of the region, the ancient city of Cosenza.[3]

In 1951 the area covered by the traditional term, *il Cosentino* had 123,000 inhabitants of whom by then about half were living in Cosenza, the metropolis of the region, seat of the government of the province and an ancient episcopal see. It was an unusually densely settled region. Its 221 inhabitants per square kilometre made it one of the most thickly settled in all of Calabria. Only the Plain of Gioia Tauro and the area on the Straits of Messina could equal it.

Traditional Cosentino contained what social scientists call a 'peasant society'. Indeed, as I shall try to demonstrate, the Cosentino had a peasant society of an almost typical kind. Evidence drawn from other parts of the world can be used to illuminate modes of behaviour there and vice versa, as if it had been designed to illustrate the ideal type. Its agriculture was, to begin with, not very specialised and its products tended to be consumed within the community. One of the greatest students of southern-Italian agriculture, Rossi-Doria, classified it in the late 1940s as 'mixed peasant agriculture',[4] mixed in the sense that it combined types of crops, say grain and olives, potatoes and figs, broad beans and grapes, even some mulberries. Its agriculture grew a bit of everything.

The Cosentino was very different from the other two types of area in this book. If you compare the three areas by type of crop, as in Table 1, you will see that the Cosentino is by far the least specialised of the three, and less even than Calabria as a whole.

The basic economic unit of the Cosentino was the peasant enterprise just as the basic social unit of the village was the

---

[3] The areas I have chosen coincide with three of the 'agrarian zones' defined by the Istituto Centrale di Statistica (ISTAT) in 1929 after a scheme devised by the Istituto Nazionale di Economia Agraria (INEA). Cf. ISTAT, *Annali di statistica*, series VI, vol. V (Rome, 1929); *Annali di statistica*, series VI, vol. XXII (Rome, 1932). The communities included within the 'hilly zone of Cosenza' were Aprigliano, Carolei, Casole Bruzio, Castrolibero, Cellara, Cerisano, Cosenza, Dipignano, Domanico, Figline Vegliaturo, Lappano, Marano Marchesato, Marano Principato, Mendicino, Paterno Calabro, Pedace, Piane Crati, Pietrafitta, Rende, Rovito, San Fili, Serra Pedace, Zumpano (see Figure 1).

[4] M. Rossi-Doria, 'La Calabria agricola e il suo avvenire', *Il Ponte*, nos. 9–10, 1950, p. 1176.

Table 1 The use of the soil in the three areas and in Calabria

	Arable		Specialised products of bush/wood		Meadow & pasturage		Forest & woodland		Uncultivated area		Total surface	
	Hectares	%	Hectares	%	Hectares	%	Hectares	%	Hectares	%	Hectares	%
Cosentino	11,724	25	8,360	18	8,252	17	18,038	38	1,000	2	47,377	100
Gioia Tauro	12,634	23	24,438	44	5,041	9	12,495	22	1,154	2	55,762	100
Crotonese	65,871	61	10,256	10	13,440	12	8,530	8	9,534	9	107,631	100
Calabria	494,000	35	228,000	16	193,000	14	384,000	27	109,000	8	1,408,000	100

Source: *Catasto agrario*, 1929

peasant family. Few other areas of southern Italy (Avellino, the Molise, parts of Abruzzo, restricted zones of Sicily and Calabria) showed so tight a correspondence between peasant production and peasant family relationships and so marked an imprint of the 'peasant mode of production' on economic and social relations, on local subculture, on the pattern of settlement and on the configuration of the landscape.

Existing official figures on the Cosentino before 1950 support this generalisation. Better than half of the total cultivated area was divided into units of less than 100 hectares. Practically all the peasant proprietors could be classed as autonomous. As an official report put it in 1929, 'there are very few cases in which they have to work as wage labour on other people's plots'.[5] The rest of the terrain was in the hands of bourgeois owners, who were very numerous and largely drawn from the members of the urban professional classes. Table 2 shows that in the Cosentino there were only four land-holdings of more than 1,000 hectares, which, in any case, only accounted for just over 12 per cent of the total.

The overwhelming majority of proprietors ran their holdings themselves. In the Cosentino there was no trace of that class of large-scale capitalist tenants so common in other parts of the Italian south. The landlords put their farms to rent or, more frequently, assigned them by a type of tenancy according to the size and productive capacity of the individual peasant family of tenants. These farms were what was called *appoderate*, that is, leased as a producing unit complete with structures and implements. Payment was fixed by a share of the crop, and the whole set-up was called the 'mixed contract of the Vale of Cosenza'. This peculiar local arrangement gave to the peasants a share sufficiently reliable to yield something 'close to rent'.[6]

There were two chief causes for the diffusion of this particular form of contract. In addition to the largely autarchic agriculture which I have already described, there was the essentially passive attitude of the Cosentino bourgeois land-owners. They wanted a

---

[5] INEA, *Rapporti tra proprietà, impresa e manodopera nell'agricoltura italiana: Calabria*, ed. E. Turbati (Rome, 1929), p. 28.   [6] *Ibid.*, p. 28.

Table 2 The distribution of landed property in the three areas, in Calabria and in the Mezzogiorno

	\multicolumn{3}{c}{Very small units (0–2 hectares)}	\multicolumn{3}{c}{Small units (2 to 10 hectares)}	\multicolumn{3}{c}{Medium-sized units (10 to 100 hectares)}
	No.	%	Total area	No.	%	Total area	No.	%	Total area	%
Cosentino	11,610	80.9	5,138	10.8	2,216	15.4	9,180	19.2	462	3.2	11,317	23.7
Crotonese	8,286	79.7	3,832	3.9	1,606	15.4	6,473	6.5	363	3.5	11,364	11.5
Plain of G.T.	22,328	87.1	9,312	19.0	2,587	10.1	10,562	21.5	694	2.7	17,746	36.2
Calabria	455,969	87.6	180,245	17.6	52,338	10.1	210,494	20.5	11,161	2.1	288,414	28.1
Mezzogiorno	3,948,189	85.4	1,869,253	20.7	551,655	11.9	2,199,457	24.4	112,239	2.4	2,888,468	32.0

	\multicolumn{3}{c}{Large property (100 to 1,000 hectares)}	\multicolumn{3}{c}{Very large property (more than 1,000 hectares)}	\multicolumn{3}{c}{Totals}
	No.	%	Total area	%	No.	%	Total area	%	No.	%	Total area	%
Cosentino	64	0.5	15,939	33.4	4	0.03	6,133	12.9	14,356	100	47,707	100
Crotonese	130	1.3	44,085	44.7	15	0.1	32,970	33.4	10,400	100	98,724	100
Plain of G.T.	29	0.1	6,932	14.1	2	0.01	4,520	9.2	25,640	100	49,072	100
Calabria	1,218	0.2	289,329	28.2	30	0.01	57,495	5.6	520,716	100	1,025,977	100
Mezzogiorno	10,486	0.2	2,364,665	26.2	204	0.01	360,359	4.0	4,622,773	100	9,028,437	100

Source: INEA 1947, *Distribuzione della proprietà fondiaria in Italia*, Rome, 1948

good income and a quiet life with which to pursue their main activities as lawyers or doctors in the capital city, Cosenza. They had none of the mercantile or entrepreneurial urges of the bourgeoisie of the Plain of Gioia Tauro, of the Salerno hinterlands, of the Adriatic region of Apulia and so on. The other main cause was the relative autonomy of the Vale. The peasants of the *Conca Cosentina* usually had a certain amount of their own livestock, seed corn, tools and agricultural implements and were hence less dependent on the owners. This gave them more leverage in negotiating terms than was available to poorer peasants elsewhere.[7]

The diffusion of the contract which we have described – *colonia parziaria appoderata* – gave to the Cosentino certain peculiar features. The most important of these was the high proportion of self-sufficient peasant cultivators. In order to get an idea of how unusual the Cosentino was in this respect, one only has to compare the percentage of the land area in the Cosentino held under such types of contracts with the percentage of similar types of contracts in the other two areas, in Calabria and in the Mezzogiorno in general. Table 3 gives such figures.

The Cosentino was, to sum up, an unusual place in the world of southern-Italian agriculture. It had its peculiar, characteristic form of share-cropping in which the whole farm made up the basis of the contract. It had a high percentage of independent peasant cultivators and it had an unusually well-balanced, mixed agriculture. It stood out especially against the general trends of agriculture in the Mezzogiorno between the unification of Italy in 1861 and the early 1950s. Against the general background the Cosentino foreground becomes clearer, so let me sketch in that background very briefly.

The agrarian system of the Italian south

The unification of Italy in 1861 nominally created one large national market. The Piedmontese, who founded the new kingdom, had nothing but the best liberal principles in mind and were determined to apply them. The Mezzogiorno was the worst

[7] *Ibid.*, pp. 26–30.

Table 3 *The diffusion of 'colonia parziaria appoderata' in the three areas, in Calabria and in the Mezzogiorno*

	%of tillable surface occupied by units held under *colonia parziaria appoderata*
Cosentino	30.0
Plain of Gioia Tauro	8.5
Calabria	8.3
Mezzogiorno	4.5
Crotonese	0.0

Source: INEA 1949, *Tipi di impresa nell'agricoltura italiana*, Rome, 1951

possible place to try them out. Its peasant agriculture was in fragments. The individual peasant had lost the last shreds of stability. There was no organisation nor market which made sure that his family had enough to eat. He had to scramble for a living by dividing his time among a variety of activities. Some part of the time he worked as a casual salaried labourer, some part on his own postage-stamp-sized property, and, finally, some part on patches of territory leased from the great landlord either as a share-cropper or as a *terratico*, i.e. one paying leases in kind.[8]

His condition was neither that of the small, pre-capitalist peasant producer nor that of the small agrarian entrepreneur in relatively moderate circumstances (the farmer) but that of a hybrid with features of both. He was always on the move in search of employment. No one job was ever adequate by itself. None assured him a secure income, none was permanent or reliable. The southern-Italian peasant put on the mask of the entrepreneur, constantly on the look out for a way to turn the odd penny, but it was a grotesque mockery of the genuine entrepreneur. The peasant of the Mezzogiorno was an entrepreneur without an enterprise. After 1861 he found himself in a larger market in which he remained at once the unique producer of

[8] M. Rossi-Doria, 'Struttura e problemi dell'agricoltura meridionale', *Riforma agraria ed azione meridionalista* (Bologna, 1948).

goods and the unique organiser of that production, yet lacked the power to influence the market in any way. As the money economy spread, he lost the pathetic residue of self-sufficiency he once had. By the late 1940s he could produce 1,000 litres of wine and get less than £20 for it, the result of five months' work. Bushels of home-grown tomatoes and peppers could not buy shoes.

Unification accelerated a process which Gramsci called the 'great social disintegration'. The spread of the market economy in the nineteenth century literally liquidated countless ancient usages and customs, customary rights to the use of the soil and ancient systems of measurement and barter. The new bourgeois class, often installed by the abolition of what early nineteenth-century liberals condemned as 'feudalism', claimed to own land which had, in the bourgeois sense, never been owned before. Peasant communities were atomised.[9] Competition for the remaining scraps of land, forest and pasturage, destroyed immemorial customary agreements, the so-called *usi civici*. There was no effective central point in peasant society to permit them to regroup, reorganise and regulate their affairs. There was no class, group, economic or political coterie which had the slightest interest in obtaining the organised consent of the peasants to the new order. The 'great social disintegration' avoided becoming utterly anarchic, because the torn fabrics of the social system were artificially 'held together' by repression: state repression, familial repression and repression by cliques of clients and dependants, the so-called *clientelismo* of the Italian south.

The damage to the fabric of society was not always obvious. Immediately after unification there was a severe crisis which hit the rural artisan class very hard and led to peasant revolt, brigandage and flight from the land. As the nineteenth century wore on, stability seemed to return to the Mezzogiorno.[10] The new class of landed proprietors gained control of the social and political systems and seemed to be securely fixed in power. The countryside was quiet.

The land-owner, medium-sized or large, the well-known figure

---

[9] E. C. Banfield, *The Moral Basis of a Backward Society* (New York, 1958).
[10] E. Sereni, *Il capitalismo nelle campagne (1860–1900)* (Turin, 1968).

of the southern-Italian *galantuomo*, is one of the best known and least understood characters in the tragedy of the Mezzogiorno. Many of the best students of the south have insisted on seeing the *galantuomo* as an embodiment of feudalism, the reincarnation of the feudal *seigneur* in the turbulence of the nineteenth century. Such a view is misleading. These 'barons' were not genuinely baronial but key figures who piloted the Mezzogiorno from the ancient world of custom to what might be called 'capitalist underdevelopment'. The way the barons operated has also been misunderstood. In the circumstances of the late nineteenth century, they had no need to transform themselves into rural capitalists. They had no incentive to try new forms of agriculture nor to improve their yields per hectare. Money rewards and yields in kind went up quite neatly without their efforts. The atomisation of peasant society, the increasing overpopulation, the disintegration of the artisan class, the fierce battle for ever smaller bits of soil yielded the land-owner ever better returns by a kind of 'invisible hand'. The more brutal the competition among peasants, the more advantageous for the barons became the annual negotiations on share-cropping and tenant-farming.

They had only one problem: keeping the lid on the turbulence of rural misery. Hence they had to count on a permanent armed force tough enough to control the peasants. The key to understanding the situation is not in concepts like feudalism nor even in discussions of parasitic ownership but in the absolutely central importance which force, repression and the monopoly of arms had for the land-owning class of the south. The new Kingdom of Italy had been imposed by force, and the 'barons' had no doubt that it would have to be maintained in the same way. It was not just the outburst of brigandage which made the 1860s so dangerous but the much longer-term centrifugal forces which the abolition of ancient rights unleashed. Immemorial customs, rights to pasture, to gather chestnuts, to sow crops on commons, had been whipped away in a moment. Peasant society threatened to burst at every seam. It was the job of the new state to prevent that.

The *galantuomo* depended on the state and the state depended on him. The deal had precisely the opposite effects of that which created the improving, Whiggish English landlord. The English gentry had used the power of the state to sweep the peasantry from the soil. Once the countryside had been cleared, the few tenants who remained were fortunate and docile. Hence the country gentleman could turn to improvements, his turnips, his new machines and his detestation of state power. Rural England was agreeably underpopulated. The country gentleman could let the market forces play freely on a situation no longer explosive.

The *galantuomo* could not chase the peasants from the soil; on the contrary, he used the state to keep them there. He forced them to stay in servile status so as to squeeze additional surplus from their labour which he could then market. The disequilibrium between population and resources was great and growing. The southern *galantuomo* needed the state to keep it tilted properly in his direction. He had to prevent what Polanyi has called the 'utopia of a society of self-regulating markets'. For that would have overthrown the baron.

The risks in this enterprise were unusually high, and shrewd observers of southern reality saw it. After all, the barons were attempting to maintain an entirely artificial set of economic relationships by using external, non-economic means. The classical students of the south, the so-called *meridionalisti*, saw it from their point of view, as did Antonio Gramsci from his Marxist one. It was, in fact, Gramsci who conceptualised the two contradictory aspects of the social structure of the traditional Mezzogiorno. In his writings he defines the Mezzogiorno both (and it is both) as the 'agrarian bloc' and as the 'great social disintegration'.[11]

Sonnino and Franchetti[12] were themselves landed proprietors. The vision of the Mezzogiorno in flames obsessed them and they foresaw the day of peasant rising which would destroy the agrarian bloc. In their writings they captured one vital element of the new structure of administration. They saw that the Piedmontese state had given enormous power to local officials and especially to the local mayor, the *sindaco*. By one of those ironies of history, the Piedmontese state, which emerged from

[11] A. Gramsci, *La questione meridionale* (Rome, 1966).
[12] Sidney Sonnino (1847–1922) and Leopoldo Franchetti (1847–1917) became famous in the 1870s for their investigations of agricultural conditions in Tuscany and the south. Sonnino, of course, later became prime minister and foreign secretary during the First World War (Translator).

the Napoleonic wars, rejected the ideology of the French revolution but adopted its administration. The highly centralised French system of prefects governing provinces, sub-prefects governing districts, and mayors governing towns, had been designed to support Napoleon's dictatorship. Applied to Italy with its millennia of separate, regional developments, it had paradoxical effects. Instead of the state at the centre issuing commands instantly obeyed at the periphery, the periphery used the centralised administrative structure to protect its local autonomy. Napoleon wanted no local autonomy and demanded order imposed from above; what the Piedmontese state achieved by unifying Italy was local autonomy protected from above.

The *sindaco* had enormous powers delegated from the centre. He was the supreme authority in the community. He could impose taxes, administer the communal property and in many cases exercise police functions. He had the rights to carry out the first stages of criminal investigation and had some powers of a magistrate.[13]

Control of such powers meant more than just directing the local administration in the interests of the exponents of the professional bourgeoisie. It was the tap from which wealth flowed. For the small but growing class of petty-bourgeois intellectuals it meant survival. This class tended to be a nuisance because its fierce acquisitive urge and its subaltern social position forced it to break more and more of the basic rules of traditional society. Anything was acceptable in the struggle for land and wealth. For example, the *sindaco* frequently violated the code of *omertà*, that honour which bound members of the community to silence when crimes had been committed. After all, the *sindaco* spied for the police and the magistrates. As the administrator of the commons, he could favour usurpers, and violate ancient communal rights. As the custodian of the communal stores in times of hardship he could deprive poor peasants of the means of survival or, more commonly, favour his own faction of clients.

---

[13] L. Franchetti, *Le condizioni economiche ed amministrative delle province napoletane* (Florence, 1875); L. Franchetti and S. Sonnino, *Inchiesta in Sicilia* (Florence, 1874).

The second great instrument of repression, parallel to and dependent on the state, was the organisation of systems of clients, the institution called *clientela*. The origins of such 'vertical relations of dominion and personal dependency'[14] are to be found in the feudal paternalism of the *ancien régime*, that is, in the society which existed until the French invasions at the end of the eighteenth century. The basis of such relationships was a delicate equilibrium between the contribution which the lord made in administering justice and in providing security against external enemies and the contribution made by the peasant in the form of products. As long as the proportion between the two contributions – and the lord's is, of course, hard to assess – remained set within certain acceptable limits and as long as the lord's part was felt as an obvious and natural thing by the peasant, the tie between lord and peasant stood firm. Revolt was unlikely.[15]

These ties snapped when paternalism gave way to competition for ownership. Indeed, it had been strained during the eighteenth century as capitalist relations penetrated the countryside. Unification in 1861 and its consequences literally pulled them apart. It was not so much the struggle for land which was in short supply, but rather the complex legal and customary tangle which surrounded land (the *usi civici*, the rights to pasture or cultivate open fields etc.). The unravelling of such tangles determined whether peasant land hunger would or would not be satisfied and to what extent. It takes little imagination to see how the birth of the modern bourgeois latifondist structure of the Mezzogiorno and even more its maintenance over a long period was accompanied by a great deal of prolonged violence, in contrast to what happened elsewhere.

The paternalistic tie between baron and peasant had rested on principles of 'redistribution'. Redistribution meant obligatory payment in material objects, monetary instruments or labour service at some socially recognised centre, which in turn redistributed some part of the produce received to furnish goods and services for the community, such as defence, the festivals, justice, free distribution of stores in hard times, as well as

---

[14] S. G. Tarrow, *Partito comunista e contadini nel Mezzogiorno* (Turin, 1972), p. 15.
[15] For a discussion of this problem, cf. Barrington Moore, *The Social Origins of Dictatorship and Democracy* (London, 1969), chap. 9, pp. 453 ff.

distribution of special products to specified persons at specified times.[16]

Capitalism ruptured the relations of redistribution and deprived the new barons of any link with ancient, legitimate authority. Their rule became, and was seen by the peasants to be, naked authoritarianism. It became a kind of 'negative reciprocity' between *galantuomo* and semi-proletarian tenant, which found its leverage in the gross imbalance within the labour market between supply and demand.

The peasants loathed the *galantuomo*, and never recognised his authority. He was, for them, fraud incarnate. He had gained his lands by theft and violence and had subjugated the peasantry. The trouble was that each individual peasant needed each individual *galantuomo*, because he was the source of work. The naked reality gradually evolved its own system of social relations within which the new class of rural petty bourgeoisie acted as intermediary and in which it saw its very rationale. Hence

---

[16] Reciprocity behavior between individuals integrates the economy only if symmetrically organized structures, such as a symmetrical system of kinship groups, are given. But a kinship system never arises as the result of mere reciprocating behavior on the personal level. Similarly, in regard to redistribution. It presupposes the presence of an allocative center in the community, yet the organization and validation of such a center does not come about merely as a consequence of frequent acts of sharing as between individuals. Finally, the same is true of the market system. Acts of exchange on the personal level produce prices only if they occur under a system of price-making markets, an institutional setup which is nowhere created by mere random acts of exchange. We do not wish to imply, of course, that those supporting patterns are the outcome of some mysterious forces acting outside the range of personal or individual behavior. We merely insist that if, in any given case, the societal effects of individual behavior depend on the presence of definite institutional conditions, these conditions do not for that reason result from the personal behavior in question. (K. Polanyi, *Trade and Market in the Early Empires*, New York, 1957, p. 25).

The analytical categories of reciprocity, redistribution and exchange were 'discovered' by Thurnewald, Malinowski and Mauss, and elaborated by Polanyi and his school. A detailed description of them and their application in concrete cases can be found in K. Polanyi, *Origins of our Time; the Great Transformation* (London, 1945); K. Polanyi, *Trade and Market in the Early Empires*, pp. 243–70; K. Polanyi, *Dahomey and the Slave Trade* (Seattle, Washington, 1966); G. Dalton, 'History, Politics and Economic Development in Liberia', *Journal of Economic History*, XXV (1965), pp. 569–91; G. Dalton, 'Economic Theory and Primitive Society', *American Anthropologist*, LVIII (1961), pp. 1–25; G. Dalton, 'Traditional Production in Primitive African Economies', *Quarterly Journal of Economics*, LXXVI (1962), pp. 360–78.

clientelism became an element shaping the structure of southern-Italian society, because it carried out functions of control or repressive integration by shackling the peasantry more firmly with links forged by the dominant class. Clientelism filled the space between the new alien administrative machinery of the state and the existing community. It took the place of any modern form of political activity and prevented the emergence of mass party-politics.[17]

The strategic variable of the social system remained the splintering of the relations of production, but its economic consequences expressed themselves through social institutions, the state or the system of clientelism. They also worked themselves out in the family, the third prop of repressive integration in the traditional Mezzogiorno.

The break-up of stable agricultural relations into all sorts of fragmentary activities made it impossible to arrive at a stable division of labour. This brought with it fragmentation of the activities of the nuclear family and often of each member. Since there was virtually no specialisation of 'professional roles', the various activities of labour reduced themselves to mere means of survival. The trades had no 'value in themselves' and could no longer be organised in a hierarchy of apprenticeship or prestige. The authority of the father in the family suffered by this process of 'de-skilling'.

The authority of the father had always been a rather precarious one, based on his alleged capacity to procure the means of subsistence. 'As soon as they had begun to earn for themselves, nothing could hold them back. They spoke to their father with curses and obscenities, as, in fact, he had always spoken to them.'[18] Paradoxically the weakness of parental authority favoured the affirmation of an extremely rigid authoritarianism within the family. Relations became 'vertical' – parents–children, husband–wife, older brother–younger brother etc.[19]

---

[17] A. Gramsci, *La questione meridionale*; G. Salvemini, 'La piccola borghesia intellettuale del Mezzogiorno d'Italia', *Scritti sulla questione meridionale* (Turin, 1955).

[18] L. Sciascia, *Le parrocchie di Regalpetra* (Bari, 1956), p. 124.

[19] G. Zappa, 'La questione meridionale: aspetti sociali e culturali', *Mezzogiorno e politica di piano* (Bari, 1964), p. 101.

The two tendencies clashed: the fluidity occasioned by the irregular, unpredictable and fragmented division of labour within the family and the authoritarian stabilisation of social roles. Economic and social roles drew apart. The domestic group divided and the family became one thing, the economic enterprise another, a tendency which, of course, became much more marked in the years after the Second World War. Here we see yet again the peculiarly dialectical and paradoxical situation of the Mezzogiorno after unification: most of the fundamental institutions were theatres of literally continuous struggle between contrasting forces.

Fragmentation of the relations of production in the family-economy generated a peasantry semi-proletarianised, 'amorphous and disintegrated'.[20] Within it there existed very high physical mobility and variety of conditions. The bourgeois strata were equally disorganised. Society became structurally complex but relatively fluid within the barriers of each class. Opposed to this extremely atomised social order stood the unusually rigid system of 'reproduction', which we have already examined. Its bases were the 'total' institutions of state, client and family. These institutions froze the fragmentation and variety of the relations of production and led to stagnation in economic development and social change.

The family-enterprise

The general background of the economy of the Mezzogiorno makes it evident at once how different the social and economic order of the Cosentino was. Take, in the first place, the role of the peasant proprietor who was self-sufficient and operated under partial lease-holding arrangements characteristic of rural areas of the Vale of Cosenza. The presence of these two features ensured that between family and farm there was a stable relationship. On such a basis all other social arrangements became themselves stable. In other words, the Cosentino was the exact opposite of the typically precarious structures of the rest of the Mezzogiorno.

---

[20] M. Rossi-Doria, *Dieci anni di politica agraria nel Mezzogiorno* (Bari, 1958), pp. 21–3.

The contract of *colonia parziaria appoderata* differed from every other peasant contract employed in the south because it went beyond simple renting or share-cropping of a piece of territory to include farm out-buildings, equipment, house and barns, calibrated precisely and fractionally by the specific characteristics and dimensions of each peasant family.[21] The farm became a unit of production tailored to the measure of the peasant family. The reverse was also true. The family was a microscopic social unit fitted to occupy precisely the economic units being offered. You could say that the 'economic' and 'social' became almost the same thing, a *unicum*, a complex socio-economic entity, which resisted separation of its parts as it opposed all change. Cultivation on such farms was dedicated to self-sufficiency. Hence the mixed agriculture. One part of the property was dedicated to arable crops, another to crops of bush, tree and vine (grapes, figs, olives). Often there were chestnut trees and usually a meadow for forage. Only a small part of produce went to market. During the 1940s roughly 75 per cent of all production was consumed in the Cosentino by the families producing it.

The family farm guaranteed to all its members of working age stable employment through most of the year. According to the official 'Sample study of peasant entrepreneurial families' published by ISTAT in 1939, more than half of all members of each family in the Cosentino worked full-time on the family farm. The enquiry also found that every square kilometre of farmed land in the Cosentino provided stable employment to 55 persons. Table 4 shows how relevant that fact was by comparing the Cosentino with other parts of Italy. In no other region of Calabria and in only 14 out of 330 agricultural zones in the Mezzogiorno was there a density of employed peasant population to equal that of the Cosentino.

The basis of the family-enterprise was the integration of economic production in the web of family relationships. Aspects which in a capitalist enterprise would be thought 'non-economic' or 'exogenous' were the very essence of the economic arrangement. Economic relationships as such could not be separated from others in the peasant enterprise in the Cosentino, and by the

---

[21] A. Serpieri, *La struttura sociale dell'agricoltura italiana* (Rome, 1947), p. 212; G. Giorgetti, *Contadini e proprietari nell'Italia moderna* (Turin, 1976), chap. 5.

Table 4 *Number of persons per peasant family employed regularly, per square kilometre of area farmed, by the three regions, the rest of Calabria, mainland Mezzogiorno and other agricultural areas of Italy*

	Male	Female	Total
Cosentino	36	19	55
Northern Italy	31	11	42
Central Italy	29	12	41
Italy	27	9	36
Mainland Mezzogiorno	23	5	28
Plain of Gioia Tauro	23	4	27
Calabria	15	4	19
Crotonese	17	0.5	18
Sicily, Sardinia	15	0.3	15

Source: ISTAT, *Indagine rappresentativa sulle famiglie contadine imprenditrici*, Rome, 1939

same token economic realities produced peculiar distortions in family structure and behaviour. The family produced more than merely goods and services. Each single cell of such rural production units had an organisation appropriate to its domestic division of labour. Family roles coincided with economic roles and vice versa. The division of labour was under the central direction of the father. He was the only subject even minimally specialised enough or 'professionalised' enough to indicate types and times of production, subdivision of tasks, coordination of non-agricultural domestic work (weaving and sewing, preserving food, preparing meat for sausages or salamis, selling surplus etc.) with field-work.

Paternal authority was thus the power of the head of the family to give direct orders. It covered all the other stages of development of the family not economic in character: the decision to send a son to study elsewhere or to marry off a daughter. It rested on the ability to organise domestic work and to negotiate advantageous arrangements with other similar family-production units in the community or with the ground landlord. It rested on the politics of the kinship and its ability to apply case by case (and to ensure obedience to) the ruling norms in the subculture.

In the typical rural family of the Cosentino, women had

Table 5 *Participation of women among those occupied full-time in the three areas, in Calabria, in mainland Mezzogiorno and other regions*

	Women per 100 occupied persons
Cosentino	34
Central Italy	30
Northern Italy	27
Italy	26
Calabria	22
Mainland Mezzogiorno	18
Plain of Gioia Tauro	14
Crotonese	3
Sicily, Sardinia	2

Source: ISTAT, *Indagine rappresentativa*

subordinate positions, relieved a little by their importance for the process of production. Their part in the domestic economy was thus vital. As will be clear from Table 5, for every hundred persons permanently employed in peasant farms in the Cosentino 34 were women. No other agricultural system in any other part of Italy – not even in central Italy dominated as it was by tenancies of the 'appoderated' type very similar to those in the Cosentino – involved so strong a female labour force. Women's participation in the full range of agricultural activity was made easier by the pattern of settlement. The Cosentine countryside was spotted with individual homesteads instead of the much commoner centralised 'rural city' so characteristic of the rest of Calabria and the Italian south in general. In the rest of the Mezzogiorno, the centralised peasant village was normally far from the places of work. Every day long columns of peasants would move out in the early hours of the morning to work the distant fields. This tended to separate 'woman' and 'home' from 'work' in the formal sense, something which never happened in the Vale of Cosenza.

The comparatively favourable position of women in the Cosentino cannot be explained merely by the fact that they worked along with men. Female labour was, of course, perfectly compatible with low social status. Indeed, in the Plain of Gioia Tauro, for example, 51 per cent of wage labourers who worked the fields were women, and precisely because they worked in that way they stood at the very bottom of the social pyramid. Work as such never settled the position of a woman in the scale of public esteem. It was the type of work and, more particularly, the degree of remoteness from salaried work, which counted. The more a family member depended on other people for his subsistence the lower his prestige.

Family hierarchy was very rigid. Children were absolutely subordinate to parents. Obedience was the main virtue and there was little room for intimacy. Children addressed parents in the second person formal *voi* and not the more intimate *tu*. Even adult children had to obey and could never decide things for themselves; they too had fixed places in the family hierarchy. Division of labour, indeed, all economic categories in the strict sense, depended on the maintenance of rigid family relationships and absolute obedience of children to parents. Inheritance, dowries, marriage arrangements would not have been possible if children had rights to decide for themselves. The hierarchy of relations and values had to be internalised if the socio-economic system were to survive.

Thomas and Znaniecki in their massive study of the Polish peasantry noticed the same family structure which distinguished the Cosentino. They coined the term 'familial solidarity' to describe such formal, normative relationships among family members.

The family is, thus, a very complex group with limits only approximately determined and with various kinds and degrees of relationship between its members. But the fundamental familial connection is one and irreducible; it cannot be converted into any other type of group-relationship nor reduced to personal relation between otherwise isolated individuals. It may be termed *familial solidarity* and it manifests itself both in assistance rendered to, and in control exerted over, any member of the group by any other representing the group as a whole.[22]

In the peasant family in the Cosentino up to the 1940s the

---

[22] W. I. Thomas and Florian Znaniecki, *The Polish Peasant in Europe and America* (2 vols., New York, 1958), p. 89.

individual characters of the members of the family were much less important than the formal positions in the family. Structure and hierarchy determined solidarity and the amount of assistance and cooperation which each member brought to the effort of all. In contrast to modern nuclear families and, indeed, to families in the other regions of Calabria examined in this study, the space for individual variation in behaviour was sharply reduced. Among members of a family there could be no gradations, as, for example, love or even friendship. Everything tended to be fixed by the type and proximity of one's family relationship.

Such families had strong control systems. Many aspects of ordinary family life, which are unpredictable or even dangerous, could be reduced to predictable limits. The circuits in such relationships were not 'overloaded'. Intense domestic relations raise the voltage and had thus to be avoided. This is particularly important if one remembers how highly charged the enclosed and taut life of a nuclear peasant family must be when it is also an economic unit. Moments of extreme tension and explosion are only too frequent.

The control system in the peasant-enterprise of the Cosentino was evident in the central relationship of husband–wife. The principle which governed it was far from that which operates in the normal urban nuclear family. The key principle was *rispetto*, only weakly captured by the English word 'respect'. *Rispetto* had little to do with the feelings of those involved. It was precise and verifiable. It had to do with obligations and reciprocal arrangements. *Rispetto* meant for the husband that he treat his wife well, keep faith, preserve her from the need to work for others, and, in general, pay continuous attention to her social position and the consideration which she might enjoy within the community. The wife owed *rispetto* too in the form of obedience, fidelity, capacity to save and to run the house, the care of the husband's health and well-being.

Affection did not constitute an essential component of *rispetto*, even if its presence was desirable. Sexual love was a purely personal thing which must not be allowed to interfere in any way with the couple's relationship. The family ignored its existence. The slightest mention of sexual relations within marriage was frowned upon. It was as if such conjugal sexual relations were beyond consideration. Unlike sexual relations outside marriage, sex-life within it was neither institutionalised nor subject to strict norms. Instead, relations between husband and wife were just part of that network of family relations which bound the complex together. There was no difference in kind between conjugal and other relations within the family.[23]

What was true within a family tended to apply and reinforce itself outside. Self-respect within each family mirrored the respect accorded it from without. The community sustained the family and the families made up the community. Each member of each family felt himself to be responsible for the acts and well-being of every other member of the same family. In the peasant communities of the traditional Cosentino each family had its public value based on the behaviour of its members and each individual had value in precise relation to the public value and esteem which his family enjoyed. Nobody could raise or lower himself without dragging with him the entire family.

Since family relations were so formal, moments of crisis would reinforce them even more rigidly. Sometimes the individual had to be sacrificed in the interests of all the family members. The writer, Corrado Alvaro, recalls in *Itinerario italiano* the family of the years before the Second World War:

If the father cannot carry out the function of raising a family, the eldest son assumes the position of the father and regards himself as having assumed the age of his father and not his own. The sisters wil be married off one after another by age ... many marriages have to be delayed because an older sister has not yet been sought. In many places a man seeking the hand of a daughter will be offered that of her eldest sister instead. This indicates how utterly the individual has been annihilated in the face of family necessity.[24]

The mode of family production

In spite of the strong dose of anti-individualism and the rigidity of the norms governing it, the traditional family of the Vale of

---

[23] Thomas and Znaniecki observed the same thing in Polish families. 'The marriage norm is not love but "respect", as the relationship which can be controlled and reinforced.' *Ibid*. p. 90, and pp. 106–10.

[24] Corrado Alvaro, *Itinerario italiano* (Milan, 1962), pp. 355–6.

Cosenza ought not to be thought of as gratuitously repressive. Its basis did not consist in blind submission of individuals to an authority without prestige, even if in moments of general upheaval it may have seemed that way to its members in revolt.

Its rigidity grew out of its multi-dimensionality. It had to be rigid because it had to meet so many different needs. Above all, it had to maintain perfect congruity between the economic and non-economic activities in which it moved. The family protected its members from market forces, not by opposing them with some sort of vague family feeling but by absorbing them. Its complex mesh of role, function and value moulded the whole activity of its members, enabling them to coordinate their economic activities.

The conditions of the relations between family and enterprise governed the stability and reproduction of the entire social and economic order of the Cosentino by reacting in a manner more rigid when it was threatened by the subversive forces of the market or the state. The content of these conditions formed a sort of interlocking set of pieces, not unlike a puzzle. However complicated it may have been in execution, the logic was simple and easily summarised in three elementary propositions:

(a) the dimensions of the family define the upper and lower limits of its activity as an agricultural producing unit and vice versa;
(b) no form of production whatever was possible on a small scale in that peasant society without a family base;
(c) family life and social life itself could not exist without a productive base.

The first point sanctioned an interdependence of enterprise and family, of economic and of social relations, which is capable of explaining both the endogenous rules of social stratification of the peasants of the Cosentino and the weakness of vertical conflict among those same peasants. Points (b) and (c) synthesise the rules of social control specific to the peasant society. Section 1 will be dedicated to an examination of point (a) while section 2 will deal with points (b) and (c).

1. For the Cosentino the strict link between enterprise and family structure can be documented statistically. If we compare the

Table 6 *Ratio of number of heads of family and number of farming units per category of peasant in the Cosentino*

Category	Family	Units	Ratio family: units
Tenants	1,000	998	100.2
Share-croppers	1,965	2,001	98.2

Source: ISTAT, *Censimento agricolo*, 1930; ISTAT, *Censimento demografico*, 1931

Table 7 *Ratio between size of family and size of unit of production in peasant farms of the Cosentino*

Size of unit in hectares	Persons per family
0.5–1	4.1
1–3	4.5
3–5	5.6
5–10	6.8
10–20	9.6

Source: Sample of 100 family-enterprises drawn from local registries and from *Catasto agrario*, 1929

Table 8 *Ratio of family size and size of farm in the Cosentino by type of tenure*

Type of tenure	Average size of farm in hectares	Average number in family
Rent	7.3	6.7
Share-cropping	4.8	6.1
Direct tenure	3.8	5.5

Source: ISTAT, *Censimento agricolo*, 1930; ISTAT, *Censimento demografico*, 1931

number of farming units recorded in the agricultural census of 1930 with the number of heads of families recorded in the population census of 1931, we get a high degree of correspondence. For the Vale of Cosenza, for 5,755 heads of families there are 6,103 units of between 0.5 and 20 hectares. For certain categories of tenant the fit is nearly perfect, as is shown in Table 6.

The relationship between family and productive unit was not merely quantitative in the Cosentino but much more profound. There was a definable link between size of unit and size of family; the bigger the family the bigger the unit of production. If we analyse the units by size and if we calculate at the same time the average size of the family which cultivated such units, we see a strong proportionality between size of unit and size of family. Table 7 shows that relationship.

A similar result is obtained if we use official figures on size of holding by type of tenure. Arranging the units on a scale based on their median size by type we see that it amounts to a scale of family size (Table 8).

The tables tell us, then, that there is a correlation between size of family and amount of economic activity but not much more. We get from these tables merely a mechanical correspondence. Now we have to look to the internal arrangement of such families to see how such matching worked in practice. One could begin by supposing (and many agricultural economists do suppose something of the sort) that peasant family size is determined by the availability of resources, that is, peasants in the Cosentino effectively furnished themselves with families equal to their material means. The opposite is, however just as plausible, that is, that family size determined the amount of farming undertaken. They would do this by acquiring units of production which matched the number of hands in the family.

What happens when families grow or contract? If the amount of land determined the size of family, was the family with a small plot to practise birth control or suffer a higher rate of infant mortality to keep the equation in balance? Clearly there must have been regulatory mechanisms which allowed for change. The system is far from being explained by stating its equilibrium conditions.

Table 9 illustrates the point. There is no indication that the

Table 9 *Percentage of children under six in the different categories of family farming units by size of unit*

Size of unit in hectares	% of children under 6
0.5–1	25
1–3	24
3–5	24
5–10	22
10–20	18

Source: Own calculations

number of children born to poorer peasants was lower than to the richer, nor that infant mortality was higher. In other words, there was neither self-regulation of family size nor any such regulation exercised by external conditions. If anything, the table suggests a reverse correlation, which is even more improbable.

There is a further difficulty in approaching this phenomenon in terms too exclusively mechanical. The two causal elements, size of farm and size of family, interact abstractly as if there were no limits in finances, in law or in economics, as if there were no markets, wars, droughts nor death. In fact, the most interesting aspect of rural society in the Cosentine basin can be revealed only when the 'constraints' are restored. The damage done by market and political forces after 1860, during depressions, wars and crises had to be repaired, and it was in the resistance to shocks from without that the true equilibrating forces within the society became obvious. How did the endogenous structures and forces of population and society react to the exogenous pressures and shocks to the system?

The first step in a more precise analysis takes us back to Table 9. At first glance the figures seem to say that the poorer peasants have more children, but in fact the results of my research suggest that, first, birth-rate is quite independent of economic level and that, second, size of unit is in part socially determined. Stratification by size of unit amounts, in reality, to a stratification by age. In the Cosentino the younger the family, the smaller its holding and

Table 10 *Size of peasant farm and age of head of family in the Cosentino*

Size of unit in hectares	% of heads of family less than 40 years old
0.5–2	50
2.5–5	30
5–10	14
over 10	6

Source: Own calculations

hence the higher its proportion of very young children. This hypothesis is confirmed if we compare the age of the head of the household with the size of the unit farmed. Table 10 shows how strong that correlation is.

Clearly the age of the family cannot be a function of the amount of land cultivated; it must be the other way round. There must be forces making the amount of land depend on the size and age of the family, and, given the high degree of formalisation of social relations in the Cosentino, that ought not to surprise us. All the processes of reproduction of families are subject to elaborate norms: betrothal, marriage around the age of 25, inheritance, and dowry obligations. The dimensions of each family can be seen to be a function of age.

If, then, the dimensions of the productive unit are strongly influenced by the dimensions of the family, then variations in size and hence the level of well-being and position in the social hierarchy of each peasant family in the Vale of Cosenza will be greatly affected by the 'natural history' of each family.

Here is a sketch of a typical family unit, a kind of average 'natural history'. It begins with a young couple on a small farm who raise a certain number of children. The farm consists of a limited quantity of soil, a few draught-animals and a small quantity of implements received either as dowry or by inheritance. The growth of the family creates a great demand for goods. The head of the family must seek to expand the operation, acquiring or, more frequently, renting more land and livestock.

As the number of sons and daughters increases, the labour potential of the unit expands, but this is paralleled by growth in the demands for consumption. There are new needs and new problems of employment. Besides, after a certain number of years, the family has to put aside a fixed amount of its income to accumulate dowries. If conditions on the land market allow it, the farm can be extended as the children reach adolescence and begin to count as full members of the labour force. Otherwise, a part of the excess labour must be allowed to emigrate.

At a certain point, normally about the twenty-fifth year of marriage, the arc of the parabola is reached and the family unit begins to decline. The first son marries and inherits a part of the farm. Normally he would also get from the ground landlord some small additional plot conceded under the customary Cosentine contracts. A few years later the second son marries and the unit contracts further. The process continues until the size of the family and the unit of production have returned to the starting point. The elderly married couple end up living with one of the married children and the cycle of ascent and descent begins anew.

The presence of the institution of *colonia parziaria appoderata* introduces an element of stability into this cycle. It makes the land relatively disposable but prevents richer peasants from transmitting great quantities of land by inheritance. It also discourages the fragmentation of units, what Friedrich List called 'the midget economy', by which sons receive ever smaller but equal divisions of land. The custom of assignment of units by size of family prevents that otherwise not uncommon outcome of close peasant social orders.

The natural history of the family and the expansion and contraction of unit size over the span of time had important consequences for the dynamic equilibrium of the entire social system. It tended to give rise to a potentially fixed distribution of family-enterprises in three fundamental categories of size and wealth. At any one point, the Cosentine basin revealed a mass of units of varied size – large, medium and small – each at a different stage of family development. If you looked again later, you might find that the number of units had varied greatly, that there had been large entries and exits in the various sectors, that each individual unit had changed radically, but the curve of the distribution of family units by size would have remained nearly constant. The specific mechanism of self-regulation in the Cosentino lay in this congruence between great individual change and equally great fixity of the overall stratification of the individual units. Two currents, one ascending and the other descending, constantly reinforced each other and maintained the balance.

The Italian economic and social statistics are too crude to allow us to isolate an individual group of families for the Cosentino or any other area. I have had to construct such series on the basis of the registers of the *comuni* and the records of agricultural holdings (*catasto*). By using these figures, it is possible to follow the progress of a sample of 100 families over the period 1929 to 1945. The intense mobility in both directions becomes evident. During a single generation practically all the families seem to have undergone movement consistent with the assumed arc of family development. These results forced me to alter the 'preanalytic image' with which I began: that peasant society was immobile, undifferentiated and without internal mechanisms of equilibrium.

A second set of calculations was made, using the dates 1930 and 1967, the two official enquiries which actually gathered data on the amount of family labour employed, a critical variable for any analysis of rural stratification. Using these two series, I constructed an analysis of social stratification by peasant productive unit, which is summarised in Table 11.

The table is worth consideration. The period which it covers saw the greatest transformation in the external conditions of peasant agriculture of any in the recent history of the Italian peninsula. There was the great depression, the disastrous Second World War, peasant unrest after it and the great emigration which literally wiped out whole segments of the peasant economy. Nevertheless the pattern of social stratification of peasant enterprise remained astonishingly stable. It would appear that the forces of self-regulation within the peasant economy continued to operate through all the turbulence of these years, and this was true of all the regions, again in spite of vast differences in relation to market forces, changes in transportation and in political structure.

Table 11 *Social stratification of the peasant farms in the Cosentino, in Calabria and of the other principal Italian regions in 1930 and 1967*[25]

	% of units of poor peasants		% of units of rich peasants		Variance
	1930	1967	1930	1967	
North Italy	49	49	51	51	–
Central Italy	46	49	54	51	–3
Mezzogiorno	65	67	35	33	–2
Calabria	77	70	23	30	+7
Cosentino	46	46	54	54	–

Source: ISTAT, *Indagine rappresentativa sulle famiglie contadine imprenditrici*, Rome, 1939; ISTAT-CEE, *Indagine sulla struttura delle aziende agricole*, Rome, 1970

What we have now isolated, important as it is, must be kept in perspective. I am not arguing that in the traditional Cosentino, and even less in the Cosentino after the Second World War, there were no profound changes brought about by purely economic factors. There were such changes, both in the stratification and number of peasant production units. What we have seen, however, is that there were, apparently, internal mechanisms for reacting to external shocks. The traditional system of correspondence between economic and social factors generated a demo-

---

[25] 1930: the figure for the percentage of units classified as run by poor peasants was derived by using the hypothesis that the distinction between peasant population occupied permanently in work on the units and peasant population occupied temporarily – a distinction quantified in table 5 of the *Indagine rappresentativa sulle famiglie contadine imprenditrici* – corresponded to the stratification among units of poor, middle and rich peasants.
1967: the figure for poor peasants was derived by using table 15, vol. II of *Indagine sulla struttura delle aziende agricole* and by considering as 'poor' peasant units those which employed less than one annual labour unit, that is, less than 300 days of adult labour. For the relevant figure for the Cosentino, the same criteria were used but modified to take account of the fact that figures in the two surveys do not distinguish anything below the level of the region. I adopted the method of calculating the difference between the supply of family labour and the quantity of such labour required by the prevailing set-up of crop cultivation.

graphic regulator which kept the balance in a system of dynamic equilibrium over time. External forces could modify or threaten to destroy that equilibrium, and it is now necessary to see how.

The rise and decline of the typical family over the span of time was not the only occasion of growth and contraction. Families could rise and fall with constant numbers, that is, pushed by forces that had nothing to do with the inherent demographic patterns of peasant life. Favourable or unfavourable economic trends might make it more or less difficult for the families to move along the endogenous arc of development. The tendency to an equilibrium would show itself only over a long period when the external turbulence had worked itself out.

Within a decade or two, market forces might move the social currents of ascent and descent towards a position of temporary disequilibrium. One current might dominate the other and within a few years shift the entire curve of distribution of family farms. Thus, the first twenty years of the new Italian state, 1861 to 1881, was a period in which the descending current dominated. Economic conditions were distinctly hostile. The new state imposed new taxes. Land was in short supply and the worldwide depression affected agricultural prices. It was harder to bring goods to market. All these adverse influences made it harder for the young family to grow by gaining land to match the increase in its offspring. The number of very small family units grew and there was a general lowering of the level of subsistence.[26]

The pressures towards the imposition of the market as the supreme regulator of all relations did not succeed. The mechanism of the family-enterprise continued to keep the plane of economic relations 'glued' to the plane of social relations, and the society of the Cosentino peasants was not destroyed.

The period between the 1880s and the First World War was much more favourable. Now market forces seemed to help the

---

[26] A. Branca, 'Relazione sulla seconda circoscrizione (province di Potenza, Cosenza, Catanzaro, Reggio Calabria)', *Atti della Giunta per la Inchiesta Agraria e sulle Condizioni della Classe Agricola*, vol. IX, fasc. 1 and 2 (Rome, 1883); D. Demarco, 'Considerazioni sulle vicende della proprietà fondiaria e delle classi rurali in Calabria, dopo l'Unità (1860–80)', *Atti del II Congresso Storico Calabrese* (Naples, 1961), pp. 481–513.

Table 12 *Stratification of peasant families by size in the province of Cosenza between 1931 and 1951*

	1931		1936		1951	
Number in family	no.	%	no.	%	no.	%
From 2 to 4	17,856	45.5	17,141	43.6	15,127	44.0
From 5 to 8	18,712	47.6	18,253	46.4	16,135	46.9
More than 9	2,705	6.9	3,937	10.0	3,142	9.1
Totals	39,273	100	39,331	100	34,404	100

Source: Censimenti demografici

community to regulate its own social mobility. Ascending currents began to dominate from the early 1880s. Market forces, in this case international labour market forces, began to attract the first great wave of transoceanic migration. Tens of thousands of young peasants left the Mezzogiorno for America. Emigration allowed the family-enterprise to grow peacefully. A new enlarged class of small cultivators grew up and a more intensive use of the soil followed. By 1920 the structure of peasant society had returned to the point from which it had declined in the early 1860s.

For the twenty years 1931 to 1951 we have figures on family size which suggest that there was a tendency for the size of family to settle at constant levels. Table 12 gives figures for the whole of the province of Cosenza and not merely for the sample villages from the Vale itself.

The table suggests that there was a slight but noticeable tendency for large families to reconstitute themselves, a phenomenon which can be verified by other means for the interwar years. The reduction of 12 per cent of the peasant population which the 1951 census recorded shows that a new cycle of urbanisation and emigration had begun to make itself felt in the last few years of the period.

There is, then, a complex interaction between demographic-social factors on the inside of peasant society, which determine the 'natural history' of the family, and the economic forces in the market from the outside. Social stratification results from the interplay of the two over long periods, and there are several important consequences of that fact. The first is the absence of any drive toward vertical social conflict within society itself. Society never lacked occasion for conflict and the ninety years after unification were charged with violence, but the conflict was very seldom between groups within peasant society. The main friction arose between the tough, integrated communities of the Cosentino and the new state. In the first decade of the new Kingdom of Italy the revolt of the peasants took the form of brigandage, an armed protest against the new powers. The Calabrian centre of the wars of the brigands was the province of Cosenza.[27] In addition, the peasants of Cosenza showed a healthy capacity to fight off the usurpation of commons, pasturage and woodland in those areas where the hill country of Cosenza began to decline toward the arid shore of the Ionian sea. The new 'barons' of the Crotonese had to suffer violent raids, kidnapping and arson.[28]

The peasants of Cosenza also had some success in fighting off the tentacles of the new market economy. They resisted the introduction of the new means of payment, the spread of money contracts, mortgages, credit offered on usurous terms and so on. In the first twenty years of this century, the Cosentino became the only region of Calabria in which a cooperative movement under Catholic auspices and almost always headed by local priests grew up. These cooperatives were very like the so-called 'white leagues' of northern Italy and rested on a solid network of small savings banks and rural cooperatives whose aim it was to free the peasants from the need to go to town for finance and marketing.[29]

These fiercely independent peasants never engaged in class conflict among themselves in spite of the manifest differences of

---

[27] M. Milani, *La repressione dell'ultimo brigantaggio nelle Calabrie* (Pavia, 1952); F. Molfese, *Storia del brigantaggio dopo l'Unità* (Milan, 1964).

[28] A. Basile, 'Moti contadini in Calabria dal 1844 al 1870', *Archivo storico per la Calabria e la Lucania*, XXVI (Rome, 1958), pp. 67–100.

[29] S. Antonioli and G. Cameroni, *Movimento cattolico e contadino. Indagine su Carlo De Cardona* (Milan, 1976); F. Cassiani, *I contadini calabresi di C. De Cardona* (Rome, 1976).

wealth and poverty which existed among them. All the 'objective' conditions existed and yet class struggle or even conflict among groups within classes remained alien to the traditional social order of the Cosentino. I have found few examples of clashes between groups of peasants in the whole period of my research. The incendiary material was there in plenty; the conflict was not.

Marxism in its classical or in its Leninist guise cannot explain such phenomena. There were, after all, many poor peasants of the type presupposed in the Leninist scheme; yet there was no tendency to accumulate wealth on a permanent basis, to form a rural petty bourgeoisie or a class of rich peasants like the Russian *kulaks*. Gross inequalities in the ownership of the means of production led neither to class formation and conflict nor to the accumulation of capital necessary for early mercantile capitalist development of the countryside.

Understanding the way the family-enterprise worked makes it possible to explain such an 'anomaly'. A stratification based, purely and simply, on differences in ownership of the means of production is not enough. The key lies in the interaction between ownership and the peculiar character of the units which owned or, more accurately, controlled these means. Two vital elements caused the difference: the passivity and parasitic character of the bourgeoisie who actually owned the means of production, and the perception by peasants within the system that differences of wealth and poverty were essentially cyclical and hence transitory. In theory each young family had the chance of improvement and could enjoy the highest position on the hierarchical scale. As long as market forces never quite imposed themselves so strongly that only economic factors dominated, the working of the social system ensured a slow but steady elaboration of a kind of redistributive justice. The slow rhythm of the family's 'natural history' assured each group sufficient chances of social mobility.

The stratification into large, medium and small tenant farmers, then, is more a statistical description than a true social classification. Organisation into social classes of the Marxian type[30] did

---

[30] Karl Marx and Friedrich Engels, *The German Ideology*. Trs. W. Lough and C. P. McGill, rev. by R. Pascal (London, 1938), pp. 63 ff.

not exist in rural Cosentino where the positions of individuals were constantly fluctuating.

Since classes in the strict sense could not form themselves, neither conflict nor social change could occur. Certainly there were many elements to cause conflict between individuals or groups, but there was no systematic struggle of classes which could give rise to large-scale social change. There was never an 'antagonistic contradiction' between two social classes which could operate as the motive for such change.

2. No doubt in a system less rigid than that of the Cosentino the relationship between the family and its business would not be so central a piece of the social architecture. For example, the entire system rested absolutely on the institution of marriage and the possession of an enterprise by every member of the younger generation. Peasant life in the Cosenza basin simply left no room for non-married persons outside the family. The 'single' could not be tolerated. The community and family jointly demanded of each member that he or she marry, unless there were physical or mental obstacles. The distinction between married and single, which is, in our society, simply a category of person, involved in the Cosentino genuine discrimination. The condition of an isolated single person came close to that of deviance. The individual could not acquire respectability except as a member of a family.

As long as he or she remained unmarried, the single person played a subordinate role in the family. The politics of the family made the single person the one to do the dirtiest work or to face the gravest risks. For example, the unmarried man was expected to face emigration, either short- or long-term, to take the blame in the case of judicial enquiries about a crime committed by another member of the same family. Even so, he rarely abandoned family life, at least in normal times. If he did so, social life became impossible. It would be a crazy act, half-way between anomie and deviance.[31] One of the neatest descriptions of the way families

---

[31] On the relationship between celibacy and deviance cf. C. Lévi-Strauss, *The Elementary Structures of Kinship*. Rev. ed. translated from the French by James Harle Bell, J. R. von Sturmer and Rodney Needham (Boston, 1969), pp. 38–41.

integrated their younger members is to be found in Corrado Alvaro's *Itinerario italiano*:

> The power of Calabria ... is in its family structure. The family is its vital thrust ... Other than that one could never grasp the parabola which each Calabrian of modest means passes through as he faces life ... while he needs to work alone, he creates responsibilities; without the weight of the family group he would see struggle as useless. If he stays alone and free to go where he likes, his fierce individualism which rises from his restless nature carries him to insane extremes. He needs the natural brake which family pressure provides. The family is the only means by which he can be settled in society.[32]

'Irregularity' or 'inconstancy' marked the lives of unmarried men and women who had to live in peasant society. Those 'without family' could not take part in the life of the community in the same way as the married. They lacked the possibility of reciprocal giving and receiving of favours and still less of cooperation, and became ever more marginal, excluded from the basic circuits of social life. Eventually they alienated themselves, becoming vagabonds, drunks or paupers.

The obligation to belong to a family in the traditional Cosentino was the obligation to run a farm or an enterprise. The economic distinction between self-employment and wage labour became a primary social category. Each individual or family which ceased to be able to run its own enterprise by ceasing to own land or hold tenancies lost status. It could no longer carry on the old relationships on a basis of social equality. The fall to the status of salaried persons ruined every member of the fallen family. Salaried labour on a permanent basis was the work of servants and dependants in the most literal sense of the word. What bearing arms had been for the free man in the middle ages, operation of the productive unit became for the traditional peasant of the Cosentino, the sign of full status in the community.

As the peasants saw it, just as there was no farm without family, so they could not imagine family without farm. It followed that the social system had no space for those without property and hence the propertyless, the salaried, simply could

---

[32] C. Alvaro, *Itinerario italiano*, p. 284.

not and did not exist. Where economic or natural disaster reduced a property-owning family to propertyless status, they became marginals, persons without rights, servants. Hence, 'without a farm' as a category coincided almost always with the group 'without family', who were not only the single but frequently the illegitimate.

The unmarried, the illegitimate, the wage labourer as categories were caught in a vicious circle. Rural proletariat could not, of course, marry, hence could not have a separate independent existence. Since relations of labour tended to coincide with family relations, the salaried person ended up by being included within a family but in the meanest domestic role, hence even further from that marriage which brought farm and family, and respectability. They ended up as farm-hands, domestics, slaughter-house porters and the like. Low-status job reinforced unmarried status and regularly led to more illegitimacy. This social fabric with its tightly knit strands is typical of much of the European countryside before modernisation. Karl Kautsky in *Die Agrarfrage* (The Agrarian Question) gave an analysis more than fifty years ago of the interconnection between family farm and the generation of rural deviance:

There are also the 'free' daily-wage earners who possess nothing and who pay rent to the peasant with whom they house, the *'Einlieger'* or 'hirelings', who sell their labour power where they can find a buyer. In some ways they are quite like the city proletariat but there are also profound differences. They form, to begin with, an appendage to the peasant family and, in a peasant's view, to live under another's roof is the very sign of dependency. Circumstances in the countryside do not favour procreation among landless labourers. The hired hand is by definition forbidden to marry. He cannot set up an independent household so raising a family is out of the question. Sexual drives do not therefore disappear but find outlets in unnatural ways in order to avoid children. If nature overcomes these artificial devices, the unhappy mother may be forced to go to extremes to rid herself of the unwanted offspring. She knows only too well why. Neither she nor her child has much to hope for in the future. Illegitimate children face the most unfavourable prospects. A large part of them die young and another, not inconsiderable, portion end in jail.[33]

[33] Karl Kautsky, *Die Agrarfrage. Eine Uebersicht über die Tendenzen der modernen Landwirtschaft und die Agrarpolitik der Sozialdemokratie* (Stuttgart, 1899), pp. 158–9.

The marriage of these deviants, social types specific to peasant society, only had to be formally forbidden in very rare cases. There existed a vast gamut of institutionalised procedures which made the peasant marriage into a 'total social fact', in the sense understood by anthropologists, that is, an economic, social, religious and even political act as a part of the politics of the family. This meant that for many marriage was unattainable. In the rural society of the Vale of Cosenza the arrangements of the dowry and the regulation of male inheritance were so complex and formalised that by themselves they automatically excluded all those not furnished with the requisite economic and social attributes. Betrothal was governed by ceremonial arrangements of the most minute and precise kind. It reflected on a smaller scale the ceremonial and contractual elements later to follow at the marriage proper. T. Tentori has described the ceremony of betrothal in Matera in the Basilicata, but it could have applied to the Cosentino before 1950 quite as easily:

> The official beginning of an engagement was symbolised by the giving of the ring. Before the official act, there had been the *parlamento* (the meeting) which always took place in the house of a neutral family, that is, related neither to the one nor the other party to the engagement. The parents of the two young people had to negotiate the agreement on the dowry and enumerate in writing with the help of a friend who was 'lettered' precisely what each family proposed to provide for the young couple. That document had the same function as the *capitoli* (marriage contracts) among the gentlefolk and was called the 'charter of the spinster' or the charter by which the dowry was established. In the contract the parties stipulated what the future husband and future wife were expected to provide. The girl would be expected to provide her own underclothes, her dresses, the sheets, bedcovers, mattresses and a linen chest. The future husband was expected to provide his own underclothes and some furniture. Besides ... he received from his parents tools, some seed and the rent for a grain-field for one year. A few days after the *parlamento*, there followed the *trasuta*, that is, the visit of the groom at the home of the bride and the presentation of the official engagement present. The *trasuta* was much more festive than the *parlamento* and involved the provision of wine and sweetmeats to the visitors. It was not uncommon that the betrothed met each other for the first time at the *trasuta* ... The day before the wedding, the relatives on both sides met and, with the charter in hand, verified that everything promised had in fact been fulfilled.[34]

[34] T. Tentori, *Antropologia economica* (Milan, 1974), pp. 492–3.

Dowry and inheritance were two central components of the process of reproduction of the family. They served to provide the new enterprise with the necessary capital and equipment to get started and to reinforce cohesion among families. But there was a snag. The very strictness of the regulations governing engagement and marriage, of dowry and inheritance, together with the norms governing farms, ended up by producing a contradiction within the system.

If the culture and the structure of the peasant social order in the Cosentino permitted no enterprises which were not families nor families which had no enterprises, it followed that the velocity, indeed the very maintenance, of the system was obstructed by the elaborateness of marriage requirements. The rigid limits of the marriageable produced the paradox that, while not everybody in the countryside could marry, life in the countryside unmarried was in fact impossible. The means by which the social order renewed itself generated a constant quota of the very deviants which it most wished to prevent. These persons, who might be called 'frictional' products of the social order, had no place in the intricate matrimonial strategies: the difficult, defective, illegitimate, lame, poor, servants, the excluded.

A peasant society as tightly knit as the Cosentino could only tolerate a limited number of such deviants and hence had to expel them. This gave rise to a particular form of emigration very different in kind from the grand transoceanic emigration which I shall talk about later. The 'frictionals' were pushed out onto the road and trickled toward the towns or along the well-trodden paths of rural homelessness. They had to be expelled lest they created social conflict or, which was the same thing, gave rise to a reserve labour force earning wages.

The diffusion of the market economy accelerated these tendencies. On the one hand, they shattered the delicate architecture of social reproduction in peasant society; on the other they forced that society to defend its structures by raising ever higher the social, economic and familial barriers which guaranteed social and economic stability. As the rules became more rigid, the number of frictionals grew. The obstacles to matrimony made emigration the only way out for the young man with no means. As Kautsky saw it in the German countryside of the 1890s,

In the countryside the foundation of an independent household or a family is only possible through the acquisition (by purchase or tenancy) of one's own independent agricultural enterprise. That is much more difficult where large land-holdings have developed and in such areas there is good reason to flee the land.

But even in areas where land has been divided into very small units, founding a household is difficult. For the agricultural wage-earner, farmhand or maidservant, it is nearly impossible to save up enough money. Such people are condemned to remain all their lives not merely propertyless but dependent hangers-on in other people's houses, forbidden to marry and have a family. Under such circumstances, only one way is open to them, the way to independence and freedom, which the defenders of home and hearth, the substantial pious peasant and the junker, deny them, and that is flight from the land.[35]

The principle of reciprocity

The 'laws' of the mode of family production have their limits. They can preserve peasant society against many of the most devastating effects of the penetration of the market economy. They can prevent the growth of social classes and class struggle. They cannot make men angels nor prevent the tendency toward antagonism among families. The inclinations toward the restricted interests of the family were given free rein, and the system of production was not adapted in itself to supply a general support to economic solidarity. The rural communities of the Cosentino were not ideal objects for romantic contemplation. In their midst there was no general harmony. Among the many cellular units which made them up, friction and conflict were inevitable and frequent. Eric Wolf argues that a certain dose of conflict acts in some small communities as an instrument of integration:

> Paralleling the mechanisms of control which are primarily economic in origin are psychological mechanisms like *institutionalised envy* which may find expression in various manifestations such as gossip, attacks of the evil eye or in the fear and practice of witchcraft ... Here, witchcraft as well as milder forms of institutionalised envy, have an integrative effect in restraining non-traditional behaviour as long as social relations suffer no serious disruption. It minimises disruptive phenomena such as

---

[35] Karl Kautsky, *Die Agrarfrage*, pp. 214–15.

economic mobility, abuse of ascribed power or individual conspicuous show of wealth. On the individual plane, it thus acts to maintain the individual in equilibrium with his neighbours. On the social plane it reduces the disruptive influences of outside society.[36]

These very socio-psychological mechanisms operated in the Cosentino but could neither eliminate nor diminish a fundamental fact: from the intrinsic character of the relations of the familial mode of production reigning in this type of society there emerged no obligation or need for sociality. The conditions of production, excluding the social division of labour as the basis of interfamilial social connection, furnished the conditions for a rather marked familial individualism whose disintegrative consequences, however, were restricted and repelled by a potent force for cohesion. That force was the principle of reciprocity, both economic and exogamic, which constituted the basis of collective solidarity in the Cosentino.

There was a real difference between the Cosentino and those societies undergoing the transformation to the market economy, such as that described by Marx in France in the middle of the nineteenth century. 'Thus the great mass of the French nation is formed through the simple addition of equal units, as a pile of potatoes fills out a potato sack.'[37] Nor was the Cosentino like the society of the great estates and atomised poor peasants described by Banfield as 'amoral familism'.[38] There appears to have been, in the traditional Cosentino, a life of relationships and cohesion which was extremely intense and marked by a complex system of exchange among its constituent units.

In such a society exchange manifested itself in the form of mutual gifts not commercial transactions. Nor did it have an exclusively nor essentially economic character. Once again we bump into one of those 'total social facts' whose significance is economic, social, legal, moral, utilitarian and sentimental. The aspects merge and cannot easily be separated, which is a sure sign of the importance of the phenomenon. Kinship, friendship

---

[36] Eric R. Wolf, 'Types of Latin American Peasantry. A Preliminary Discussion', *American Anthropologist*, LVII (1955), p. 460.
[37] Karl Marx, *Der 18. Brumaire des Louis Bonaparte*, Sammlung Insel (Berlin, 1960), p. 124.
[38] E. C. Banfield, *The Moral Basis*, pp. 10–11.

and neighbourliness were the social fluids through which reciprocity worked.

Some examples will illustrate the point. Families of equal standing would exchange days of work during the periods of pressure in the rural year, especially at harvest time. Marriages would take place between members of families on a balanced, mutual basis. The festivities on the occasion of the killing of a pig might be exchanged among families of equal standing. Invitations to visit, births, deaths, engagements, formal calls from house to house, were all moments for the exchange of courtesies and goods. The point to notice is that on every one of these occasions there was circulation either of goods or of labour in the guise of gifts more or less spontaneous: hours of labour, dowries, inheritances, food, drink, implements etc. Note too the ceremonial aspect as well as the non-economic implications.

Let us take the case of the slaughter of a pig, an event which revealed a basic assumption of traditional society in the Cosentino. Whereas property must never leave the family, food must be shared. Food must be shared in a way precisely regulated, collectively, and organised according to rituals of great formality:

> How could one not think of the slaughter of the family pig as a truly grand occasion, a kind of domestic liturgy? Not only the immediate family took part but relatives and friends expressly invited. January was, in any case, the month most suited to such gatherings, the most joyous month of the year, for the slaughters were very many and so were the invitations.
>
> The most vigorous and important of the guests would lay hold of the animal and immobilise it under the pressure of many hands: ears, tail, hooves, snout, anything and everything which gave a grip was seized solidly and voluptously held tight. The victim stretched and howled . . . stretched among the hands, arms and legs of the peasants, who were gripped by an orgiastic fury. The ceremony reached its height when the blood was spilt and the beast poured it out from the jugular vein . . . But it was not just to share in this splendid ceremony that the guests had come. The pig, torn into pieces, was stripped of the fatty parts and those which would not keep. These were then roasted and eaten amidst cries and utter confusion of hands and feet, pieces of flesh and children. Later, when the work of preparing the carcass had been done, they feasted on meat, bread and wine.[39]

---

[39] P. Trupia, *Ezzito. Uno studio d'ambiente nella Calabria nord-orientale* (Rome, 1961), pp. 24–5.

The slaughter of the family pig was but one of many such moments, part of a vast system of gift and counter-gift, which seemed to encompass the whole social, economic and personal life of Cosenza's peasants. Corrado Alvaro recalled it years later: 'When I was a lad in Calabria, I saw that all social life turned about these seasonal gifts: sending the first crops, gifts of fruit and of animals which went not only from neighbour to neighbour but from village to village.'[40] All of life for these peasants, as Marcel Mauss put it, 'was as if it were a perpetual giving and receiving, across a kind of current, uninterrupted and flowing in all directions, of gifts offered and received, reciprocated, obliged and with interest, to show greatness, to compensate for services rendered, as challenges, as pledges.'[41]

These gifts and counter-gifts were regulated by the obligation *to give*, *to receive* and *to repay* in a form which was apparently voluntary but in reality obligatory with the eventual sanction of private and public war.

Nobody was free to reject a gift or an alliance through marriage which had been offered him. The objects, courtesies, gifts, festivities, banquets which circulated within the channels of reciprocity, had to be repaid at once with equivalent goods. They could be accepted only on the tacit understanding that they would be repaid with counter-gifts whose value should at least equal that of those received and thus acquire the right in turn to expect repayment later with yet more goods.

Our 'obsolete' market economy finds this ceaseless flow of goods and gifts incomprehensible. Often the gifts exchanged were, in fact, of equal value and seemed to bring no material gain whatever. After all, the essence of market transactions is that they are carried out for gain only. Why exchange pieces of pork for pieces of pork, offered, moreover, at precisely the same ceremony? The answer is that it was this system which enabled the peasants of the Cosentino and central Calabria to avoid a Hobbesian chaos and to form a genuine society.

The constant movement of goods and services cannot be

---

[40] C. Alvaro, *Calabria* (Florence, 1931), p. 48.
[41] M. Mauss, *Sociologie et anthropologie* (Paris, 1950); Italian translation *Teoria generale della magia* (Turin, 1965), citations from Italian edition, p. 200.

understood outside the social context of which it is a basic part. As M.D. Sahlins observes in his 'Sociology of Primitive Exchange':

> What are in the received wisdom 'noneconomic' or 'exogenous' conditions are in the primitive reality the very organization of economy. A material transaction is usually a momentary episode in a continuous social relation. The social relation exerts governance: the flow of goods is constrained by, is part of, a status etiquette.[42]

Hence the entire economic system in a peasant society like the Cosentino can be said to be 'immersed' in the social system. All the characteristic features of economic life for the peasants of the Cosenza basin had a sociological and qualitative aspect. They lacked that general principle which marks a more developed economy that a thing must be paid for by an equivalent quantity. They lacked 'calculation', and sometimes appears to us stupid, but the stupidity of such deals rests on the assumptions of the outside observer. We expect economic exchanges to have certain rational features and we mistake what is primarily a social ritual for an economic act.

Yet the economic aspect is not missing; it is linked in a bilateral way to the social. It could be put this way. If a given social relationship determines certain economic exchanges, the economic exchanges condition the social relationships. The saying sums it up: 'If friends give gifts, gifts make friends.' Corrado Alvaro writes: 'These are the signs which initiate friendship and adoptive kinship (*comparaggio*) . . . Nor should you imagine that you can remain indifferent to gifts which have been offered . . . The means by which you conquer a person could be the subject of a little treatise on primitive courtesy.'[43] The overwhelming majority of exchanges between family farms in the traditional Cosentino had that aim. They were attempts to guarantee or initiate social relations. This is the more important because the community lacked other means of integration. The atomism of the family unit weakened ties of solidarity, as we have seen, but there is no real infrastructure in the modern sense.

---

[42] Marshall D. Sahlins, 'On the Sociology of Primitive Exchange', *Stone Age Economics* (Chicago, 1972), pp. 185–6.
[43] C. Alvaro, *Itinerario italiano*, pp. 285–6.

... persons and (especially) groups confront each other not merely as distinct interests but with the possible inclination and certain right to physically prosecute these interests. Force is decentralized, legitimately held in severalty, the social compact has yet to be drawn, the state nonexistent. So peacemaking is not a sporadic intersocietal event, it is a continuous process going on within society itself. Groups must 'come to terms' – the phrase notably connotes a material exchange satisfactory on both sides.[44]

Peasant society in the Cosentino was a segmented society, in which there were only extremes. People approached each other in a strange state of mind ..' of fear and exaggerated aggressiveness and with a generosity likewise much exaggerated ... trusting entirely or distrusting entirely; laying down their arms and renouncing magic or giving their all: from fleeting hospitality to the offer of daughters or goods. In such a state man has given up his own status and depends entirely on exchange, on giving and receiving.'[45] Hence social relations were rendered stable, and peasants preferred the festivity and the acts of exchange to war and to isolation within their little domestic groups.

It is, perhaps, easier to see now why Cosentine peasants were prepared to put aside such a proportion of their goods for the circulation of gifts, festivities and reciprocal loans. 'He who eats alone chokes', says the old proverb. Even in cases where discernible economic motives pushed the individual toward economically determined exchange of goods or services, the operation was never carried out in entirely economic terms. Even when the exchange appeared in the form of an unsolicited gift, a pure act of giving governed by the unwritten laws of generalised reciprocity, there was always an extra-economic dimension. Offers and counter-offers circulate according to the laws of 'balanced reciprocity':

'Balanced reciprocity' refers to direct exchange. In precise balance, the reciprocation is the customary equivalent of the thing received and is without delay. Perfectly balanced reciprocity, the simultaneous exchange of the same types of goods to the same amounts, is not only

[44] Marshall D. Sahlins, 'On the Sociology of Primitive Exchange', pp. 186–7.
[45] M. Mauss, *Teoria generale della magia*, pp. 289–90.

conceivable but ethnographically attested in certain marital transactions. 'Balanced reciprocity' may be more loosely applied to transactions which stipulate returns of commensurate worth or utility within a finite and narrow period. Much 'gift-exchange,' many 'payments,' much that goes under the ethnographic head of 'trade' and plenty that is called 'buying–selling' and involves 'primitive money' belong in the genre of balanced reciprocity.[46]

Balanced reciprocity was well understood consciously by the members of each peasant community. Matrimonial exchanges of the type we have seen were regulated by it. Goods of the same type and quality were exchanged and verified. The field of action of the principle of reciprocity was vast and existed as a separate, definable category of action which governed both individual and collective behaviour. There was even a word for it, sure sign of its importance as a conscious principle of social control: *la ritenna*. P. Trupia in his study of an individual Calabrian village found *la ritenna* at work almost everywhere:

If you asked what the term meant, they would reply: 'If we don't help one another, how shall we manage to live?' So you work *a ritenna*, you give or receive gifts *a ritenna*. It is something different and more fundamental than barter. Barter, after all, presupposes the immediate disponibility of actual goods and can take place with the first person you meet at almost any time or place. *La ritenna* presupposes instead the existence of cordial relations among the parties, without which the pledges given and received could not be maintained.

There are basic economic activities in which all families participate but there are a few specific to individual families, and these make it possible to operate *la ritenna*. A few families have herds of sheep; a few have oxen; a few have grain-fields more extended than the others and, at certain times of year, extra hands. By means of *la ritenna* all enjoy these goods. He who has a lot of hay to bale calls on him who has time to help. He who needs to carry a wounded man on a stretcher or carry a corpse can easily find seven men willing to help, silently obliging himself to carry seven future loads. So everything circulates and all benefit.[47]

These are not market exchanges in the usual sense of the word. They relieve all the actors in this microcosm of the functions of securing and maintaining social cohesion. The *ritenna* is the

[46] Marshall D. Sahlins, 'On the Sociology of Primitive Exchange', pp. 194–5.
[47] P. Trupia, *Ezzito*, pp. 26–7.

thread which runs through the fabric. What would otherwise be a world of Leibnizian monads without doors or windows is transformed into a social order. The knowing game of exchange consists in a complex agglomeration of moves, some conscious, some less so, directed at transforming antagonism into alliance, hostility into cooperation, feud into matrimony.

Negative reciprocity and the crisis of the family-enterprise

Stable relations with the land, family-enterprises, and the principle of reciprocity formed the stitches in a tightly knit network of social relations. The social whole was held together by a network which tied it together at many levels over and over again. Violence was the last resort, the ultimate sanction against those who transgressed against the basic norms of the sub-culture. It was not, as in the 'ideal type' of southern agrarian system described at the beginning of the chapter, an essential element of social integration. Authoritarianism of the state, *clientela* or family was superfluous. There was no need for a coagulant to force society together from outside.

Nevertheless, peasant society in the Cosentino showed itself extremely sensitive to subversive influences from outside. It turned out to be vulnerable to the historical penetration of the market. The attempt to gain control of the self-sufficient peasant community by market forces took two forms. In the first the 'balanced reciprocity' of traditional society was overturned and replaced by 'negative reciprocity'; in the second the reproductive mechanism of the family farm was broken.

As we have seen, reciprocity covered an entire class of exchanges. As Sahlins puts it, there is also a reverse kind of reciprocity, which he calls 'negative':

'Negative reciprocity' is the attempt to get something for nothing with impunity, the several forms of appropriation, transactions opened and conducted toward net utilitarian advantage. Indicative ethnographic terms include 'haggling' or 'barter,' 'gambling,' 'chicanery,' 'theft,' and other varieties of seizure.

Negative reciprocity is the most impersonal sort of exchange. In guises such as 'barter' it is from our own point of view the 'most economic.' The participants confront each other as opposed interests, each looking to maximize utility at the other's expense. Approaching the transaction with an eye singular to the main chance, the aim of the opening party, or of both parties, is the unearned increment. One of the most sociable forms, leaning toward balance, is haggling conducted in the spirit of 'what the traffic will bear.' From this, negative reciprocity ranges through various degrees of cunning, guile, stealth, and violence to the finesse of a well-conducted horse raid. The 'reciprocity' is, of course, conditional again, a matter of defense of self-interest. So the flow may be one-way once more, reciprocation contingent upon mustering countervailing pressure or guile.[48]

In the primitive societies described by Sahlins, negative reciprocity normally worked against outsiders to the tribal group, against those alien to 'the world of men', represented by the community in which one lived. It had, thus, the effect of strengthening the internal ties and reinforcing balanced and general reciprocity within the community. It encouraged a system of double morality, one for use within and one for the foreigner.

In the Cosenza basin and the high valleys of the Crati, and presumably in many rural communities of the Mezzogiorno, the unification of Italy began with a heavy dose of negative reciprocity. The new state led to large-scale fraud, usurpation and violence. Commons were unjustly seized. Church land was grabbed and sold for gain. The space within which traditional reciprocity had operated became narrower. Individuals began to act independently of the prevailing norms. Quick gains without communal advantage tore holes in the fabric of society. Members of the community were now tempted, forced perhaps, to practise double morality, not on outsiders but on each other. This, in turn, further liquidated old ties and led to further reprisals, feuds and violence.

Many family farms lost land by expropriation. The intense and integrated social–economic hierarchy shattered. All the old institutions crumbled. Respectable families could not provide for their children. The sons became *braccianti*. Sometimes they earned more than their fathers, which eroded the old hierarchy of authority. They rebelled against the old ways, now apparently senseless and rigid. They assaulted parental authority. Daughters no longer married by age. Suddenly there were young single

---

[48] Marshall D. Sahlins, 'On the Sociology of Primitive Exchange', p. 195.

men in the village with money. Sexual attraction, 'love', replaced the older system of *rispetto*. Institutions like dowries, *parlamento*, *trasuta* went on; indeed, paradoxically in a spasm of self-defence, the old families clung to them ever more fiercely. Yet their internal logic had lost purchase. In fact, they frequently worked against the interests of the family-undertaking and led to impoverishment, debts and sometimes ruin. The delicate economic equilibrium had been jarred and the institutions now gave rise to endless litigation and quarrel, because the units could no longer carry out the promises. The normative and the practical had split. Out of the tension between what ought to be and what was, a new social institution grew up: *la fuiuta* or 'flight', that is, an elopement in which the young couple simply went off, spent at least one night together and confronted their families with the fact. This 'short cut' had great economic and social advantages for hard-pressed peasant families. It presented all concerned with a *fait accompli*; face and *rispetto* were, more or less, preserved and much money saved. *La fuiuta* was an adaptation to a new reality. It avoided the long ritual, the heavy burden and the mutual responsibilities. It also meant that the young couple began life much, much poorer than their parents had done.

Institutions torn from their context, social roles undermined and destroyed, were the fruits of the unified state and its liberal market economy. Something very like it happened, of course, elsewhere in the Mezzogiorno. The astonishing difference between the Cosentino and other areas of the south was its powers of recovery. The reaction in the Cosentino was so intense that within a cycle of thirty years it led to a nearly complete reconstitution of the traditional social and economic order. This remarkable recovery distinguished this area and requires yet deeper explanation.

When market forces hit the valley of the Crati, they met a society without painless means to expand production nor to engage in large-scale commercial farming. Hence the money economy led to an extremely violent reaction. The Cosentino could be destroyed, broken in its fundamental features, blown up, but it could not be made to adapt gradually. It could not be slowly 'opened' to the market. There was no line of development from self-sufficiency to production for market.[49] This is the single most important difference between the Cosentino and the 'society in permanent transition' of the Plain of Gioia Tauro. As we shall see in the next chapter, the wounds opened in that society in the nineteenth century never healed. The clash between market forces and peasant society separated forever the family from the farm.

The reaction of the society of the Cosentino was, from the beginning, much more global. The Cosentino was an 'all or nothing' proposition. The wounds healed. The social groups threatened by the disintegration of the market turned to rebuild the economic foundations of their world. The fundamental instrument in this process was emigration.

Emigration

The great wave of emigration carried the peasants of the Cosentino to North and South America. It began in the last two decades of the nineteenth century and continued up to the First World War. Its protagonist was the individual peasant, solidly anchored in the culture and society of his traditional community, who, in spite of his own efforts, had been pried loose from the community and forced into economic exile. The new state began to take taxes equal to as much as 25 per cent of peasant income. It drafted the sons for its military service when they were at the most productive ages. The common lands of the Sila mountains and the goods of the ecclesiastical establishment had been sold to private persons. Possession and management of the traditional family-farming unit became more and more difficult for more and more peasant families.[50]

The culture resisted. Economic conditions might worsen. Individuals might be separated from the system of family-enterprise. Families lost farms and farms were stripped from

---

[49] On the relationship between the market and pre-industrial societies, cf. K. Polanyi, *Primitive, Archaic and Modern Economies*, ed. G. Dalton (New York, 1968).

[50] R. Ciasca, 'Le trasformazioni agrarie in Calabria dopo l'Unità', *Atti del I Congresso Storico Calabrese* (Rome, 1957), pp. 357–74.

families. The material basis of Cosentino society was threatened, but there was no parallel crisis of culture.

All the resources of traditional society were mobilised to resist the new threats. The first opposition was frontal. The peasants took to the hills and turned into the famous 'brigands' who made life so difficult for the new administrators. When after the defeat of the brigands it became evident that reconstitution was impossible by political and military means, attempts to emigrate began, at first very tentative, then with increasing confidence.

> At first only the most ardent emigrated, those who earlier would have stalked the Sila as brigands. You might even say that brigandage was destroyed less by the government troops than by America. Besides, the hunt for the last 'Kings of the Sila' was so brutal and relentless that many were persuaded that it was more convenient, bearing in mind the dangers and the benefits, to take a chance on America than on the woods.[51]

It was the very nature of Cosentine communities, based as they were on reciprocity and the family farm, which gave the individuals who wanted to emigrate their chance. The system of reciprocal exchange made it far easier in the Cosentino than elsewhere to raise the passage money and to acquire the kit needed before going away. Traditional institutions supported the non-traditional activity in traditional ways and made possible an ever larger stream of expatriates. The flow of departing people was composed not only of the marginal figures who managed autonomously to scramble their money together but of young men and women fully integrated into the communal systems. They used the 'obligations' implicit in the system to raise passage money, *il peculio*.

If the family and reciprocity 'reinforced' emigration, emigration actually reinforced recriprocity and the family-enterprise. Marriage, family, kinship, friendship, exchanges were not weakened but strengthened by emigration. Contrary to what one might expect and, indeed, what one finds in other types of emigration, the rate of marriage did not fall during the years of

---

[51] L. A. Caputo, 'Di alcune questioni economiche della Calabria', *Il giornale degli economisti*, no. 2, 1907, p. 1175.

heaviest emigration.[52] To some extent, marriage was 'used' as a way of acquiring the necessary means and money to be able to emigrate but, more profoundly, marriage became the pledge of inclusion in traditional society by those about to embark on the great adventure of long years away from home. It reaffirmed the commitment of those who left and of those who stayed behind. Observers at the time noticed the phenomenon and described it:

For some time in the Italian Mezzogiorno and especially in Calabria, a new tendency has been spreading ... the men who have decided to go off to America, who are for the most part between 20 and 35 years of age, give a ring to the woman of their choice a month or so, sometimes only fifteen days, before facing the great ocean crossing. Many influences would appear to be working to produce this abnormal phenomenon. My personal enquiry leads me to believe that, together with the attractiveness of a small dowry which will produce the hotly desired *peculio*, there is the other motive, the desire to leave at home, in the native village, a secure correspondent to whom to address and entrust one's savings. So too those who remain home and have not yet married hurry to get married themselves.[53]

The essential element to bear in mind to explain the 'abnormal custom' is the way it reinforced reciprocity. It was the process by which the emigrant integrated himself into the community and bound himself to it. Hence emigration from the *Gemeinschaft* of peasants in the Cosentino became a way of restabilising the economic and social bases of a threatened society.

Emigration became an undertaking of limited duration. Its spirit was embodied in the transformation of reciprocity while maintaining its character. The individual emigrated to preserve or improve his position within the traditional hierarchy of the community of origin, not to better himself by the standards of the place to which he was going. He married because he thought of his expatriation as purely temporary. The point of reference remained the village.

This was their place, the place where it would be good to live if only one had the money. The new 'host' society was inferior in their eyes except for one point: that one could work and earn money there. For that

---

[52] D. Taruffi, L. de Nobili and C. Lori, *La questione agraria e l'emigrazione in Calabria* (Florence, 1908), pp. 123–30; L. A. Caputo, 'Di alcune questioni', p. 1179.
[53] D. Taruffi et al., *La questione agraria*, pp. 125–6.

reason the emigrant thought of his time abroad as temporary. It would last only as long as it might take to earn enough to re-enter society in the old place, to realise himself in the old society. The host society was alien. He never understood it or its values. He merely adjusted to it because he was forced to do so by economic necessity ...

The idea was to 'raid' the host society of its wealth for as long as was necessary to become rich oneself and to be esteemed on one's return. This type of emigration took the place in modern times of the plundering campaign of an earlier day.[54]

Evidence of the temporary character of emigration can be found in the official statistics. The figures show that the emigrants were overwhelmingly individual males in early manhood. Approximately 75 per cent of those who emigrated took no family with them, and the percentage of those who returned was correspondingly high. According to the study made by L.A. Caputo published in 1907 in the *Giornale degli economisti*, based on a village-by-village study of every community in the province of Cosenza, the percentage of those who returned for the period 1890 to 1905 amounted to about three quarters of those who had emigrated. For Italy as a whole the figure was about half. As Caputo summed it up,

Looking at the phenomenon of migration as a whole, as well as in the individual villages, I have noticed that, if the emigrant takes his family with him, he is most unlikely to return. Vice versa, it is hard not to return if he has left his family.

But I never supposed that there would be a correspondence between the percentage of women who emigrate and the numbers of men who do not return. The percentage of women to the total number of emigrants remained more or less constant throughout the period 1880 to 1905 at about 25 per cent. So from my hypothesis, from the figures, from direct observation I have come to the conclusion that our emigrants in general come back. Those who take wives with them when they leave or marry someone from home when they get to America do not return: that is, the non-returnees equal the number of women who emigrate, roughly 25 per cent.[55]

The Cosentino had an unusually high percentage of returnees. This was partly due to the relatively brief time spent in North America. F.S. Nitti, the southern economist and later prime

[54] F. Alberoni and G. Baglioni, *L'integrazione dell'immigrato nella società industriale* (Bologna, 1965), pp. 212–13.
[55] L. A. Caputo, 'Di alcune questioni', p. 1171.

minister, wrote of this aspect in his famous enquiry into the conditions of peasants in the Basilicata and Calabria which he carried out in the years 1906 to 1910: 'Emigration has lost its quasi-dramatic character. People come and go from America with the greatest ease ... The peasants are not going to an unknown place. Many have been three or four times. They go; they come back and then go again.'[56] The available studies, both Italian and American, confirm that view. The average length of residence in the USA was about three years, followed by a period in the home village of between three and five years.[57]

The Cosentino is in some ways very unusual but, as far as the temporary quality of emigration goes, it is quite characteristic of other areas and of Italian emigration as a whole. It was not characteristic of the other ethnic groups who made their way from central, southern and eastern Europe in increasing numbers during the years 1870 to 1914. R.F. Foerster wrote a study of Italian emigration which was published after the First World War in which he tried to explain it. As he put it,

> Between 1860 and 1880, as the fresh arrivals increased, the immigration assumed a much more definite character. Where before there had been individuals there were now types and classes. From small beginnings the contingent from South Italy had swelled to substantial proportions. After 1870, for the first time, it became evident that, following a somewhat indeterminate stay, many repacked their chattels and went home again. No previous immigrants into this land of promise had done that![58]

The 'birds of passage syndrome' was the name commonly given to the behaviour of the typical young labourer from the Italian south, here today, gone tomorrow. There was none of the usual commitment to 'make a new life' which marked other

---

[56] F. S. Nitti, *Inchiesta sulle condizioni dei contadini in Basilicata e Calabria* (2 vols., Bari, 1968), vol. I, p. 154.

[57] F. S. Nitti, *Inchiesta*, chap. 7; R. F. Foerster, *The Italian Emigration of Our Time* (Cambridge, Mass., 1919), chap. 2; T. Kessner, *The Golden Door. Italian and Jewish Immigrant Mobility in New York City, 1880–1915* (New York, 1977), pp. 26–39.

[58] R. F. Foerster, *The Italian Emigration*, p. 324; B. Boyd Caroli, *Italian Repatriation from the United States, 1900–14* (New York, 1973), chap. 2; G. Florenzano, *Dell' emigrazione italiana in America* (Naples, 1874), p. 289; L. Carpi, *Delle colonie e dell'emigrazione d'italiani all'estero* (Milan, 1874), vol. I, p. 75.

groups. He came to earn as much as possible as quickly as possible. Once in America he took the heaviest and most precarious work, which others shunned. Accustomed to a very low standard of living, he survived on the barest minimum. Foerster quotes an account of Italians in New York in 1907:

'Men, women, dogs, cats, and monkeys eat and sleep together in the same hole without air and without light.' They buy stale beer at two cents a pint from a rascally Italian in a basement, and they break into endless brawls. During the summer they work on the railroads and in the fields; 'in the winter they return to fill the streets of New York, where the boys are bootblacks and the men either are employed at the most repulsive tasks, scorned by workmen of other nationalities – carrying offal to the ships and dumping it in the sea, cleaning the sewers *et similia* – or they go about with sacks on their shoulders rummaging the garbage cans, gleaning paper, rags, bones, broken glass' ...

'And while the workmen fag from morning to evening, the bosses smoke tranquilly and superintend them with rifles at their sides and revolvers at their belts. They seem – and are – real brigands.' Whoever tells these natives of Avellino, of the Abruzzi, of Basilicata, that they are being cheated, loses his words. '*Signorino,*' they reply, 'we are ignorant and do not know English. Our boss brought us here, knows where to find work, makes contracts with the companies. What should we do without him?' The Camorra flourishes as in the worst Bourbon times and 'the Italian, illiterate, carrying the knife, defrauded and fraudulent, is more despised than the Irish and the Chinese.'[59]

It is well to remember that it was not only young men integrated into village society at home and bent on returning who emigrated. A certain quota of emigrants came from the 'frictional' types we mentioned earlier: single salaried workers, illegitimate sons and daughters, rebels, deviants, criminals, peasant families 'declassed' by sudden impoverishment, all sorts and conditions of outsiders, sometimes with considerable cash in hand. What they had in common was the fact that society had no place for them. In effect, they had been expelled.

It is impossible to furnish figures for this category. This group distinguished itself from the others in only one evident respect: the lack of desire to return. For these were the people for whom the village had few charms and evoked no nostalgia. By contrast with the 'birds of passage', their American adventure took place

---

[59] R. F. Foerster, *The Italian Emigration*, p. 326.

without the safety net in case of failure. From this there developed a strong urge to assimilate to American society, marked even in the old world by a kind of 'anticipatory socialisation'.[60] It is reasonable to assume that even of those who for various reasons stayed, settled and prospered in America, the deviants made up only a small segment, but they were certainly there and influenced the early history of the Italo-American permanent community.[61] The deviants appear to have been the first to seek entrepreneurial activities, to have entered politics, founded businesses and organised crime. Within a short period they had grabbed the leadership of the community.[62] It is striking, if you read the biographies of first generation Italo-American politicians or businessmen or of the founders of the mafia 'families' how often there is clear evidence of some 'break' with traditional society which led to the decision to emigrate. Sometimes the break was personal, sometimes it arose out of a conflict between or within kinship networks, or with the law or the state. The progressive assimilation of the Italian-American community into the mainstream of American life was much coloured by the high proportion of such men amongst its leaders, often fierce and unscrupulous types who during the 1920s and 1930s made the first breaches in the isolation of the Italo-American community and became the first examples of social mobility.[63]

The effect of emigration on the Cosentino was from a demographic point of view rather modest. The high level of returnees ensured that the population went through only temporary fluctuations, as, for example, during the years of most massive

[60] On the concept of 'anticipatory socialisation', see F. Alberoni and G. Baglioni, *L'integrazione dell'immigrato*, chap. 2, p. 77.
[61] The sheer scale of the exodus of migrants was so great that in spite of the fact that the quota of emigrants who remained in the new world only amounted to a third of all emigrants from Italy in the years 1867–1914, the migratory movement generated an ethnic community which by 1911, according to Foerster, amounted already to four million two hundred thousand persons, more than two thirds of whom came from the regions of the Italian south.
[62] W. F. White, *Street Corner Society* (Chicago, 1943).
[63] D. Bell, 'Crime as an American Way of Life', *The End of Ideology* (New York, 1965), pp. 127–50; H. Nelli, *The Italians of Chicago. A Study in Ethnic Mobility* (New York, 1933); A. De Conde, *Half Bitter, Half Sweet. An Excursion into Italian American History* (New York, 1970).

movement before the First World War.[64] The birth rate fell sharply but only for brief periods and the sharp fall in rates of mortality brought about by improvements in sanitation and the gradual rise in the standard of nourishment caused the population of the Cosentino to grow even during the years 1871 to 1911 by some 20 per cent.[65]

The reconstitution of the socio-economic system of the Cosentino did not remain merely a dream of the emigrants. Emigration was not one of many ineffective or more or less desperate devices tried by the peasants to restore the old equilibrium. Emigration made it possible to restore the essential economic cells of the old system and, by reconstituting on new bases the ties of reciprocity and by reaffirming the central importance of the family, the family-enterprise itself could be rebuilt. After two or three periods in the USA, say, some ten to fifteen years, the emigrant would have enough savings to realise 'the hope which first drove him across the ocean', that is, the rejoining of family and farming unit.

> The first thing is the house which he buys or constructs. Every village in the province has a group of new houses, clean and spacious, which stand out by contrast with the filthy, narrow old huts in the place, for these are the houses of the *'americani'* ...
> Once he has the house, he emigrates again and saves for the completion of the great hope, for the idea which contains the whole world of our peasants: to become the owner of a piece of land.[66]

The development of emigration was accompanied by the growth and formation on a large scale of new larger family-farming units. Each census recorded an increase in the average size of the family in the Cosentino, which grew from 4.2 members in 1901, to 4.4 by 1911 and to 4.8 by 1921. The emigrants finally and definitively back from America gave the main thrust to this movement, which after the First World War became so marked that a special government enquiry into the growth of the small property-owning peasantry was carried out by the *Istituto Nazionale di Economia Agraria*. The enquiry showed that there had

---

[64] V. Bruno, 'La diffusione territoriale delle migrazioni', *Rivista italiana di economia, demografia e statistica*, nos. 1–2, 1960.
[65] See Table 13, p. 68.
[66] A. Serpieri, *La struttura sociale*, p. 164.

been a transfer of property to the *americani* of almost two million hectares. These pieces of territory had been acquired by the peasants for cash. They appeared to the investigators to be capable of sustaining a stable agricultural activity, giving rise to an increase both in productivity and in intensity of cultivation.[67]

[67] INEA, *Inchiesta sulla piccola proprietà coltivatrice formatasi nel dopoguerra*, vol. II, *Calabria*, ed. E. Blandini (Rome, 1931), pp. 52–4.

2

The society of permanent transition of the Plain of Gioia Tauro

The Plain of Gioia Tauro covers a surface area of 587 square kilometres and includes the territory of 19 *comuni* with a population of 123,926 in the year 1951. Its demographic and territorial proportions are slightly more ample than those of the Cosentino and its density of population is also slightly higher (235 as opposed to 221 inhabitants per square kilometre).[1]

One can certainly assert that the similarity between these two important areas of Calabria, at least for the period under consideration here, stops at that point. As we shall see in the course of this chapter, the Plain of Gioia Tauro presents an economic system, a set of social relationships and a diachronic movement of its fundamental variables which is completely different and, in many respects, opposed to that which we have noted in the Cosentino.

Let us begin by examining the type of dynamic in the demography of the Plain in the ninety years preceding 1950 and then let us compare it with the situation in the Cosentino and in Calabria in general. From Table 13 and from Figure 2 we can observe a noticeable irregularity within the general growth trend by comparison with the trends of the other two regions where growth was weaker but steadier.

The average annual rate of demographic increment stayed at a

---

[1] The *comuni* of the Plain of Gioia Tauro are those listed under Zone XXII in the ISTAT classification and are: Anoia, Candidoni, Cinquefrondi, Cittanova, Feroleto della Chiesa, Galatro, Giffone, Gioia Tauro, Laureana di Borello, Maropati, Melicucco, Polistena, Rizziconi, Rosarno, San Giorgio Morgeto, San Pietro di Caridà, Serrata, Taurianova, Varapodio.

Table 13 *Population present in the Plain of Gioia Tauro, the Cosentino and Calabria from 1861 to 1951*

	1861	variation	1871	variation	1881	variation
Plain of Gioia Tauro	60,867	100	68,775	113	71,270	117
Cosentino	65,545	100	64,194	98	66,284	101
Calabria	1,140,396	100	1,206,302	106	1,257,883	110

	1901	variation	1911	variation	1921	variation
Plain of Gioia Tauro	86,177	141	97,273	160	110,247	181
Cosentino	74,416	113	78,190	119	82,983	127
Calabria	1,370,208	120	1,402,151	123	1,512,381	133

	1931	variation	1936	variation	1951	variation
Plain of Gioia Tauro	123,459	203	116,651	192	131,837	217
Cosentino	93,887	143	100,509	153	123,926	189
Calabria	1,668,954	146	1,721,077	151	1,982,473	174

Source: ISTAT, *Censimenti della popolazione*

level in the Plain superior to that in the Cosentino and Calabria for the entire period from 1861 to 1921. Ten-year averages often exceeded 1 per cent and there were periodic strong jumps, as, for example, from 0.4 per cent for the decade 1871–81 to 1.3 per cent for the twenty years between 1901–21.

For the entire arc 1861 to 1951 we can distinguish three fundamental phases. The first covered the twenty years im-

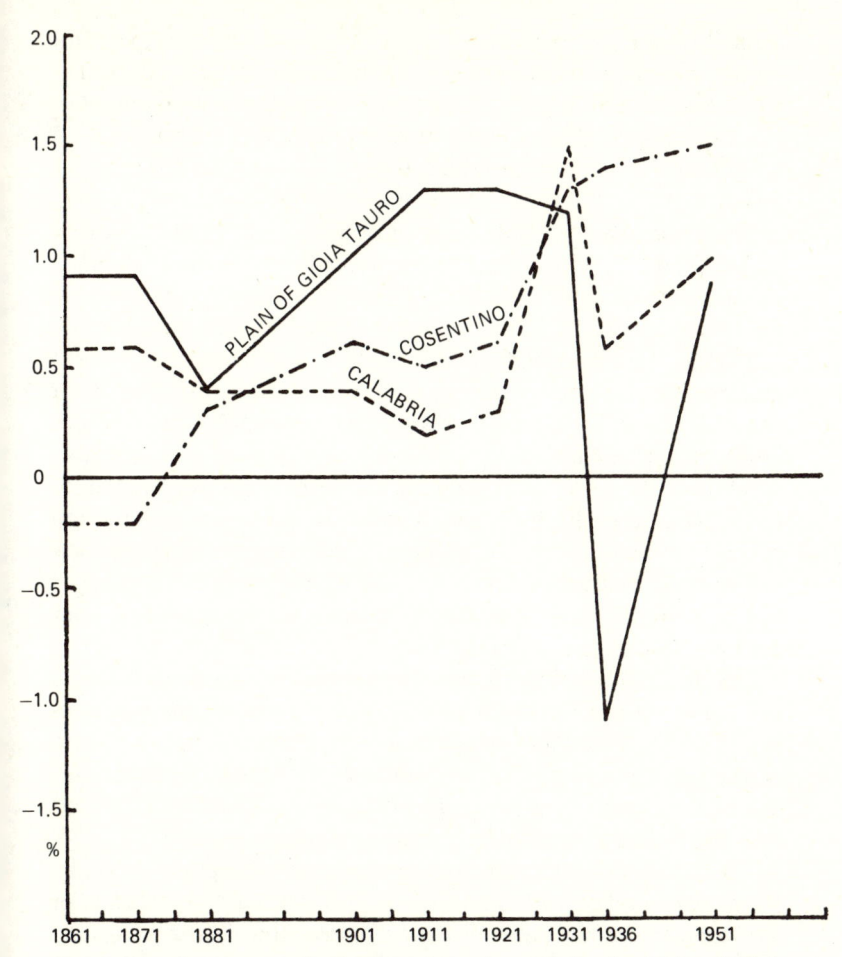

Fig. 2 Population growth in percentages by year for the Plain of Gioia Tauro, the Cosentino and Calabria

mediately following unification and was marked by an average increment which was rather weak. The population of the Plain grew at a rhythm of 0.6 per cent per annum by comparison with a nearly analogous regional pattern and complete stagnation in the Cosentino, which, indeed, saw the absolute amount of its population diminish in the first decade.

The second phase went from 1881 to 1931 and was characterised by a rhythm of increase more than double (1.5 per cent annual rate of growth over the entire half century but 3 per cent to 4 per cent in certain years) as opposed to a regional movement of population growth and a local movement in the Cosentino which were much weaker (respectively 0.6 per cent and 0.8 per cent per annum).

The third phase was the most complicated. It began in the first half of the 1930s with a sharp inversion of the preceding tendency to increase and which led in the Plain to an absolute decrease in the total population. The population of the Plain fell from 123,000 in 1931 to 116,000 in 1936, that is, a rate of decrease of 1.1 per cent per annum. In the same quinquennium the Cosentino went through one of its sharpest upward movements (1.4 per cent per annum) while Calabria as a whole experienced a discernible slowing of its rate of demographic increase. In the second half of the 1930s and in the 1940s the Plain of Gioia Tauro recovered the preceding demographic flexibility and returned to a level of +0.9 per cent per annum. By now it had been surpassed in respect of rate of growth by the Cosentino and Calabria (respectively 1.5 per cent and 1 per cent annually over the period 1936 to 1951).

On the most general level, the reasons for such an atypical demographic evolution are to be sought in the particular physiognomy of the economic structure of the Plain. For more than a century it constituted, in fact, the 'richest' zone of Calabria and one of the zones of the Mezzogiorno most profoundly integrated into the national and international market for goods.[2]

The Plain of Gioia Tauro is characterised by the presence on its territory of a relative diversification of productive activities and of 'an intensive agriculture for export', according to the classification of Rossi-Doria.[3] The domain of the fruit tree and the market gardener contrasts with 'naked' Mezzogiorno of extensive agriculture and of the cereal–pastoral economy of the Ionian slopes as

---

[2] U. Caldora, 'La "Statistica" murattiana del Regno di Napoli: le relazioni sulla Calabria', *Quaderni di geografia umana per la Sicilia e la Calabria*, no. 5, 1960, pp. 9–113; G. Pasquale, 'Relazione sullo stato fisico–economico–agrario della Prima Calabria Ulteriore', *Atti del Reale Istituto di Incoraggiamento delle Scienze Naturali* (Naples, 1863) sections I and XI; F. Arcà, *Calabria vera. Appunti statistici ed economici della provincia di Reggio Calabria* (Reggio Calabria, 1907).

[3] M. Rossi-Doria, 'Struttura e problemi', pp. 31–6.

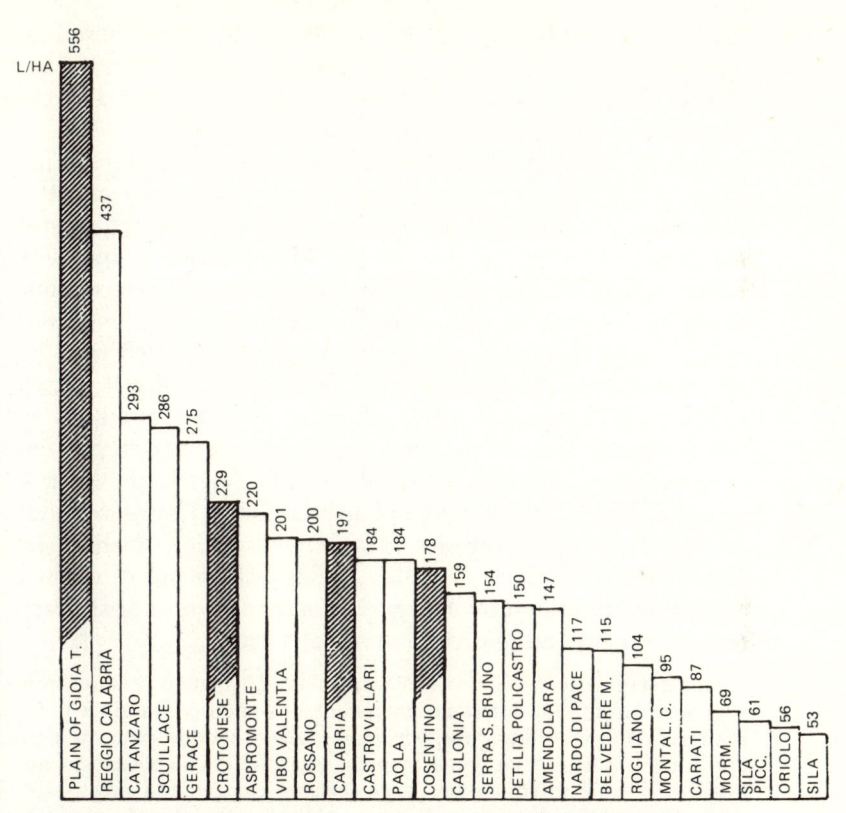

Fig. 3 Distribution of agricultural zones in Calabria by taxable yield per hectare cultivated measured in lire per hectare (L/HA)
Source: INEA, *Inchiesta sulla distribuzione della proprietà fondiaria in Italia*, Rome, 1948

much as it contrasts with the peasant agriculture of autoconsumption of the internal valleys.

In a ranking of the types of agrarian zones into which Calabria has been divided by ISTAT and INEA, carried out according to the criteria of quantity of taxable income yielded by hectare of cultivated surface, the Plain of Gioia Tauro occupied the top place with a yield of 566 lire per hectare, three times higher than the corresponding average regional amount, more than three times the values registered in the Cosentino and more than twice that recorded in the territory of the *latifondo* of the Crotonese (see Figure 3). Although the Plain of Gioia Tauro represents only 7 per cent of the productive surface of the region, it produces 20 per cent of the agricultural income of all of Calabria.[4]

The development of specialised commercial agriculture in the Plain took place in the main during the first twenty years after unification. It followed the same rhythms as the impressive reconversion of production in the Mezzogiorno countryside which took place after the fall of the ancient protective economic apparatus of the Bourbon kingdom. Between 1860 and 1880 intensive southern agriculture was suddenly inserted into the world market by the free-trade policies of the new state. It reacted to the great demand for olive oil, wine and citrus products by specialising in these crops. Land area devoted to such crops went up five times, involving almost 850,000 hectares in the Mezzogiorno of which 150,000 were in Calabria alone.[5] The initiative for this transformation, 'the one, great transformation of which the Mezzogiorno has been capable', as Rossi-Doria put it, did not arise only from the rural bourgeoisie or land-owning aristocracy but from many, more diverse strata of society:

> The first move to develop new plantations and irrigation systems came sometimes from a local trader or merchant, or sometimes from the petty bourgeois and middling bourgeois land-owners, who leapt at the new opportunities. These bourgeois owners, as so often in the Mezzogiorno, lived in the big towns or the larger coastal villages and practised a profession in a desultory way. They reread the finer print in old contracts and demanded improvements on their property from their tenants. Occasionally the lust for gain pushed them to pay for the improvements themselves, at their risk. Very often – and this was especially true of the vineyards and market gardens – it was the peasants themselves on their own properties or on those taken in tenancy on long, harsh contracts, who from nothing created flourishing market gardens by stubborn and tenacious hours with hoe and spade.[6]

At the end of this process, the relationships between the two great economic and territorial units into which the traditional

---

[4] INEA, *Inchiesta sulla distribuzione della proprietà*.
[5] M. Rossi-Doria, *Dieci anni*, pp. 267–8; C. Rodanò, *Mezzogiorno e sviluppo economico* (Bari, 1954), pp. 84–5; N. Zitara, *L'Unità d'Italia: nascita di una colonia* (Milan, 1971), pp. 45–51.
[6] M. Rossi-Doria, 'Struttura e problemi', p. 32.

Mezzogiorno has often been divided were reversed: it was the 'pure' commercial structures of the coast which had come to dominate, in terms of quantity of wealth produced and in occupational density, the latifondist and peasant structures of the coastal hills and internal mountains.[7]

If we return to our initial observation about the great irregularity and velocity of growth of the demographic curve of the Plain, we now have a most important explanatory element. The highest rate of demographic increase which began to be registered at the end of the 1880s can be related to an increase in the demand for labour induced by earlier investment in typically labour-intensive agriculture, such as the cultivation of citrus fruits, olives and grapes. In a similar way, the fall in population of the years 1931 to 1936 was tied to the body blow dealt the people by the closing of international outlets for such products as a result of the fascist policy of autarchy and by the world exchange crisis of the early 1930s. The weak recovery of population growth in the fifteen years 1936 to 1951 can be correlated with a situation of scarce activity in international commerce which depressed the 'Ricardian physiognomy' of the agricultural economy of the Plain of Gioia Tauro and strengthened, by contrast, the autarchic economy of the Cosentino.

Toward the end of the 1880s the great wave of agricultural investments died down. In the economy of the Mezzogiorno a regressive dynamic sparked itself off, which tended 'to turn backwards' the relations of production and of exchange within rural society,[8] restricting the physical and economic space occupied by specialised commercial cultures. Notwithstanding all that and in spite of the fascist policy of incentives to cereal cultivation, the territory of the Plain remained solidly characterised by its dominant form of production for high return throughout the entire span of years from 1861 to 1950.

According to the investigation of F. Milone on the use of the soil in Calabria, the Plain of Gioia Tauro produced at the beginning of the 1950s 13.5 per cent of the entire regional production of olive oil, with yields much higher than the

[7] M. Rossi-Doria, *Dieci anni*, p. 260.
[8] M. Rossi-Doria, *Dieci anni*, pp. 269–85.

Calabrian average (18 quintals per hectare of specialised cultivation).[9] The dominance of olive cultivation gave the entire zone 'the aspect of a huge olive-oil factory', around which, as we shall see, the basic economic and social circuits were organised.

One important consequence of the domination of intensive cultivation was that there were few very large holdings of the absentee or latifondist type of more than 1,000 hectares and also very few small holdings of independent cultivators in the Plain (see Table 2, p. 13). On the whole of the Plain of Gioia Tauro there existed in 1947 only two private properties which extended beyond 1,000 hectares (one of 1,952 and the other of 2,568 hectares), which, in any case, only took up under 10 per cent of the surface under cultivation. These two holdings were situated on the edge of the Plain, in the two *comuni* on the lower slopes of the Aspromonte.

Even the presence of large properties between 100 and 1,000 hectares was rather limited, in all 29 units which occupied 14 per cent of the territory, whereas the largest quota of productive territory (36.2 per cent) was held by 694 properties between 10 and 100 hectares (see Table 2). If we analyse this last fact a little more deeply, we see more clearly how it relates to the broad diffusion of intensive, export-orientated agriculture. From Table 14 it emerges that in the four 'central' *comuni* of the Plain, whose territory was covered up to 90 per cent by orchard and other tree crops, the incidence of medium-sized property expands sharply at the expense of the categories at the extremes; the medium-sized unit occupied roughly half of the cultivated ground in the *comuni* of Gioia Tauro and Taurianova.

Table 14 also makes evident a phenomenon already obvious from Table 2, that is, the relevance assumed in the Plain of Gioia Tauro by parcellisation of holdings. Nearly one sixth of the cultivated surface was occupied by micro-units of less than 2 hectares. Such units in an environment by now almost without resources, rights and institutions of a collective type, which might have tended to support and integrate families by providing a subsistence yield even on a tiny holding, were hence placed at the ultimate edges of the economic flows.

[9] F. Milone, *Memoria illustrativa della carta di utilizzazione del suolo della Calabria* (Rome, 1956).

Table 14 The distribution of landed property in the central communities of the Plain of Gioia Tauro

Comuni	Very small (0–2 hectares)				Small (2–10 hectares)				Middle-sized (10–100 hectares)			
	No.	%	Total area		No.	%	Total area	%	No.	%	Total area	%
Rosarno	2,265	89.4	1,092	21.1	209	8.2	785	15.2	55	2.2	1,614	31.2
Taurianova	2,166	83.4	810	14.7	318	12.2	1,366	24.8	113	4.3	2,820	51.3
Rizziconi	984	81.6	409	10.5	159	13.2	707	18.1	60	5.0	1,669	42.7
Gioia Tauro	1,041	79.6	390	10.3	188	14.4	764	20.3	74	5.7	1,896	50.2
Total	6,456	84.4	2,701	14.7	874	11.4	3,622	19.7	302	4	7,999	43.6

Comuni	Large Units (100–1,000 hectares)				Totals			
	No.	%	Total area	%	No.	%	Total area	%
Rosarno	6	0.2	1,682	32.5	2,535	100	5,173	100
Taurianova	1	0.03	504	9.2	2,598	100	5,500	100
Rizziconi	3	0.2	1,124	28.7	1,206	100	3,909	100
Gioia Tauro	4	0.3	727	19.2	1,307	100	3,777	100
Total	14	0.2	4,037	22	7,646	100	18,359	100

Source: INEA 1947, Distribuzione della proprietà fondiaria in Italia

Table 15 *The distribution of landed property in the Plain of Gioia Tauro according to classes of taxable income*

	% of units	% of income
Very small (up to 2,000 lire)	89.5	20.7
Small (from 2,000 lire to 10,000 lire)	8.2	27.6
Medium-sized (from 10,000 lire to 100,000 lire)	2.2	44.2
Large (from 100,000 lire to 500,000 lire)	0.1	7.5
Very large (above 500,000 lire)	—	—
	100.0	100.0

Source: INEA 1947, *Distribuzione della proprietà fondiaria*

Even small property, between 2 and 10 hectares, can, for the most part, be placed in that peripheral productive area to which corresponded the high level of labour supply provided by such smallholders. From the investigation of INEA on 'The Relations between Property, Enterprise and Labour in Italian Agriculture' and 'Types of Enterprise in Italian Agriculture' we learn how, notwithstanding the remarkable diffusion of the enterprise under direct cultivation which occupied 36 per cent of the cultivable terrain of the Plain, the peasant-proprietors were not in the full sense independent: 'They are unable to absorb all the labour of which they dispose in their own enterprises and, as a rule, assume either a *partitanza* [a collective tenancy with rent in kind] or work as wage labour on other holdings.'[10]

In the zone which we are analysing, therefore, the fulcrum of the social relations was not represented as in the Cosentino by a robust class of self-sufficient peasants but by a broad but unstable band of medium-sized proprietors who managed their holdings by making use of salaried labour, or by the *colonia parziaria* (partial tenancy) not *appoderata* or by any of the various forms of share-cropping.

An examination of the organisation of landed property by a subdivision based on categories of economic breadth, that is, on

[10] INEA, *Rapporti tra proprietà*, p. 120.

taxable income for purposes of the land tax, confirms again more clearly the observations made so far about the fundamental agrarian structures of the Plain of Gioia Tauro.

From Table 15 it is clear that
(1) the category of very large property, whose economic and juridical significance we have already established as rather limited, does not exist as an economic element;
(2) large property had an economic weight less than its juridical extent (7.5 per cent of income from 14.2 per cent of the total surface);
(3) the area of 'pulverised' micro-holdings earned more income than its share of surface (20.7 per cent of income from 18.9 per cent of surface);
(4) medium-sized property constituted the most important economic category by a long way (44.2 per cent of income from 36 per cent of surface), followed by small property.

The elementary unit of the agrarian system based on medium-sized property and medium-sized enterprise was the garden, that is, a piece of territory thickly covered by fruit trees and specialised in the production of one crop only, whose sale on the market furnished a median yield among the highest in Italian agriculture: from 60,000 to 100,000 lire for olives, between 300,000 and 1,000,000 for citrus crops, compared to 20,000 to 30,000 per hectare for land devoted to cereal culture.

The interaction of these elements at the base of the productive structure and the natural environment produced a peculiar form of rural scenery and human settlement. The Plain of Gioia Tauro was a classic case of the 'Mediterranean garden'[11] and of centralised settlement.[12] Even the spatial signs of the old grain-and-pastoral economy had been utterly wiped out. The greatest evidence of its subjugation to market forces consisted, from the point of view of territorial structures, in the snapping of the 'circular relationship of exchange' established with the mountains in other zones (especially on the Ionian coast), in traditional Calabria by the cycle of the *transumanza* – the annual

---

[11] The 'Mediterranean garden' is one of the types of rural landscape in Italy defined by E. Sereni in his *Storia del paesaggio agrario italiano* (Bari, 1961).
[12] R. Biasutti, *Carta degli insediamenti rurali in Italia* (Rome, 1932).

cattle drive to the hills – and by the periodic movements of the economy from cereal to pasture and back.[13] Expansion of mercantile cultivation chased the shepherds from the land and invaded the coastal pastures of the Plain of Gioia Tauro, bringing about, from the end of the eighteenth century, a slow but steady 'return' of population to the coasts after fifteen centuries of mountain settlement. The only sign of the old economic equilibrium remained in the 'stretched-out' topography of a few *comuni* of the Plain.[14]

Market and social structure

Another important characteristic of the Plain of Gioia Tauro, a characteristic which serves to distinguish it from the other Calabrian areas studied here, was the existence of a consistent commercial bourgeoisie, which developed at the beginning of the nineteenth century and which was in the first period exclusively composed of non-native elements. Amalfitani, Apulians and Genoese maintained for years a monopoly of trade in olives, wine and citrus products, until the action of market forces in the period after unification and the effects of certain mechanisms of reproduction typical of families of commercial strangers 'opened' local society and generated a layer of indigenous entrepreneurs, who by 1950 had become the centre of gravity of local economic life.

For the entire first phase, the relationship between the 'merchants who come from outside' and the society of the Plain taken as a whole was not much different from that typical of any agrarian pre-industrial community which encounters long-distance commerce.[15] Its base was reciprocal hostility, which burst out in periodic clashes and open struggles.[16] Its effects tended to reinforce traditional social cohesion rather than to spark off indigenous mercantile tendencies.

It was not that the Plain of Gioia Tauro did not know the market

[13] On this point see p. 131 in Chapter 3 where this theme is developed.
[14] M. Palumbo, *I comuni meridionali, prima e dopo le leggi eversive della feudalità* (Montecorvo Rovella, 1910); L. Gambi, *La Calabria* (Turin, 1965), chap. VIII.
[15] See note 49, Chapter I.
[16] A. Basile, 'Incitamenti a violenze contro i commercianti genovesi di Gioia Tauro nel 1848', *Archivio storico per la Calabria e la Lucania*, XXXII, 1963, nos. 1–2.

as an institution. On the contrary, there appear to have been markets in the zone from very early times, but these were local affairs based on the exchange of complementary articles: wool, cheese and other goods produced in the pastoral economy of the Aspromonte mountains were exchanged frequently for the oil and wine of the coastal centres. There also existed conspicuous currents of exchange with the Ionian territories in grain and meat products.

The existence of markets based on natural facts such as geographical distance and climate played no fundamental role in the regulation of social relations, which remained based on principles and institutions of their own kind. There did not develop, that is, any tendency *within* the society of the Plain of Gioia Tauro towards further expansion of such markets, even if it would be natural to presume on the basis of the mythology of *homo economicus* of classical economics that from the individual acts of barter and exchange taking place in the markets themselves there would have been a push towards the constitution of a competitive regional and interregional system of marketing.

The local markets of the Plain of Gioia Tauro were essentially 'markets of the neighboring zone',[17] which, even if important to the life of the community, never gave the slightest sign of reducing to their model the social system or the economic one. As regards the formation of prices, for example, the actions of supply and demand were heavily conditioned in such markets by a variety of social factors: family relationship, lineage, geographic origin or other indicators of rank in the buyers; traditional norms about the 'just price', anxieties among the market women not to sell everything too quickly since the market was a place of entertainment and social exchange.

In such markets, there were, it is true, seasonal price fluctuations and other changes not entirely foreseeable, but within variations not fully determined by costs of production or demand. The chief category of sellers was, in any case, that of small rural producers frequently incapable of calculating in money terms their costs of production because they had not had to acquire anything for the process of production. Another

---

[17] K. Polanyi, *Origins of our Time; The Great Transformation*, chap. 5.

important aspect of prices formed in such local markets of the Plain was the fact that they performed none of the functions – crucial in all the market economies of the West – of allocating the resources and factors of production among alternative production processes. Although the products which came to market might be sold at prices fixed by a rough game of supply and demand, the feed-back effect on resource allocation, which makes the interdependent formation of market prices – the so-called 'market system' – of such great importance in the economy and formal economic theory of industrialised societies, was entirely lacking. The prices in the local markets of the Plain of Gioia Tauro had the same influence on productive decisions that auctions have on the antiques sold in our economy.

Local markets in the Plain of Gioia Tauro, moreover, never implied any real competition. They were often disorganised by the appearance of such competition, and were strongly regulated by the political and social authorities who set the dates, places and duration. Within a week, for example, a rotation of the place of the market used to take place (and to some extent still does) among the principal centres of the Plain. In each of these centres a complicated procedure for beginning and closing transactions obtained, and the whole activity maintained a strong ceremonial significance as a collective festivity which *contained* (in both senses of the word) the economic character of the event.

The non-competitive, local markets of the Plain of Gioia Tauro provided no point of departure for national and international commerce. Long-distance trade was created in this zone by individuals who came from other regions, who put themselves into direct opposition to the social organisation and existing institutions. The local society in turn reacted initially by isolating the aliens. The 'foreign' traders of the early years of the last century were forced to form their own little 'society' in whose ambit they met, conducted business and intermarried.

The growth in the volume of their business meant that many eventually transferred their own families to the Plain, and this fact was one of the most important reasons for the emergence of that layer of local entrepreneurs whom we found among the protagonists of mercantile development in the years after unification.

The mercantile enterprises of the 'foreigners' were organised, in fact, on a family base. Business relations tended to transform themselves into family ones and vice versa. Very often there were not enough members of the patron's family to manage the various offices, warehouses and shops. The ancient usage became widely diffused among such families of giving the management of such units to trusted persons called *commessi* or 'agents'. *Commessi* came from local families, frequently poor. They had been taken on when children as apprentice-boys and in time included within the familial orbit of the boss's family almost on the same footing as his own male heirs.

At the moment when a *commesso* married, which generally took place rather late and usually after the age of 25 to 30, he would receive from the head of the family the ownership of a shop or warehouse already set up and operating. The institution of the *commesso* by multiplying the number of professional traders of local origin was an important vehicle of penetration for competitive market forces into the society of the Plain. It created the conditions for the diffusion of a native entrepreneurship from below, which expressed itself in two crucial historical moments: in the course of the massive conversion which took place in the first two decades after unification, about which we have already spoken in the preceding section; and during the Second World War with the rise of the black-market phenomenon.

Between 1943 and 1945, when Italy remained divided in two by the events of the war, there occurred in the Mezzogiorno a true native speculative, entrepreneurial boom, which saw in the Plain of Gioia Tauro the rise of a new layer of traders and small-scale industrialists. The significance of this was, as often happens, better caught by the writers of the time than the social scientists. In the special number of the review *Il Ponte* of 1950 dedicated to Calabria, the novelist Corrado Alvaro made a contribution which described the phenomenon in the following terms:

> During the course of the Second World War . . . Calabria has seen the rise of a type of small merchant, who, coming from a people in process of disintegration, has made a little pile and begun to try his hand at buying and selling and maybe a little manufacturing. The black market is one of the most important social facts about that society. Practically all the new rich from the black market, the sly speculators who spend their nights on

trains from Capo dell'Armi to Genoa and Milan, smuggling oil and bringing back wire, textiles, shoes, medicines and finished goods, are pioneers of the modern world in Calabria. They have broken the old prejudice in favour of the degree and diploma ... By virtue of this new category of self-made men, here and there you can see the odd factory chimney, the occasional small- or medium-sized workshop in Calabria ... If you watch one of these new figures ... you see at once that he acts knowing that everybody and everything is against him, the state, the local community, the traditions and the laws.[18]

The development of a commercial bourgeoisie in the Plain of Gioia Tauro found its origin in a series of changes brought about, as Alvaro rightly observes, 'not by a spontaneous creation from the environment but under the pressure of external elements and national upheavals'.[19] The development itself followed essentially native lines and finished at the end of the 1940s by creating a situation of complete domination of the economic structures of the Plain of Gioia Tauro by competition in the market. Dealers in oil, citrus traders, and wholesalers constituted the figures *internal* to the relations of society on the Plain. Their warehouses stood along the principal thoroughfares of the main towns next to the warehouses of their former bosses. The most interesting and distinctive trait of this new commercial bourgeoisie was, as we have seen, its popular origins. The greater part of its members rose from families of workers, artisans, little peasant farmers, testifying to a possibility of economic mobility unknown in other parts of the Mezzogiorno.

Even the artisans of the Plain of Gioia Tauro displayed a physiognomy quite different from that assumed in the other Calabrian or southern productive systems. They became differentiated and highly developed almost to the level of simple manufacture. About a third of the active population were occupied at Gioia Tauro in small- and medium-sized enterprises which reached, in several cases, 100 to 150 employees. Processing olives, manufacturing the barrels for olive oil and wine, construction of means of transport, a certain liveliness within the building trades, the multifarious activities connected to an economy based on exchange and long-distance commerce gave the push towards

[18] C. Alvaro, 'L'animo del calabrese', *Il Ponte*, nos. 9–10, 1950, pp. 971–2.
[19] C. Alvaro, 'L'animo', pp. 971–2.

a production no longer integrated into the circuit of small rural autarchies but already instead partially specialised and subject to the mechanism of market prices.

The presence of such a manufacturing apparatus gave precise form to aspects of the social structure. The division of labour here showed relatively distinct outlines; that is, there was none of that mixture of trades and social types, that blurring of function typical of the world of the peasant and landless labourer. There were no peasant-shoemakers, no peasant-blacksmiths, no peasant-tailors, no peasant-carpenters in the Plain, the type which Saverio Strati describes in the Ionian zones of the great estates and which formed the soul of the whole system of non-mercantile exchange in large areas of the Cosentino.[20] To the diverse processing activities there corresponded a professionalisation made necessary by the competition of elements coming from other regions. The separation of rural production from manufacturing activity had been almost completely achieved.

A contribution of great significance to the rise of non-agricultural employment was in addition provided by a group of agrarian industries owned by central- and northern-Italian interests (refineries, factories for processing the citrus-fruit juices etc.) which employed, in addition to a quota of seasonal workers who flooded in from other areas of the region, a certain percentage of qualified and specialised local workers.

This greater productive diversification of the Plain with respect to the other Calabrian areas, did not mean naturally that we find ourselves confronting a system of professional roles so consolidated as to do away with that general fluidity of occupations characteristic of the labour market of the Mezzogiorno.[21] It meant rather that alongside the very high *horizontal* occupational mobility of the latter, there was added in the Plain of Gioia Tauro a consistent vertical mobility of ascent and descent, based on the *stratification* of the labour market itself. At the base of this market we find an undifferentiated magma of precarious employment, of the pre-industrial proletariat (landless labourers, poor

---

[20] S. Strati, 'Contadini del Sud', *Quaderni calabresi*, no. 33, June 1974.

[21] On the subject of precarious employment as a condition of the labour market in underdeveloped agricultural economies, see P. Sylos Labini, 'Precarious Employment in Sicily', *International Labour Review*, March 1964.

peasants, artisans competing with industry, travelling salesmen, tiny traders etc.) but whose central fibre was constituted by much more decisively modern figures.

Social mobility and 'ethnic' stratification

So far I have attempted to demonstrate by means of an analysis of some basic 'peculiarities' of the Plain of Gioia Tauro the fact that we do not confront in this case an elementary society governed by the reproductive mechanisms of the family-enterprise and by the various forms of mechanical solidarity in a perpetual clash with the logic of economic commercialisation, but a complex entity based on the autonomous development of its components and of a complex interdependence of its categories.

Such elaborate internal articulation represented also the product of a very intense exchange of populations with other Calabrian and southern zones. From the point of view of its 'ethnic' configuration, the society of the Plain was, perhaps, the most varied in the entire south of Italy.

The periodic disturbances in the labour market connected with the alternating vicissitudes of high-quality agriculture for export brought to the territory intense waves of migration from the inland mountains and the Ionian areas. The olive-crop harvest generated a strong demand for a female labour force which could not be satisfied by the local supply, and brought onto the Plain a work force drawn from relatively distant areas (certain zones of the province of Cosenza and western Sicily, for example).[22]

In time, the repetition of such floods of migratory labour finished by laying down a sediment of unskilled labour which occupied the lowest positions of the occupational hierarchy and thus created the base from which the upwardly mobile people born in the area, whom we have noticed, tended to rise. A good half of the native population of Gioia Tauro in about 1950 seems to have settled down in positions of middle-class employment of a dependent kind (*commessi*, warehousemen, book-keepers, public employees, bank clerks, administrators, supervisors,

---

[22] J. Meyriat, *La Calabria* (Milan, 1960), p. 223; L. Franchetti, *Le condizioni economiche*, p. 227; V. Padula, *Persone in Calabria* (Rome, 1967), pp. 164–7.

railway employees etc.) or in ownership of commercial artisan or small industrial enterprise.

The labour market for unskilled workers presented, therefore, a tendency to scarcity of supply, which found only the most infrequent parallel in other zones of Calabria and the Mezzogiorno. As a result, there was a very high proportion of women and children in the unskilled labour force. In the demographic census of 1951 the percentage of women in the total employed population of the Plain of Gioia Tauro amounted to 51 per cent. This in turn pushed up the percentage of the actively employed within the total population to 46 per cent compared to 38 per cent for the regional average.

Aside from the currents of seasonal migratory labour, the Plain was the site of a permanent immigration of a mixed type: cowherds and farm foremen, fishermen and artisans from the coastal centres along the Straits of Messina, workers and technicians who came with central- and northern-based refinery industries, besides the 'foreigners' in trade whom we have already mentioned. This stratification based on geographical mobility of the population 'cut across' the hierarchy based on income and power, producing within each sub-group further subdivisions and breaking each category into a series of little 'ethnic' sub-cells. An example of the minute network of cultural reticulation which broke the solidarity founded on purely economic and social elements and prevented political mobilisation may be found in the waterfront neighbourhood of Gioia Tauro, the 'Marina':

> The Marina of Gioia Tauro is divided politically and socially. These divisions have roots in the origins of the neighbourhood. The main causes which have led to the present state of disintegration arise from the different places from which the inhabitants come. A large part is formed by citizens of Bagnara who live in the northern section of the quarter; the other part is composed of people from Palmi who live in the southern half.
>
> Different customs and habits and the different sorts of economics in their home communities have split the neighbourhood into Bagnaroti and Palmesi. The Bagnaroti devote themselves and all their resources to coastal fishing, from which they derive a wretched and primitive living. The Palmesi look down on coastal fishing and coastal fishermen as humble. They involve themselves in petty commerce and look for quick rewards. They began as proper sailors and then passed to employment

on steamers when sail gave way to steam, so the Palmesi are not unacquainted with the life of the sea nor were they exempt from the exploitation and slavery practised by the big bosses of merchant shipping. Nevertheless the Palmesi think of themselves as above the Bagnaroti.[23]

Such movement of the population took place in various phases and in different forms in different villages or groups of villages. It was highest in the development of Gioia Tauro whose population increased by ten-fold between 1861 and 1951, quintupling in the first forty years after unification. The growth of the other three 'central' communities of the Plain was also very rapid. In the period 1861 to 1951 they tripled or quadrupled their inhabitants also as a result of entirely new settlements created in the previous decades. Such was the case of San Ferdinando di Rosarno, an agricultural settlement established in 1818 by a great local landlord who was forced to have recourse to the poorest peasants of the inland zones of Calabria and to a supply of prisoners put at his disposal by the Bourbon government because of the scarcity of local agricultural labourers prepared to transform themselves into small settlers.

The rapid population growth of these new centres – San Ferdinando had already passed 5,000 inhabitants by 1891 – placed as they were in the fertile zones of the Plain, now free of malaria, further accentuated the composite character which the population of the zone had assumed in the decades after unification. This genetic element was sensed, if a bit crudely, in a rural history essay on the origins and development of San Ferdinando:

> If you consider the various origins of the inhabitants or, should I say, means of recruitment of the various settlers drawn from every part of Calabria (not to mention those drawn from penal servitude who came from all over Italy), you will grasp the fact that the people of San Ferdinando have a character all their own. The inhabitants of the village are full of the spirit of initiative. They lack that deep hatred of novelty normally found in rural communities and especially in the Calabrian countryside. Instead they are quick to face new challenges, to try new

---

[23] *Marina Oggi*, only edition of the information magazine, published by the FGCI (Federazione Giovanile Comuniste Italiana). Circolo Lenin, Marina di Gioia Tauro, September, 1976, p. 1.

experiences and, above all, to see if they cannot draw some personal gain from the business to raise their own position.[24]

In the subsequent history of the Plain, immigration has almost always surpassed in quantitative terms and in social importance emigration. Emigration never achieved the enormous proportions and the sustained intensity over nearly a half century which we have noticed in the Cosentino and in Calabria in general. Emigration in the Plain began two decades later than in the other areas and stayed at extremely modest levels. Until 1891 official statistics do not record any departures from the Plain, compared to a rate of emigration which in the same period exceeded 10 per thousand in the Cosentino and 6 per thousand in the rest of Calabria. Only between 1902 and 1913 at a time when the Cosentino, Calabria and the Mezzogiorno seemed to be emptied by the 'flight' of whole blocks of the population did the Plain of Gioia Tauro register a wave of departures which was statistically consistent (19 per thousand against 28 per thousand for Calabria and 34 per thousand for the Cosentino).[25]

Even the social identity of the emigrant from the Plain was different from that of the peasant areas of inland Calabria. The enquiries into emigration carried out in the early years of the century revealed how much the sociological composition of those leaving the Plain reflected the greater economic and social diversification of the region. The protagonist of the phenomenon was frequently a skilled worker or at least semi-skilled in the building trades, in agriculture or in the tertiary sector, the sort of person who emigrated with greater ease, given his greater economic resources, and also for periods much shorter than those of the peasants of the Cosentino.[26]

The effects of the formation of a national market for goods and capital assumed a different importance in the Plain than elsewhere. Instead of provoking the disorganisation of the preexisting socio-economic systems, it favoured forms of real accumulation of cash, land and trade. Dividing up the domain

---

[24] F. Nunziante, *La bonifica di Rosarno ed il villagio di S. Ferdinando. Saggio di storia agraria* (Florence, 1929), p. 57.
[25] Ministero di Agricoltura, Industria e Commercio, Direzione Generale della Statistica, *Statistica dell'emigrazione all'estero*, published annually.
[26] D. Taruffi et al., *La questione agraria*, chap. 8.

and common lands (which everywhere else in the Mezzogiorno in the period after unification contributed to reduce the rural masses to a wretched level and which provoked fierce, armed opposition) furnished yet another occasion on the Plain of Gioia Tauro for a not inconsiderable proportion of the population on the lower levels of the socio-economic scale to transform themselves into a class of small- and medium-sized capitalists.[27]

Even the special laws favouring Calabria served frequently to consolidate or bring to birth entrepreneurial fortunes. The Plain of Gioia Tauro can, moreover, be considered one of the few areas of Calabria in which during the years after the First World War there was a real growth in the category of small peasant-proprietors. The difference between it and the Crotonese with its huge estates was truly remarkable:

Between 1922 and 1926 ... 28,000 hectares passed into the hands of peasants, above all at Cittanova, Nicastro, at Palmi and at Paola on the one hand, and to peasants in the Crotonese in places such as Cirò, Savelli and Strongoli. In the first group of *comuni*, the new pieces of land were capable of becoming plantations which yielded a genuine profit and permitted the new proprietors to raise their standard of living, even if at the price of ferociously hard work. The story in the second group of *comuni* was very different. The new proprietors ran into grave difficulties and were soon disappointed ... Not even constant labour could grant them the barest means of subsistence.[28]

The very high level of social mobility and the notable rate of 'replacement' of the population had a decisive impact on the socio-cultural structure of the zone, forcing it, as we shall see further on, to elaborate particular forms of control over its transforming dynamism. The strategic element in this dynamism was the intense vertical mobility which impeded in the Plain the crystallisation of that set of social relations typical of the 'meridional`agrarian bloc'. There existed a constant movement up and down along the hierarchy of social stratification. There was open to all the hope of some little deal, some sort of small investment which would improve the status of an individual or a family

---

[27] V. Ricchioni, *Le leggi eversive della feudalità e la storia delle quotizzazioni demaniali nel Mezzogiorno*, published by the Cassa per il Mezzogiorno in the series *Problemi dell'agricoltura meridionale* (Naples, 1953).

[28] J. Meyriat, *La Calabria*, p. 51.

within the span of even a few years. Just as open to all was the way down.

Such accentuated inter-class mobility ended by producing a social disintegration even more acute than that dominant in the areas typical of the 'meridional agrarian bloc' where the mobility was above all *intra*-class and social conflict found its outlet in class struggle. In the Plain of Gioia Tauro the whole concealed caste system was blown up, giving place to a war of all against all, families against families, groups against groups.

The very structure of stratification favoured disintegration. Among the four fundamental 'class aggregates' – pre-industrial proletariat/*braccianti*, workers, small artisans/petty-bourgeois land-owners, traders and intellectuals/medium-sized and large land-owners, professional men, industrialists and traders – there were no rigid limits. In place of Gramsci's classic analysis in three parts of the agrarian bloc we find in the Plain a complex of numerous subcultures in perpetual de- and re-composition.

The central axis of social relations was always the broad layer of middle commercial and agricultural bourgeoisie which we analysed roughly in the preceding pages, but that only within an ambit of general movement which permitted no establishment of a stable framework of classes and status groups nor lasting coagulations within each class. The Plain of Gioia Tauro was the zone in Calabria which had the weakest cooperative and associational traditions. In all the statistics about the rural cooperative movement, the province of Reggio Calabria, of which the Plain of Gioia Tauro makes up the most important economic and demographic unit, ended up regularly in last place (see Table 16). The contrast with the situation in the Cosentino is marked. There the most intense social cohesion was reflected in a much more extensive diffusion of associational activity.[29]

Instability of the market and circulation of elites

To this point we have observed only a few, admittedly fundamental, features of the economic and social circuits of the Plain

[29] Associazione per lo Sviluppo dell'Industria nel Mezzogiorno (SVIMEZ), *La cooperazione agraria nel Mezzogiorno* (Rome, 1955), pp. 181–5.

Table 16 *The rural cooperative movement in Calabria: types of cooperative*

	Production/ labour		Provision of tools, implements		Processing/ sales		Economic integration		Totals	
	Coops. (No.)	Members (No.)	Coops. (No.)	Members (No.)	Coops. (No.)	Members (No.)	Coops. (No.)	Members (No.)	Coops. (No.)	Members (No.)
Catanzaro	70	13,913	1	6,067	1	300	3	129	75	20,409
Cosenza	85	15,242	2	3,331	—	—	14	734	101	19,307
Reggio Calabria	32	4,346	1	5,316	—	—	3	2,022	36	11,684
Total	187	33,501	4	14,714	1	300	20	2,885	212	51,400

Source: SVIMEZ, *Cooperazione agraria nel Mezzogiorno*, Rome, 1955

of Gioia Tauro. Now we must try to explain their connections by discriminating better among the dynamics of their functioning. That will permit us to proceed in the analysis and to hazard a much wider-ranging interpretation of the phenomena examined so far. We have seen how, from the point of view of the market economy, the social division of labour, the increase of manufacturing and tertiary activity, the Plain stood as an area of economic 'development' with respect to the regional norm and to the Cosentino. But we have also seen how it was at the same time a zone of the most extreme disorganisation and atomisation of social relations, hence of the most profound 'underdevelopment'.

It is necessary to avoid the temptation to explain this contradiction by using one of the conceptual formulations which are to be found in 'the sociologist's tool-kit' or that of the anthropologist. The intrinsic evolutionism lurking within the concept of 'modernisation', for example, can prevent our comprehension of the most original trait of the temporal dynamism of this society: it based itself on a social mobility within a *closed circuit*, not inserted in a wider movement of reconstitution of a defined system of roles and relations, nor in any tendency in the short or long term to move from *Gemeinschaft* toward *Gesellschaft*.

There was no 'progress' in the Plain of Gioia Tauro. New social types were not created. Society restructured itself from time to time without breaking into pieces, by continually rotating around itself. This movement of *corsi e ricorsi* gave rise to a situation which I have termed the 'permanent transition', and which I shall try to define more closely in the succeeding sections of this chapter.

The specifically economic component of the state of permanent transition consisted in the phenomenon of instability of markets. The economic bases of the *corsi e ricorsi* which characterised the society on the Plain must be sought, I think, in the first instance, in the qualities proper to a market society (that is, in the continuous oscillation in production, in anarchic price movements, in the separation of production itself from distribution, in the dependence of agriculture on a demand external to the local economic system etc.), and, in the second instance, in the peculiar dynamics of the specialised monoculture of the Plain.

Table 17 *Cultivation of olives in Calabria, 1880–1953*[30]

	Area in thousands of hectares							Production of oil in thousands of quintals (quintal = 100 kilos)		
	1880	1929		1939		1953				
	Specialised	Specialised	Mixed	Specialised	Mixed	Specialised	Mixed	1880	1939–40	1948–52
Cosenza	16	45	33	46	33	47	36	56	78	54
Catanzaro	28	51	25	51	25	51	26	115	72	96
Reggio C.	40	49	31	49	31	50	31	188	103	96
Calabria	84	145	89	146	89	148	93	359	253	246

Source: F. Milone, *L'Italia nell'economia delle sue regioni*, Turin, 1955

Let us examine as an example the movement of the cycle of the olive. Within the ambit of Calabria, after Apulia the most important Italian producing region for the crop, the Plain of Gioia Tauro represented the zone of greatest extent and specialisation of olive cultivation. After the rapid expansion of investment in the twenty years after unification, the crop faced a declining market. From Table 17 it can be seen how, notwithstanding a remarkable expansion of surface under cultivation, the production of oil diminished by almost a third in the entire region and by 50 per cent in the province of Reggio Calabria alone. The reason for this obvious decline was the inadequate renovation of the plantations, above all in zones like the Plain where they had been most exuberant. In 1940 it was estimated that one third of the total

---

[30] The raw figures were derived, for the period about 1880, from the Jacini investigation; for 1929 and for the prewar period from the *Annuario statistico dell'agricoltura italiana*, 1936–8 and 1939–42; for the period 1948–52, from the *Boll. di stat. agr. e for.* (November, 1949) and the *Boll. mens. di stat.* (May 1951 and May 1953). Figures for production around 1880 were converted from the original hectolitres using a coefficient of 93 kg for each hectolitre, the standard conversion in use in Italy. Elsewhere 90 kg is considered the norm.

Table 18 *Average annual production of olives for oil in Apulia, Calabria, in the Mezzogiorno and in Italy from 1923 to 1950*
(thousands of quintals)

	1923–8	1929	1936	1937	1938	1939	1940	1941	1942
Apulia	3,580	3,756	2,692	6,175	3,054	7,157	2,189	4,898	3,168
Calabria	2,901	5,564	769	2,393	859	4,390	892	2,682	1,491
Mezzogiorno	12,165	15,736	6,077	13,782	6,692	17,477	6,143	10,750	7,960
Italy	16,028	19,167	9,538	16,770	10,255	20,019	10,082	12,365	11,050

	1943	1944	1945	1946	1947	1948	1949	1950
Apulia	2,847	2,219	1,990	2,979	4,532	2,127	3,095	3,591
Calabria	2,242	1,104	1,847	882	2,669	746	2,189	528
Mezzogiorno	7,737	6,564	5,638	5,980	11,959	4,706	8,788	6,807
Italy	8,853	9,589	6,328	8,284	15,092	6,206	10,775	9,481

Source: SVIMEZ, *L'economia dell'olivo*, Rome, 1952

of olive trees were in an advanced stage of vegetable senescence.[31]

Among the most important consequences of this regressive trend one turned out to be of decisive importance for our analysis: an increase in the already high irregularity of the olive crop.[32] As will be clear from Tables 18, 19 and 20, Calabria, because of the extreme backwardness of its horticultural techniques, was the region in which the most extreme variations in production from one year to the next were registered.

The annual variations in the olive harvest were markedly superior to the southern and Apulian averages where the development of modern techniques of olive culture have acted as a brake on the olive cycle. From 1936 to 1950, Calabrian olive production passed from a minimum of 76.1 per cent below the median for the period to a maximum value of 98.5 per cent above. The average negative variance in the entire period 1923–50 was 48.9 per cent and the average positive variance 32.4 per cent. In 1939 production leapt to a level four times that of the year before, compared to only 1.6 times for the south of Italy as a whole. In Apulia not only were the average variations above and below the median (from +21.3 to −25.6 per cent) much narrower but the annual variations never once touched a level more than one and a half times that of the previous year's crop.

As far as the situation on the Plain of Gioia Tauro is concerned, I have collected and synthesised the statistics from the local chamber of commerce in Reggio Calabria and put them into tabular form in Table 20. It is clear that irregularities there were even greater than those of the regional average. In the period of time considered, the median positive annual variation of production on the Plain of Gioia Tauro was 53.9 per cent and the median negative variation reached the really remarkable figure of 80.8 per cent. From 1938 to 1939 production leapt from 110 per cent below the median of the entire period to 236 per cent above.

Such oscillations in production were not, in addition, balanced by adequate compensating variations in prices, because the olive

---

[31] SVIMEZ, *Economia dell'olivo* (Rome, 1952), p. 11; F. Milone, *L'Italia nell'economia delle sue regioni* (Turin, 1955), pp. 915–16.
[32] *Atti della Conferenza Nazionale del Mondo Rurale e dell'Agricoltura* (Rome, 1965), vol. VIII, p. 124.

Table 19 *Average percentage variations in the production of olives for oil with respect to the average of the period 1923–9 and 1936–50 (average × 100) in Apulia, Calabria, in the Mezzogiorno and in Italy*

	1923–8	1929	1936	1937	1938	1939	1940	1941	1942	1943
Apulia	+ 1.0	+ 6.0	−24.0	+74.3	−13.8	+102.0	−38.2	+38.2	−10.6	−19.7
Calabria	+31.2	+51.6	−65.2	+ 8.2	−61.2	+ 98.5	−59.7	+21.3	−32.6	+ 1.4
Mezzogiorno	+24.0	+60.4	−38.1	+40.5	−31.8	+ 78.2	−37.4	+ 9.6	−18.9	−21.1
Italy	+25.9	+50.6	−25.1	+31.8	−19.4	+ 54.3	−20.8	− 2.9	−13.2	−30.4

	1944	1945	1946	1947	1948	1949	1950	percentage fluctuation positive	percentage fluctuation negative
Apulia	−37.4	−43.8	−15.8	+27.9	−40.0	−12.6	+ 1.4	21.3	25.6
Calabria	−50.1	−16.5	−60.1	+20.7	−66.3	− 1.0	−76.1	32.4	48.9
Mezzogiorno	−33.1	−42.5	−39.0	+21.9	−52.0	−10.4	−30.6	32.2	32.7
Italy	−24.7	−50.3	−34.9	+18.6	−51.2	−15.3	−25.5	31.1	26.1

Source: SVIMEZ, *L'economia dell'olivo*

Table 20 *Percentage variations in the production of olives for oil with respect to the average production (where 1925 to 1950 = 100) in the Plain of Gioia Tauro from 1920 to 1950*

1920	+43.1	1937	+ 22.2
1921	+68.4	1938	−110.3
1922	− 125	1939	+236.9
1923	+40.5	1940	− 61.5
1924	−25.2	1941	+ 40.3
1925	+55.5	1942	− 56.2
1926	−52.3	1943	+ 8.4
1927	+40.8	1944	− 70.1
1928	−65.3	1945	− 30.4
1929	+73.3	1946	− 60.8
1930	+ 8.1	1947	+ 39.1
1931	−62.3	1948	−180.2
1932	−28.7	1949	− 30.3
1933	+68.5	1950	−270.3
1934	−67.1		
1935	+10.2		
1936	−77.2		

Average percentage fluctuations	
positive	negative
53.9	80.8

Source: Chamber of commerce, Reggio Calabria

market was effectively an 'oligopsony'. In fact 80 per cent of the harvest was bought up by the seven or eight local wholesalers in the Plain, who were, in part, acting as agents for the central and northern refining industries and in part on their own account, since many had become modern entrepreneurs in the olive processing branch. To the high variability of supply, constituted by a stratum of many small- and medium-sized producers, there was no corresponding elasticity of average price at wholesale level.[33] In the province of Reggio in the period 1947 to 1950 an average oscillation in production of roughly 55 per cent resulted in an average variation of price of only 12 per cent.

[33] *Atti della Conferenza*, pp. 172–5.

It is easy to imagine what such an alternation of productive activity meant in terms of oscillation and uncertainty of income for the cultivators. To have some idea of the variation of yield on an individual holding, it is enough to bear in mind that, in a typical unit of the Plain of Gioia studied over the space of four years, yield went from 105,000 lire per cultivated hectare in a good year to 11,000 in a bad year.[34] In such conditions economic activity comes to resemble a game of chance.

It is also easy to imagine what the consequences of such a game of chance must have been for a territory whose agricultural income, whose commerce and industry depended up to 75 per cent on the cultivation and processing of olives and the remaining 25 per cent on citrus fruits, an agriculture equally unstable for reasons of climate, backwardness of productive techniques and of marketing:

> In the periods of prosperity, in the good years with high prices, the agriculture of this zone seems to be able to provide a living for a vast population and unemployment disappears. Money circulates and revives every sort of economic activity. No sooner have bad periods begun, either for reasons of climate or market, than immediately a terrible unemployment emerges ... One sees at once that the economic structure of this zone lacks internal equilibrium.[35]

It ought now to be much clearer why there was the intense social mobility, dishomogeneity and disintegration which we have identified as the peculiar attributes of the Plain of Gioia in the preceding pages. Each social group in the course of its history had passed many times through the see-saw of rags to riches, a process which had progressively modified its character, fracturing its internal cohesion and decomposing it into its elementary primary units. In ever-increasing numbers from the decades between unification and 1950, the landless labourers of the Plain had periodically become small tenants, share-croppers or small holders of some sort. Earnings and savings had allowed them to acquire a small piece of ground, to build a house and to buy a few animals, but the violent oscillations of production and yield had also frequently forced them to sell out again. In the course of such

---

[34] *Atti della Conferenza*, p. 395.
[35] M. Rossi-Doria, 'Struttura e problemi', p. 35.

a process each became more separate from the other, more committed to the harsh competitive struggle for work or for a chance to cultivate a few strips of earth, less and less to class solidarity and collective life, becoming ever more individualist and 'familialist'. The two great moments of class struggle in Calabria and the south in general, the brigand period of the 1860s and the struggle for the soil of the 1940s, found a very weak echo in the Plain.

This highly unstable economic dynamism favoured the development of a 'circulation of elites' unknown in other parts of Calabria. Informal groups held power and wealth for a while, forming and disintegrating to be replaced by analogous groups who had risen to the top. The great anxiety about social rank so marked on the Plain is tied precisely to this sort of mobility. Social rank measured the position of a family on the economic scale and gave rise to a type of attitude which was the exact opposite of the reserve and 'camouflage' required by the mechanisms of social control operating in the village of the Cosentino. On the Plain the attitude to wealth and show was based on a proud awareness of the symbols of prestige, and unfolded itself in the ostentatious exhibition of objects acquired for cash and in the exaltation of power and the virtues of self and family.

Here is the source of that aggressive tendency in the basic personality type of the Plain, which Rohlfs noted as an anthropological feature of the 'Greek' part of Calabria south of the Isthmus of Catanzaro and which he tried to trace to ancient historical and cultural matrices.[36] A little later, in the pages devoted to the mafia and *mafioso* behaviour, I shall attempt to offer a less remote explanation of the undoubted presence in the Plain of Gioia of this type of personality.

This 'open', highly unstable society exploited its continuous interaction with the outside world and tied its fortunes to the fate of that world. The peasant society of the Cosentino prevented accumulation and, above all, flaunting of wealth, and took great pains to reduce the effect of both on the structure of the community. It set up a tough resistance to any form of change and defended the traditional equilibrium. The composite society

[36] G. Rohlfs, 'Le due Calabrie', *Almanacco Calabrese*, 1962.

Table 21 *Average size of family resident in the Plain of Gioia Tauro and in the Cosentino*

	Number in family
Plain of Gioia Tauro	4.2
Cosentino	4.6

Source: *Censimento demografico*, 1951

Table 22 *Average size of families of persons employed in agriculture and of persons employed in non-agricultural work in the Plain of Gioia Tauro and in the Cosentino*

	Number in family	
	agricultural	non-agricultural
Plain of Gioia Tauro	4.5	4.6
Cosentino	5.5	4.7

Source: *Censimento demografico*, 1951

of the Plain, on the contrary, not only permitted but encouraged accumulation and ostentation, especially during years of rising demand for its products from outside. It gave to these new evidences of wealth a decisive influence in the periodic reconstitution of social ties.

Familialism and civil society

The very outlines of the fundamental social institutions of the Plain turn out to be apparently coherent with the economic and social circuits we have described. We see first a smaller average size of family compared to the Cosentino (Table 21). The reduced numbers of family members typical of the Plain was a function, in the first instance, of the much smaller domestic, agricultural nuclei. There was hence not much difference in size between the rural and the urban family. From Table 22 we can see how much

Table 23 *Average size of families of dependent labourers and of independent labourers in agriculture in the Plain of Gioia Tauro and in the Cosentino*

| | Number in family ||
	Dependent labourers	Independent labourers
Plain of Gioia Tauro	4.4	4.8
Cosentino	4.8	5.8

Source: Censimento demografico, 1951

Table 24 *Average size of families divided by the professional or economic status of the head of the household for agricultural and non-agricultural activities in the Plain of Gioia Tauro and the Cosentino*

| | Number in family ||
	Plain of G.T.	Cosentino
Agriculture		
Proprietors not cultivating	4.3	4.6
Proprietors cultivating	4.8	5.8
Directors and employees	5.2	4.9
Assistants of independents	4.7	4.2
Others (labourers etc.)	4.4	4.8
Other sectors		
Administrators, and people in professions	4.9	4.8
Self-employed workers	4.7	4.8
Directors and employees	4.1	4.4
Assistants of independents	5.0	4.7
Others (labourers etc.)	4.7	4.7

Source: Censimento demografico, 1951

smaller the difference is between the two types of family in the Plain than in the Cosentino.

Within the agricultural sector itself there existed, in addition, a much less accentuated distinction between the size of families of independent proprietors and those of dependent labourers. Here too, as we see in Table 23, there is a contrast with the Cosentino.

Finally, Table 24 offers us a picture of family size arranged by diverse categories of employment which, in spite of its roughness and its imprecise basis of classification, turns out to be very useful for the sort of analysis we are carrying out, as a static comparison, because it highlights the divergences between the two zones.

One element emerges clearly from the table: the difference in size of the rural families in the two regions is due very largely to the marked difference in the size of the peasant family of the Cosentino, on average formed of 5.8 persons compared to 4.8 on the Plain. This piece of evidence confirms our previous reflections on the marginality of the peasant economy in the Plain of Gioia. As we have seen in the previous chapter, the dimensions of peasant families are strictly correlated to the volume of their economic activity.

One has to be careful not to neglect another element of the situation in the Plain of Gioia Tauro which also emerges from a reading of Table 24: the evident approximation in size of family of all four main categories by number and importance. The average family size for families of 'self-employed labourers' and of 'others in the non-agricultural sectors' is 4.7; for 'agricultural proprietors who cultivate themselves' 4.8; and 4.4 for 'others in the agricultural sector'. Loosened from the terminology of ISTAT the figures mean that there were no great differences of size among families of peasants, landless rural labourers, artisans and small tradesmen of the Plain and that, on the contrary, there existed a high degree of homogeneity and interchangeability of conditions, which, in turn, concurs with the preceding observations about the accentuated horizontal and vertical social mobility of the Plain itself.

Another fundamental difference between the institution of the family on the Plain of Gioia and in the peasant community of the Cosentino can be seen in the pronounced instability and internal disorganisation of the former. Traditional institutions of social reproduction, such as the status of majority, marriage of offspring by fixed order of age and sex, the need to possess a farm etc. had lost their efficacy on the Plain and by the 1940s had become little more than memories. No alternative familial system of control had replaced them. Permanent conflict among the members of the family group became the norm.

The attractive force of family ties was hence rather weak. The number of bachelors, persons living alone, of those 'without family', was always much higher on the Plain than in the Cosentino. Progressive individualisation had steadily undermined that patriarchal power as the rigid basis of all authority which governed family life in the Cosentino. The typical family of the Plain of Gioia Tauro showed a strong lack of homogeneity and a variability in the professional activities of its members which further contributed to the progress of individualism and of conflict.

Diversity of productive activity and the dominion of market forces had profound effects on the organisation of the family of the Plain. Women in labouring families took part in the seasonal labour market. Young sons of artisan and proletarian families took jobs as salaried employees in industry, trade or transport, and hence received their own wages independent of the cooperative work of the family. It was not unusual to find families whose members participated in three or four different types of external specialised activity. With the exception of a small number of artisan families, on the Plain the family had ceased to be the centre of the individual's working life. 'Home' and 'work' had become separate. Home was no longer the place of collective production but only of collective consumption.

The absence of the typical patriarchal authority and of an internal hierarchy of family roles based on the needs of a productive familial economy was not accompanied on the Plain of Gioia, as we have already briefly noted, by the emergence of an alternative set of norms and values or of roles opposed to those hallowed by sanctions in the Cosentino. On the contrary, we can observe a type of *exaltation* of the traditional patriarchal institutions or, perhaps, a kind of exaggerated idealisation of the social set-up of the traditional peasant family of the Cosentino type. This form of exaltation served to favour the development of a rigid authoritarianism of a male, paternal type. The family of the Plain appeared to be dominated, even more than the general southern type described in the preceding chapter, by 'vertical' relationships and by a paternal autocracy, which no longer rested on the entrepreneurial capabilities of the head of the family, but on much more basic needs for 'defence' amidst the fluidity of roles and internal functions no less than against the clashes and threats from outside.

It is vital to avoid thinking of the family on the Plain as some sort of caricature of the peasant family of the Cosentino. The content of its social relations was entirely different from the traditional model, but also no less distant from the relational model typical of the modern urban nuclear family unit. Within the domestic units of the Plain the norm which regulated intra-familial relations was neither family solidarity as in the peasant family of the Cosentino nor the intimacy and solidarity of the modern nuclear family, but subordination, that is, the complex of duties and values which highlighted the prerogatives of each position of power obtaining within the domestic hierarchy.

The family of the Plain of Gioia Tauro, structurally well on the way to disintegration, was 'held together' by the violence of a harsh, internal authoritarianism based on the need for security, arising from the disorganisation of family roles as well as by the external 'compression' caused by the anomie of the extra-familial social space. This latter point needs to be further examined. In my view, the crucial fact is not the pure and simple loss of the economic functions of the family as a productive unit, nor even the separation of enterprise from home and the consequent evolution of the individualisation of its members in response to the possibilities of salaried work or extra-familial activity in general.

The differential element specific not just to family relations on the Plain must be sought on the other 'slope' of the sociological typology of the transformation of domestic relations. Wherever it has occurred, the decline of the productive functions of the family has been accompanied by a decline in many other functions as well and, in the first place, of those connected to the guarantee of physical and legal security and safety. These latter functions have been transferred to a series of supra-familial institutions, such as the state, the bureaucracy and so on.

The increased weight of central power conceded a wider protection to its subordinate members than the domestic community could offer, and assumed many of the welfare and disciplinary functions of parents. This growth determined that 'liberation from parental authority' which constituted a fundamental transformation of the Western family. As Lawrence Stone writes, 'The most remarkable change inside the family was the shift away from paternal authority, a shift made possible by the extension of the power of the central government. As the state and law courts came to provide greater protection to wives and children, the need for subordination to husband and father declined.'[37]

The strengthening by external solidarities of the restricted circle of family life and the multiplication of intermediate institutions between the individual and society make a part of that much wider process of development which we call 'civil society' and which has brought not only the qualitative and quantitative 'simplification' of the family community but also a drastic limitation of primary bonds and ascriptive relations in the lives of individuals. As Max Weber described the process,

> An individual no longer gets protection from the household and kinship groups but rather from political authority which exercises compulsory jurisdiction. Furthermore, household and occupation become ecologically separated, and the household is no longer a unit of common production but of common consumption. Moreover, the individual receives his entire education increasingly from outside his home, and by means which are supplied by various enterprises: schools, bookstores, theaters, concert halls, clubs, meetings, etc. He can no longer regard the household as the bearer of those cultural values in whose service he places himself.[38]

In the 'permanent transition' of the Plain of Gioia this linear passage of roles and functions from the family to civil society never took place. The social structure was characterised precisely by the absence of this transfer of powers to civil society and central authority. Although it was both the seat of a market economy and the home of a family of the nuclear type, the Plain of Gioia presents an extra-familial web of social relations both extremely thin and very limited. Relations among families and individuals were those of sovereign powers in conflict. There Sahlins's rules of 'negative reciprocity' held sway (see Chapter 1, pp. 54–5).

---

[37] Lawrence Stone, *The Crisis of the Aristocracy, 1558–1641* (Oxford, 1965), p. 669.
[38] Max Weber, *Economy and Society. An Outline of Interpretive Sociology*, ed. Guenther Roth and Claus Willich (New York, 1968), vol. I, pp. 375–6.

The whole set-up of the social system resembled in many ways that described in *The Leviathan* of Hobbes without, however, the presence of the Leviathan itself. The Plain of Gioia was the zone of the *faida*, of clans, of violent political and family feuds. The social aggregate there was formed of a multitude of monads without doors or windows. No pre-established harmony could prevent either their proliferation or their antagonisms. Each blood group was almost completely free of the laws of the territorial community. The respect of each for the rights of the others was assured by the recognition that any injured party had the absolute right to obtain redress by force and by the support of his relatives in any such action.

Artificial kinship and instrumental friendship

The most ancient 'right to the *faida*', which re-emerged when traditional society was penetrated by the market, is only a part of the general 'impact' of the logic of the market on cultural structures in the society itself.

The encounter between the market and the specific culture of the society of permanent transition translated itself into a clash of values and in a consequent state of disorientation and anomie both individual and collective. Given the instability of the activity of the market and the 'permanence of the transition' connected to it, the clash could never resolve itself in one direction or the other. The modern logic of the market was never able to get control totally of traditional culture, and the latter for its part never had the force to expel or neutralise the forces, values and modes of behaving dictated by the market.

The result of this conflict did not, however, consist in a schizophrenic division of social action but in an interesting, if highly complicated, modification of its 'sense'. There emerged a double reaction which both exalted the traditional culture and instrumentalised, on a selective basis, certain traditional values, of which mafia behaviour represented the most complete synthesis.

Honour, friendship, masculinity, fidelity, family, kinship and localism were exalted in this zone to the paradoxical point at which to the casual observer they seemed to be the exclusive models of behaviour and morality. This ostentatious enthusiasm for tradition ought neither to annul nor conceal the fact that to this block of values – as we have seen – there was no corresponding social structure nor homogeneous economic structure. A conflict opened up between the goals prescribed by the culture and the socially structured possibilities available to individuals to act in conformity with them.

This potential menace to the linearity of action was in part overcome precisely by the selection and instrumentalisation of the very traditional values themselves. The selection took place (a) by transferring into daily behaviour those themes – such as 'honour' – functional for the stimulus toward competition and struggle which originated either in the economic sphere or from the extra-familial arena; (b) by letting drop those other themes – such as the solidarity of village and neighbourhood, the various forms of mutual aid rendered without the expectation of immediate repayment which one was held to offer to friends and relatives – too strictly tied to situations of *Gemeinschaft*. The instrumentalisation took place, in addition, by opening a space for the commercial and conflictual use of the duties and values connected with friendship and kinship.

Even the relations of kinship were subjected in the Plain of Gioia Tauro to the cycle of *corsi e ricorsi* of the social hierarchy. They could, however, not be 'overloaded' beyond necessity. Each domestic unit needed its own space for 'possible' relations within which to play its chances and in which it did not have to be obliged by 'closed', predetermined systems of duties among blood relatives. In the *Gemeinschaft* of the Cosentino such opportunities were reduced to a minimum. There was a system of basic relationships which conceded very little room for individual variation. In the Plain of Gioia, by contrast, the possibility of employing such individual variations by slackening all relations of an ascriptive type when the needs of social realignment demanded formed the central nucleus of family politics.

Natural kinship presented a different 'sense' here than in the Cosentino. It did not give rise to profoundly interiorised relations whose prescriptive character constituted merely the 'appearance' in front of a very solid structure, but to a 'fan' of channels of communication which often found themselves out of phase with respect to the changeable structural evolution and hence had to be continuously redefined. Such a redimensioning of the fundamentality of kinship never signified, however, the cessation of all tendencies to enlarge the relations based on it. On the contrary, it signified that a larger space was now open for the phenomenon of individual and family manipulation of the links of kinship itself. This phenomenon consisted in a restriction of the field of natural kinship. One kept alive only those blood relations which demonstrated, at least potentially, that they might be useful, independent of the elementary structures of affinity. It created, instead, a number of relations of artificial kinship, so defined, that is, by the fact that they had been chosen and not inherited.

The institution of *comparaggio*,[39] was in this respect the most precise example. It was certainly not exclusive to the Plain of Gioia, as indeed were very few of the phenomena we have analysed, but it experienced in that zone the largest and most varied diffusion and evolution. From our point of view it is interesting to observe how the exchange of *compari* between members of two nuclear families produced a tie whose normativity and importance was considered to be superior to those generated by consanguinity. It gave the impulse to a chain of formalised, interfamilial alliances which played a decisive role in the unfolding of many conflict phenomena, especially the *faida*.

The condition of permanent transition of the Plain of Gioia influenced not only the form and function of family and kinship but also other important primary institutions, such as, for example, the associative relations based on friendship. Relations between two individuals here did not symbolise, as happened in the peasant society of the Cosentino, the respective roles of the two interested persons but also implied an entire series of relations which must be valued and adapted at the slightest sign of change. In this area too there developed that type of manipulation we have already noticed. The 'politics of kinship' was allied to the 'politics of friendship'. To the pairs of opposites formed by natural and artificial kinship there corresponded the pairing of emotional and instrumental friendship.

---

[39] 'Co-parenthood' is the nearest English equivalent and the one generally used by English-speaking social scientists (Translator).

Friendship of the emotive type is an interpersonal relationship which occurs most frequently in situations in which the individual finds himself strongly tied to 'mechanical solidarities' of various types and where the arrangement of the socio-economic structures prevents geographical and social mobility. In this regard the village of the Cosentino represents an excellent example. The function of emotional friendship there was simply to reduce the costs of village life and to give a positive content to that mechanism of regulation and levelling of individual comportment which assured the 'simple reproduction' of the system. The profound emotional involvement implicit in such 'brotherhood' acted as a counterweight to the envy and suspicion which characterised neighbourly relations.[40]

In contrast to emotional friendship is what I have called instrumental friendship. Instrumental friendship may not have been entered into for the purpose of attaining access to resources – natural and social – but the striving for such access becomes vital in it. In contrast to emotional friendship, which restricts the relation to the dyad involved, in instrumental friendship each member of the dyad acts as a potential connecting link to other persons outside the dyad. Each participant is a sponsor for the other. In contrast to emotional friendship, which is associated with closure of the social circle, instrumental friendship reaches beyond the boundaries of existing sets, and seeks to establish beachheads in new sets.

Ruben Reina, whose Indian material I have described, contrasts the Indians in Chinautla with the Ladinos. 'To the Ladinos, friendship has practical utility in the realm of economic and political influence; this friendship is looked upon as a mechanism beneficial from the personal viewpoint. *Cuello*, a favorite expression among the Ladinos, indicates that a legal matter may be accelerated, or a job for which one is not totally qualified might be secured through the personal influence of an acquaintance who is in power or knows a third party who can be influenced. The *cuello* complex depends upon the strength of friendship established and is often measured in terms of the number of favors dispensed to each other. It finds its main support in the nature of a convenient social relationship defined as friendship. It follows that, for the Ladinos of Chinautla, the possession of a range of friends is most favorable' (Reina, 1959, pp. 44–45).[41]

---

[40] Max Weber, *Economy and Society*, vol. 1, p. 362.
[41] E. R. Wolf, 'Kinship, Friendship, and Patron–Client Relations in Complex Societies', in M. Banton (ed.), *The Social Anthropology of Complex Societies* (London, 1966), p. 12.

It is important not to ignore the fact that, notwithstanding the instrumental character of this relation, it is still friendship. A quantum of emotional involvement remains an important but unstable ingredient. It often happened that if the instrumental ends of friendship gained the upper hand too manifestly, or if there arose between the two parties a permanent disequilibrium based on too marked inequalities of power or income, the relationship broke up, yielding place either to declared hostility or to subordination of the client type. Even an equilibrium founded on a restricted and balanced reciprocity implied considerable inconvenience because of the excessive formalisation of actions which it required.

The society of the Plain of Gioia Tauro was an ideal territory for the development of relations of instrumental friendship. The chains of liaison there achieved a diffusion so accentuated as to supplant and render 'antiquated' the closed, linked systems based on a fixed number of relations. The prestige of an individual was measured by the number of 'adherences', the number of his 'accounts' with other people. This is how that relational form has been described by an entrepreneur on the Plain:

The *pillari*, the bumpkins from the inland zones, don't know anything but the little circle of friends and relatives in their village (which are really the same thing).
Here at Gioia we are more advanced. Here we can *select* a friendship on the basis of our preferences... You make a trip and you meet somebody who is valuable, or you have a shop and you have a group of clients who respect you, or a friend introduces you to somebody else and so on.
So a person can always count on a circle of other people who respect him and consider him a friend and whom this person thinks of as friends and respects... You never know what will happen in life. You might need them. I mean, you don't choose your friends for that reason; it's just that a true friend will always give you a hand...
If somebody does not know how to pay back a favour, well, that means he doesn't know how to be a true friend...[42]

Instrumental friendship played a part in the normal functioning of social relations in a traditional society of a complex type. Based as they were on a rather broad form of reciprocity, they

---

[42] Oral testimony, collected in Gioia Tauro, July, 1975.

possessed a strongly positive content not tilted toward the external reality. By contrast with other types of 'manipulated' social relations, they contained few marked elements of subordination and were at bottom a mode of social action which served to achieve first and more easily those 'natural ends' of a mercantile society with high mobility.

The problem of social integration

From the analysis carried out in the preceding section it ought to be abundantly clear how the 'twisting' of values and traditional institutions which we have verified in the Plain of Gioia facilitated social mobility and market exchange. What it could not do was to provide an achieved order of institutions, norms and values capable of giving some unity to the various aspects of individual and collective life.

Ties of artificial kinship and instrumental friendship constituted intrinsically limited attempts to safeguard a minimum of social cohesion. Their nature as compromises among counterpoised forces brought it about that the reconstruction of interindividual solidarity which they achieved remained, in large part, casual, episodic, lacking in coordination or general logic. For this reason they produced perverse effects even encouraging the game of fragmentation and realignment instead of slowing and controlling it, increasing the polycentrism and acephalia typical of the Plain.

One great problem remains to be explained. In the system we have been describing, the great institutions of social cohesion and traditional stability – the family-enterprise, reciprocity, elementary structures and prescriptive duties to one's kin, mechanical solidarities of various types – have all been compromised in their existence or diverted in their functioning without being substituted by any new mechanism of regulation of social relations. How, in the last analysis, can such a society be 'held together'? What prevented the characteristic war of all against all which marked interpersonal and interfamilial relations on the Plain from 'exploding'? Why did the system not generate centrifugal forces leading to mass emigration or urbanisation?

To answer this question we have to turn our attention to an

unusual phenomenon, whose relevance as an aspect of the comprehensive reintegration of traditional social cohesion has been greatly undervalued. The behaviour and power of the mafia constituted in fact the specific reaction of the society of permanent transition to the powerful centrifugal forces generated within the sphere of its economic life. The essential feature of the mafia phenomenon was not that it was an organisation nor a social movement with specific ends and programmes – as some journalists would appear to believe and even some superficial students of the phenomenon, not least some politicians – but it was the point of convergence of a series of diverse tendencies in the society itself: the self-defence of a traditional society against threats to its traditional mode of life; the aspirations of the various groups which composed it towards a 'freezing' and control of the undulating movements which distorted every institution and destroyed all security; personal ambition and the hopes of active and ruthless individuals.

Mafia behaviour and mafia power

What does it mean to 'behave in the manner of the mafia'? It means 'to make oneself respected', 'to be a man of honour' capable of revenging by his own force any sort of offence done to his own personality and capable equally of dealing out offence to an enemy. Such behaviour, be it defensive or aggressive, was not only justified but encouraged and even idealised by the society of permanent transition of the Plain of Gioia, even if it risked a frontal clash with the authority of the state. In fact, a significant part of the power and prestige of a mafia action derived precisely from the fact that it constituted an open infraction of the official judicial norms and institutions.

To comport oneself in the mafia manner meant to behave in an *honourable* way, in a way, that is, which conformed to those rules of courage, cunning, ferocity and the use of force and fraud which played a crucial role in the culture and society of the Plain of Gioia Tauro. 'He was truly valiant and nobody could face up to him.' 'Usually he was not violent but on the occasions when he was forced to it, he stunned people and astonished his enemies. It happened six or seven times and people still talk about it as if it were a legend.' This is the way the *mafioso* of a village is described in a book which might serve as a species of popular tract on the traditional mafia. To the members of the society described in *La vera storia del brigante Marlino Zappa*,[43] the word 'honourable' denoted little more than an affirmation of superior force. 'Honourable' meant 'exceptional', 'worthy', 'arrogant'. An honorific act was, in the last analysis, an extremely successful act of aggression, and it made no difference if it was in response to a previous act or was an autonomous initiative of the aggressor.

Mafia behaviour was part of a system of culture centred on the theme of honour achieved by means of individual violence. In the permanent transition of the Plain of Gioia, the personal force of each individual had more obvious and immediate influence than elsewhere in determining the distribution of honour among the diverse members of society. Neither birth nor institutions had a determining influence on that distribution. You become a man of honour; you aren't born one. Competition for honour is free to all, and anyone may enter the lists. The elite of men of honour formed itself by a harsh process of selection which took place on the basis of ruthless competition among individual persons. In the society of the Plain, unlike many other traditional societies, such antagonistic confrontation was a habitual fact, and success in the struggle became an end in itself and the basis of popular esteem and admiration.

The competition for honour was not accurately delimited nor institutionalised as happens in modern forms of sporting, scholastic or mercantile competition or in the struggles of classes or organised groups. All means were good. The most archaic forms of battle between man and man were employed: robbery with violence, devastation, kidnapping and slaughter. Aggression became the accredited form of action and the booty the most immediate proof of victorious aggression.

Given the importance of honorific conflict in the strategy of mafia values, taking a life, especially killing a fearful enemy, was honorific in the highest degree. 'X is an exceptional man; he "has" five killings.' 'Y is a man of respect; he has "stubbed out" four Christians.' These sorts of phrases recur in mafia conversa-

[43] P. Familiari, *La vera storia del brigante Marlino Zappa* (Vibo Valentia, 1971).

tion. Among the *mafiosi* of the Plain of Gioia Tauro the act of homicide, if carried out in a competition for supremacy of any sort whatever, indicated (and still does, for these attitudes persist in the flourishing mafia of today) courage and the capacity to impose oneself as a man. It brought an automatic opening of a line of credit for the killer. The more awesome and potent the victim, the more worthy and meritorious the killer. There was an important form of conversion between illegal and mafia action. Breaking the laws of the state was honorific inasmuch as it hurled defiance and expressed contempt for powerful institutions and persons. The careers of many *mafiosi* of the Plain began in common criminality.

The honorific dimension of murder, as an expression of the arrogance and capacity for revenge of the killer, wrapped in an aureole of glory every act of homicide, all the apparatus and accessories of the act. To get an idea of the resonance which an act of homicide still has for the population of the Plain, you only have to open the pages of the most widely read daily newspaper of the zone the day after the homicide itself. The pages are filled with photographs. All the events and particulars, no matter how minute, are tinged with the symbolic grandeur of the event. The report emphasises the most ferocious and violent episodes of the act, how much blood was spilt, the mutilation of the corpse, the routine of the victim's last days, the despair and wailing of the relatives.

The possession and the use of arms constituted on the Plain of Gioia an honourable fact. In 1950 there were several hundred authorisations to bear arms, a much larger number of cases of illegal possession of arms of all sorts – rifles, pistols, knives, projectiles – and an enormous number of imprisonments for 'illegal possession'.

So far, we have considered the violent and individualistic aspect of the mafia phenomenon, the anomic competition among rivals for a supremacy which was the source of esteem and public regard. If one considers the careers of the principal *mafiosi* of the Plain, one is astonished by the sheer number of conflicts from which they emerged victorious, especially during the early days of their apprenticeship.

There is a second aspect of the mafia phenomenon which has

even greater relevance for our analysis than the first and illustrates the opposite side of mafia as a social institution. This aspect may be described in terms of a process of *institutionalisation of honour* and the transformation of it into power recognised as legitimate.

What happened, in fact, when the competition for supremacy ended with the victory of a very strong competitor who thus succeeded in reaching the highest levels of honourability? Such a victor would seek to impose his patronage over territory and population by establishing a monopoly of physical violence stable enough to permit him to preserve his own position for as long as possible. He would try to 'freeze' the existing distribution of honour and to attenuate the war of all against all by regularising and controlling it. As we have seen, such a Hobbesian war was already basic to the society of the Plain.

To achieve such fundamental social control, the archaic virtues of courage, ruthlessness and force, which favoured his rise to power, were no longer enough. The *mafioso* had to be able to exercise the activities of a government if he wanted to die in bed honoured and revered as a gentleman. To the lion he had to add the fox. Now he had to prove his prudence, balance and astuteness if his power were to be accepted and recognised by the population. The people had to see in his person not only the strong, victorious man capable of annihilating any adversary whatever but also a form of superior authority. He had to act as father of all, friend of all, the protector, mediator, counsellor and judge.

As we have seen, the society of the Plain was subject to a continuous, very real menace of disintegration. There was, therefore, a strong need for a power above the individual, a public power capable of creating at least an appearance of collective order. The encounter between the needs of the system for self-regulation and the needs of the men of honour for respect ended by investing these men of honour with a variety of important public functions as the guardians of traditional values and the established order. *Mafiosi* became the civil and criminal judges, mediators, protectors, arbitrators, subsuming in themselves many delicate functions normally exercised by the power of the state. Honour transformed itself into authority, and finally into legitimacy. The legitimacy, then, in its turn, turned into a further source of confirmation and amplification of honour. Legitimacy, that is the general acceptance of mafia authority, grew not so much out of esteem and spontaneous admiration of the crowd for bold gestures carried out by the man of honour during the period of his self-assertion; honour acquired in this way put too much social distance between a hero capable of exceptional acts and the ordinary person to be able to constitute a lasting basis for identification. The mechanism of *mafioso* 'representativeness', while always keeping that elitist dimension in view, based itself on anti-heroic and anti-charismatic propaganda. The man of respect who had made it, did not seek legitimacy by presenting himself as somebody gifted with extraordinary qualities given only to the select few; but, on the contrary, he presented himself as an ordinary man, gifted in the highest grade with the basic characteristics of everybody, as a valid model for all.

The aggressive and predatory component of mafia comportment must then be understood on the basis of a marked institutionalisation and auto-limitation, which circumscribed its expressions. Mafia action is characterised by its striking conformity to the ruling cultural norms and not by a tendency to subvert them. The simple man, who nevertheless speaks for all, that was the typical *mafioso*. The chap who kept faith with his friends, who knew how to repay a favour, who exalted honour and recognition and who was ready to use violence to make sure that such values were respected, was a citizen honoured in his community. He could not be defined in any way as a delinquent, a marginal, a rebel.

There are no significant differences ¯ from this and other points of view – between the physiognomy, function and propaganda of mafia power as we have met it in the Plain of Gioia Tauro and the phenomena described by Hess in western Sicily. Hess cites two famous *capo-mafia* figures:

Momo Grasso of Mislimeri every year interpreted the role of Jesus in the traditional Passion Play ...

Genco Russo was startled by the accusation that he was a delinquent and rejected the idea; with such accusations journalists and politicians are just trying to ruin honest fathers of families. The acts carried out by him are in his eyes not criminal, but a natural 'social behaviour', a way of behaving entirely necessary in Sicilian society. Among sacrifices and troubles, largely of an altruistic kind, he assumes the role of orderer and protector ... which anyone can deduce from the wholesome course of his life.

This is a most important aspect in understanding the mafia. 'I was born this way. I act without ulterior motives. Anybody can ask a favour of me and I am willing to do it, because that's my nature ... Somebody comes along and says, "Look, I've got this problem with X; see if you can get him to agree." I call the person in question or I go to find him, depending on our relations, and I get the agreement. But I wouldn't like you to think that I am telling you all this to make myself big ... I say these things to you purely out of courtesy, because that's the way I got where I am. I am not vain nor ambitious.' This is the way the *mafioso* Genco Russo sees himself.[44]

The centrality of the *mafioso* as type and of mafia actions within the society of permanent transition must be sought in its multi-functional dimension, in its capacity to move on various planes, composing and synthesising contradictory thrusts.[45] The 'functional necessity' of mafia power was contained in its capacity to satisfy both the needs of order and of mobility at the same time, the need for cohesion and the drive toward competition which we have seen as present in the society of the Plain of Gioia Tauro. If one does not hold on to its public aspect as representative of threatened collective interests which the mafia assumes at the very moment in which it pursues its own ends of conservation and enlargement of its power base, one will never understand the nature of the traditional mafia.

It is also important to notice how all the fundamental activities of the mafia did not take place, save at a few moments of official rigidity, in frontal opposition to the tasks and functions of the organs of the state. Weber's definition of the state as 'the monopolist of violence' in a given territory was one which operates at a very high level of abstraction and takes no account of the concrete mediation through which the needs for the maintenance of social order expressed themselves. The reality of the Plain of Gioia demonstrated again and again how mafia and

---

[44] H. Hess, *Mafia* (Bari, 1973), pp. 100 and 100–101.
[45] E. Hobsbawm, *Primitive Rebels. Studies in Archaic Forms of Social Movement in the 19th and 20th Centuries* (Manchester, 1959), pp. 52–3.

organs of the state, theoretically competitors for the monopoly of the control of violence, in fact collaborated, often with very similar methods, in the repression of the most serious malfunctions and threats to the established order. In many episodes of banditry or common criminality, as in other cases of organised political dissent or trade-union activity, the intervention of the armed power of the *mafiosi* on the side of the official forces of order was decisive in the killing, capture or neutralisation of the deviants.

Since there did not exist in the Plain a proper ruling class 'traditionally' dominant but only a circulation of elites produced by the congeries of groups, families and individuals in a cycle of blind molecular movement, the dominant interests and values of the society almost never coincided with those of the group momentarily at the top, and that, in turn, reinforced the impartiality and prestige of mafia authority. The fundamental complementarity of the power and authority of the mafia and the legal authority of the state was well revealed in the gravest crisis of the latter. Between 1943 and 1945 *mafiosi* were nominated by Anglo-American military government as mayors of various towns of the Plain of Gioia Tauro, and it does not appear that their records as administrators gave rise to any particular inconveniences.

Between 1860 and the fascist period, the Italian state had in any case granted the mafia a blank cheque for the exercise of its function of public order in large areas of southern Calabria and western Sicily. The benefit from this delegation of power was that through the *mafiosi* local political groupings were drawn into national politics.[46] The system of 'notables' had already made use of the *mafiosi* to gather votes in zones not easily integrated by the normal devices of electoral consensus. The *capo-mafia* of the Plain of Gioia Tauro was almost always a great local electoral force,[47] whose support was necessary for all candidates for local and national elections. Many Calabrian members of successive governments between unification and the 1950s owed a good part of their political success to ties with mafia groups.

[46] S. F. Romano, *Storia della mafia* (Milan, 1966), p. 190.
[47] P. Familiari, *La vera storia*, pp. 30–3.

In exchange for their support at elections, which was guaranteed both by 'legal' means through political clienteles, through ties of friendship and family, and by 'illegal' means such as threats, extortion and in some cases even of kidnapping of electors, the *mafiosi* of the Plain of Gioia Tauro and of southern Calabria received from the men of government favours for themselves and their friend- and kinships groups, that is, for their *cosca*.

The exercise of the functions just described ended up by creating a sociologically rather precise standard model of the *mafioso*. There was an 'ideal type' which can be defined on the basis of a series of criteria such as (a) popular origins; (b) membership of the middle stratum of society; (c) the possession of a local, territorial power very specifically delimited.

The most important *mafiosi* of the Plain of Gioia all came from the lowest strata of society. Many of them were sons of poor peasants or even peasants themselves at the beginning of their careers. 'Don Mommo' Piromalli was a cowherd before becoming the most powerful 'man of honour' of the entire Plain. The ranks of most of his colleagues are filled with ex-*braccianti*, ex-shepherds and illiterate former carters. The subaltern strata of the Plain never developed an ideology of their own nor an autonomous complex of institutions designed to stabilise and justify their own position.

There was no trace of the 'culture of poverty'[48] in the Plain nor was there any stable stratification of internal cultures within the social structure. The values which guided the actions of discontented individuals, of local deviants in search of liberation from their misery, were thus always those of the better-off, all concentrated on the acquisition of honour. The pressure to enter the competition for honour was therefore much more intense among the members of the less honoured categories of society. This was the more true because success as a man of honour normally brought with it wealth. The man of respect usually enriched himself by means of mafia behaviour and power. Honorific ascent on the social hierarchy of the Plain was

---

[48] Oscar Lewis, *La Vida. A Puerto Rican Family in the Culture of Poverty – San Juan and New York* (London, 1967), pp. xxxix–xlviii.

accompanied by the social promotion of the *mafioso* and his family.

Whether in the popular value-system or in that of the *mafioso* himself, honour and wealth *accompanied* each other but were *never identical*. Even if normally the qualities of 'man of honour' and 'man of wealth' are to be found in the same person, there were verifiable cases in which there emerged a hierarchical difference far from negligible between the two criteria of social stratification. It could happen that a position on the top of the scale of wealth did not carry a corresponding honourability. The 'foreign' merchants, who for a long time held a near-complete monopoly of large-scale export trading and constituted during an entire phase of the history of the Plain of Gioia the local economic elite together with the large and medium-sized rural entrepreneurs, never held in any sense a position which could be defined as esteemed or 'honoured' socially.

The fundamentality of honour in the structure of mafia action brought it about that the pure-and-simple economic motive, understood either in terms of the vulgar thirst for gain or of a 'religion of accumulation', never succeeded in establishing itself as the supreme regulator of social relations and position. Accumulation, and, even more, the concentration of wealth on the part of *mafiosi*, once it reached a certain and rather conventional level, slowed down and halted. Beyond a certain limit, in fact, wealth and the power associated with it became 'incumbrances' for the *mafiosi*, difficult to defend and to justify.

The ownership of land could be the product of a good position in the hierarchy of honour and itself a source of honour, but the scale of that ownership could never surpass a certain threshold; beyond it the honorific position of the *mafioso*-turned-proprietor became difficult to maintain. In order to confront with security the aggressiveness of his numerous rivals, he would have to furnish himself with a salaried armed guard; he would have to ally himself increasingly with regional and national power elites and hence renounce a large part of his function as mediator within his own socio-cultural universe. All three of these conditions or consequences of landed wealth were within the context of the society of the Plain anti-honorific in the highest degree and required the abandonment of a gratifying style of life not least through the surrender or substitution of values which the traditional *mafioso* had no incentive to carry out.[49]

This 'imperfect conversion' between honour and wealth influenced noticeably the physiognomy and proportions of mafia power. It presented itself in the society of permanent transition almost always as a concrete power, local to a village and never in the trappings of impersonal, abstract power of a regional or national type.

The social classification of the *mafioso* was thus middling. He stood neither at the foot nor at the apex of the social pyramid. The authentic vocation of the traditional *mafioso* was neither proletarian/peasant nor aristocratic/grand bourgeois. The hostility of the mafia was often turned against both extremes even if, obviously, with much more caution and less frequency against the upper orders.

Mafia and the society of permanent transition

The mafia phenomenon, in so far as it was an attempt to guarantee and stabilise the social, economic and cultural order, constituted an original form of social integration whose efficacy ought not to be undervalued. In a static comparison of systems of integration, it would be classed in an autonomous position, distinct from that of a 'pure' traditional society like the Cosentino but also from that of modern-market society.

The mafia phenomenon had little or nothing do with either feudalism or the *latifondo*. It had instead everything to do with the profound nature of the reigning social relations in a mobile, mercantile universe like the society of permanent transition and with the 'selection' of useful relations determined themselves by a situation of generalised conflict and instability of social authority.

All typical struggles and modes of competition which take place on a large scale will lead, in the long run, despite the decisive importance in many individual cases of accidental factors and luck, to a selection of those who have in the higher degree, on the average, possessed the personal qualities important to success. What qualities are important

---

[49] P. Arlacchi, 'Mafia e tipi di società, *Rassegna italiana di sociologia*, no. 1, 1980.

depends on the conditions in which the conflict or competition takes place. It may be a matter of physical strength or unscrupulous cunning, of the level of mental ability or mere lung power... of qualities which are unusual or of those which are possessed by the mediocre majority. Among the decisive conditions, it must not be forgotten, belong the systems of order to which the behaviour of the parties is oriented, whether traditionally, as a matter of rationally disinterested loyalty (*wertrational*), or of expediency. Each type of order influences opportunities in the process of social selection differently.[50]

If the 'conditions' and the 'establishment' of the competitive struggle which unfolded in the society of permanent transition were those defined by encounter and clash of the market with the traditional cultural structure, what was the role of the power and behaviour of the mafia with regard to the market?

It is not difficult to deduce it. It is sufficient to reflect on what has been said about the two aspects of the mafia as a social phenomenon, that of struggle and that of institutionalisation. The mafia phenomenon was born out of a situation of anomic competition for honour, and represented an excellent instrument of social ascent in a system of commercial capitalism, where risk, fraud, and the absence of scruples were indispensable qualities for success. Although 'caused' by a situation of mass competition, mafia power tended 'to react on the cause' in the direction of the introduction of control over this competition. The regulation of the economic activities effected by the authority of the mafia constituted a tenacious deterrent with respect to the content of struggle, war, blood feud and generalised conflict implicit in the logic of the anomic competition of the market. Mafia power guaranteed the reciprocity of transactions. It defended consolidated commercial positions and guaranteed the places of the market. It introduced an element of direct discipline into the clash – precarious perhaps in the long run, but effective in the short run – which acted as a sort of 'visible hand' of the market itself. The cunning reformism of the *mafioso* who 'mediated' between market forces and society halted the potentially disruptive impact of the attempt to impose the market as the supreme regulator of all relations in the society.

[50] Max Weber, *Economy and Society*, vol. I, p. 38.

3
The system of 'latifondo' of the Crotonese

In the preceding chapters we have looked at two societies in no sense typical of the Mezzogiorno as a whole. There is scarcely another community which presents in such purity and rigour the peasant mode of production as the Cosentino did between the unification of Italy and 1950. There may be some similarities between the Plain of Gioia Tauro and parts of western Sicily and the Adriatic coast of Apulia, and it is possible that close analysis would uncover the same process of disintegration and recomposition which marks the peculiar social cohesion of the Plain of Gioia Tauro. These exceptional features do not, I think, weaken the paradigmatic value of the undertaking. I believe, on the contrary, they provide one of its principal advantages. It allows the observer to see in great clarity social patterns which occur but are less easily discerned in average, regular or usual situations. In such cases the statistics may be eloquent but qualitative evidence mute and hence comparison becomes difficult.

The area known as the Marchesato of Crotone (there is no easy English rendering of *Marchesato* or 'Marquisate') was also an exception.[1] There were elsewhere in the southern part of Italy great estates, worked by landless labourers called *braccianti*. Indeed, the great estate or *latifondo* (from the Latin *latifundium*) has sometimes been (wrongly) made the characteristic of all southern-Italian agriculture. The exceptional quality of the

---

[1] The villages of the Crotonese include those listed in zone XII of the ISTAT classification: Belvedere di Spinello, Carfizzi, Casabona, Cirò, Crotone, Crucoli, Cutro, Isola di Capo Rizzuto, Melissa, Roccabernarda, Rocca di Neto, San Mauro Marchesato, San Nicola dell'Alto, Santa Severina, Scandale, Strongoli.

Crotonese lay in the extent of inequality of ownership of land. There was in the Crotonese a concentration of great landholdings absolutely 'anomalous' and without parallel in the rest of the country, north or south. There existed a percentage of 'pure' rural proletariat only to be found in parts of the Po Valley and a few areas of the Capitanata. In that one sub-region of the Ionian coast of Calabria there existed a set of social relations so extreme that nothing quite like them can be found anywhere.

The exceptional quality of the Crotonese derived from a peculiar combination of geographical harshness and man-made exploitation which came to characterise the *latifondo* of the Crotonese. George Gissing, who spent an unhappy time in Crotone in 1897, could not believe the bleakness of the landscape.

> Driven inland by the gale, I wandered among low hills which overlook the town. Their aspect is very strange, for they consist entirely – on the surface, at all events – of a yellowish-grey mud, dried hard, and as bare as the high road. A few yellow hawkweeds, a few camomiles, grew in hollows here and there; but of grass not a blade. It is easy to make a model of these Crotonian hills. Shape a solid mound of hard-pressed sand, and then, from the height of a foot or two, let water trickle down upon it; the perpendicular ridges and furrows thus formed upon the miniature hill represent exactly what I saw here on a larger scale. Moreover, all the face of the ground is minutely cracked and wrinkled; a square foot includes an incalculable multitude of such meshes.[2]

On this barren soil the great estate owners of the area raised cereal crops and employed peasantry perhaps the most wretched in all Italy.

Property relations and production

The exceptional nature of the Crotonese began in the relations of property ownership. Here was the seat of the most spectacular concentration of landed property in the entire country. The INEA enquiry revealed that 1.4 per cent of the units of property covered 78.1 per cent of the surface. Fifteen individual holdings – that is, 0.1 per cent of all units – extended for 32,970 hectares, that is, a third of all the land area in the district. Each property amounted, on average, to some 2,000 hectares. The Marchesato of Crotone

---

[2] George Gissing, *By the Ionian Sea*, p. 60.

had an overall surface area of just under 100,000 hectares, equal to 9.6 per cent of all Calabrian land surface and 1 per cent of the Mezzogiorno as a whole. It contained 57 per cent of the largest land-holdings in Calabria and 9 per cent of those of the south as a whole (see Table 2, p. 13).

A large estate can cover much ground but mean little in the economy. It can be so unproductive that it influences only the margins of local production and employment in a given zone. It can, so to speak, be much less important than sheer size would indicate. This was not the case in the Crotonese where, if anything, the economic weight of the huge estates was greater than their already enormous share of the land surface. This becomes clear if, instead of land area, income per hectare is taken as the measure. The INEA enquiry of 1947 broke down the great estates of Italy by yield and in Table 25 there is an enumeration of all such estates with gross taxable incomes above 500,000 lire (worth in those days a multiple of today's lira).[3] These were great units from an economic point of view.

Table 25 shows the following:
(a) In all Italy there were only six agrarian zones in which the taxable income of macro-property exceeded four and a half million lire. The first of such zones of 'maximum concentration' was the Crotonese, where the five largest estates in all of Italy were to be found and which produced a taxable income of 7,600,000. Next came the nine biggest estates of the Milanese plain with incomes of 7,300,000 and then the six largest units in the plain of Ferrara with 'only' 4,550,000. The taxable income of the macro-estates of the Crotonese was greater than that of all the great estates of Piedmont put together. It was greater than that of Abruzzo-Molise and Lazio put together and was just below the total income of Apulia, among the most notoriously unequal regions of Italian agriculture.
(b) These five macro-estates made up 91 per cent of all the very large estates of Calabria and 30 per cent of the whole continental south (18 per cent if Sicily and Sardinia are

---

[3] The official rate of exchange in 1947 was 900 lire to £1, a raw taxable income in 1947 pounds of £555, worth roughly ten times that today (Translator).

Table 25 *The distribution of private land-holdings of more than 500,000 lire taxable yield by zones of maximum concentration, by region and by general area*

	(a) number of holdings	(b) taxable yield (000s)	(b)÷(a) average yield (000s)
Zones of maximum concentration			
Crotonese	5	7,674	1,535
Plain of Milan	9	7,306	812
Plain of Pavia	9	7,161	796
Plain of Bologna	10	5,645	564
Plain of Vercelli	6	4,998	833
Plain of Ferrara	6	4,550	758
Regions			
Lombardy	30	22,799	760
Veneto	25	19,604	784
Emilia	25	16,531	661
Sicily	20	14,720	736
Tuscany	15	12,390	826
Calabria	6	8,398	1,400
Puglia	9	8,204	912
Piedmont	9	7,011	779
Lucania	5	5,408	1,082
Abruzzo and Molise	3	3,841	1,280
Lazio	3	2,768	923
The Marches	3	1,810	603
Campania	1	612	612
Umbria	1	592	592
Liguria	—	—	—
Trentino Alto Adige	—	—	—
Sardinia	—	—	—
General area			
South Italy	44	41,183	936
Mainland Mezzogiorno	24	26,463	1,103
Italy	164	134,095	818

Source: INEA 1947, *Distribuzione della proprietà fondiaria in Italia*

included in the reckoning). In addition, it must be borne in mind that the number of proprietors is less than the number of estates measured by the INEA enquiry, because of the special inheritance system typical of the 'barons' of the Crotonese, and because joint ownership was common. The lands owned in the Crotonese by no means exhausted the holdings of the great proprietorial families. Their holdings in other parts of Italy, combined with these vast estates in the Crotonese, make it difficult to conceive of how much economic, social and political power lay in the hands of six or seven groups of families. The most important, the Barracco, the Berlingieri, the Lucifero, the Gaetani, became notorious during the post-1945 struggles and battles for land. Here is an excerpt from *Il Ponte* of 1950: 'Don Giulio Berlingieri possesses, as everybody knows, 22,500 hectares. Alfonso Barracco has only 17,000.'[4] In one community of the Marchesato, Isola di Capo Rizzuto, the barons owned 9,655 out of 12,401 hectares. The Barracco family had 5,460, the Gaetani 2,227, Giuseppina Galluccio 1,300 and the Berlingieri 668. Alongside these very large holdings there were, in addition, some thirty of about 500. The remaining twenty-seven hectares were subdivided among 437 families. In another typical community of the Crotonese, Cutro, two proprietors possessed about 8,000 hectares. Thirteen owned another 3,600. Roughly thirty had holdings of between 10 and 100 hectares, while 799 *families* possessed 349 hectares, seven of which were shared among 414 proprietors. If you turn back to Table 2 (p. 13) you will notice another fundamental feature of the Crotonese: the unimportance of the small and very small land-holdings, which occupy respectively 6.5 per cent and 3.9 per cent of the cultivated surface. The other areas have percentages two or even three times as high.

From the point of view of our analysis, the element constituted by the absence in the Crotonese of the phenomenon of agrarian parcellisation constitutes a specific difference between it and the other zones, as relevant as the existence of the dominion of large-scale ownership itself. The landed structure of the

---

[4] L. Repaci, 'Baroni controluce', *Il Ponte*, nos. 9–10, 1950, p. 1235.

Crotonese does not present that polarisation between concentration and parcellisation typical of agrarian regimes based on medium-sized and, even more, on large-scale proprietorship. Concentration of land-holding was as absolute as the dominance of the large enterprise over the relations of production.

In contrast to the meridional agrarian system, in which a relative concentration of proprietorship corresponded to a general fragmentation of the productive organisation, and equally in contrast to the capitalistically advanced rural systems, where there is a clear division between forms of ownership and forms of cultivation of the soil, between rent and profit, the agrarian set-up of the Crotonese presented a marked correspondence between property relations and relations of production. To a structure of land tenure characterised by the dominion of very few extremely large units there corresponded a productive structure based on large enterprises. A large part of the specificity and originality of the *latifondo* is to be sought precisely in its nature as a productive enterprise. It represents a qualitatively distinctive 'type' of utilisation of the factors of production not merely a simple territorial extension of vast proportion which could be run in any number of ways.

The dominating labour relations on the *latifondo* were relations of salaried labour. Almost half of the cultivated surface (see Table 26) and more than 60 per cent of the agricultural labourers registered by the census in 1936 (see Table 27) were involved in 'pure' salaried relationships. To this group, already very numerous, of agricultural proletarians we can add without hesitation the following categories:

(a) the persons listed in the census as small tenants or small share-croppers because such people represent a disguised addition to the supply of and demand for wage labour, in short, belong unequivocally to the rural proletariat;
(b) a large part of the 8 per cent listed in Table 27 as proprietors cultivating their own lands. The enquiry carried out in 1939 by ISTAT supports that assumption. It looked at the number of family members employed full-time in peasant agriculture in family-enterprises and arrived at a figure for the Crotonese of 30 per cent. The remaining 70 per cent really belong therefore to the category of wage labour. If you add the 70 per

Table 26 *The distribution of surface under cultivation by type of enterprise in the Crotonese*

	Hectares	%
Peasant enterprises		
owned	10,505	13.4
rented	26,973	34.4
Enterprises in share-cropping		
total	1,788	2.3
of which *appoderata*	0	0
Enterprises on joint basis	1,355	1.7
Enterprises using wage labour	37,873	48.2
Total	78,494	100.0

Source: INEA, *Tipi di impresa nell'agricoltura italiana*, Rome, 1951

Table 27 *Persons employed in agriculture in the Crotonese by type of employment*

	Persons	%
Direct owners	1,106	8.1
Tenant farmers		
pure	1,461	10.6
varied titles*	1,842	13.4
share-croppers	47	0.3
Wage labour		
daily hired	6,841	49.9
annual contract	1,531	11.2
Others **	874	6.5
Total employed in agriculture	13,702	100.0

Source: *Censimento demografico*, 1936
* The category includes persons listed in the census under the headings *conduttori coltivatori e fittavoli, terraticanti, enfiteuti ed usufruttuari*.
** The heading includes persons with joint tenure, owners not cultivating their own lands, employees in offices etc., miscellaneous.

cent of family members who went out to work elsewhere, you arrive at something like 12,300 of a total of 13,700 employed who can fairly be considered as essentially a wage-earning rural proletariat.

Table 26 underlines how rare other forms of contract were in the Crotonese. Aside from wage labour and small tenancies, there was very little else. These two forms of rural employment dominated the region and exercised a kind of attractive force on all the other relations of production. There is a precise relationship between the territorial diffusion of a certain type of tenure and the 'quantum' of decentralisation implicit in it. In this case that relationship is inverse. The Crotonese is the reverse of the Cosentino. Hence *colonia parziaria appoderata*, the partial tenancy with farm, which we saw as the characteristic form of tenure in the Cosentino and which gave rise to a society based on self-sufficient, self-regulating peasant agriculture, did not exist in the Crotonese. Similarly, the small peasant farm, which in any evaluation of economic and social independence must come second to the *colonia parziaria appoderata*, is also under-represented at 13.4 per cent among the types of tenure in the Crotonese.

'Latifondo', feudal land-holding and capitalist enterprise

From the point of view of the structure of the relations of property and production, therefore, the salient characteristic of the Crotonese consisted in the presence of a very sharp schism between proprietors and proletariat. The 'peasant pole' of the social order did not exist, and the Crotonese represented the antithesis of the traditional peasant society which we identified in the Cosentino in the years before 1950. Let us now try to clarify the nature of that type of productive unit around which a social structure organised itself and which was so rigorously dichotomous, so close to the pure state of a class society.

What was a *latifondo*?

It is not easy to answer that question because we still know very little about the subject. Even today there are still no studies in depth which examine the development of the fundamental economic dimensions of that type of enterprise. We still know too little about its economic calculations, about its investment policies, its wage dynamics, its productivity and so forth. We know even less about the social structure of the *latifondo* itself. The only comprehensive sketch which attempts to show the structure and dynamic complexity of the southern-Italian *latifondo*, is still that carried out by Rossi-Doria in 1944 and from which I cite here its most important traits. According to Rossi-Doria, the *latifondo* consisted of

a large productive unit devoted to cereal crops and pasture based on capitalist principles. All necessary labour is provided by salaried persons either fixed or casually employed. The type of entrepreneur was and is varied. At one extreme there is the great estate owner who runs the estate himself making use of agents or sub-agents and only in part, generally the pastoral part, makes use of tenancies or rent agreements. At the other extreme ... are tenant entrepreneurs generally risen from pastoral or mountain backgrounds ...

Latifondo enterprises have their centres sprinkled across the countryside and grouped around sets of farm buildings – the *masseria* – and embody a high level of technical rationalisation.

All south-Italian plains suffer the continuous threats of aridity on the one hand or malaria on the other ... Until a few years ago agrarian technology had no other use for the soil than an alternation between sheep herds and a precarious and intermittent cultivation of grain. The changing combination of grazing sheep or goats and extensive cereal cultivation – the most primitive types of agriculture – seemed to be an obligatory use of the terrain, which permitted owners to exploit the advantages of the mild winters, to escape, in part, the threat of drought and to leave the countryside as empty of people as possible during the summer months when malaria predominated.

In spite of the difficult conditions which make extensive rather than intensive agriculture unavoidable ... the entrepreneurs have made much progress. They have been in the van of agricultural improvement both in the techniques of grain production and in improvements in stock and herding. Nevertheless they have never been able to escape the vicious circle of this kind of agriculture because prices move so capriciously. The whole history of southern agriculture, of this type in particular, has been dominated by oscillation in the prices of wool and cheese on one side and grain on the other. Whenever the one set of prices is markedly superior to the other, the entrepreneur has no choice, lest he go broke, but to switch from pasturage to arable or the reverse. Switching from herding to sowing grain quickly can only be guaranteed if the enterprise is kept as simple as possible. Fixed investment must be avoided because it impedes rapid switching of capital investment from one sort of agriculture to the other. The more primitive the agriculture, paradoxically, the closer the units approach rationality in market terms.

The *latifondo* carries out another crucial function; it integrates vast areas of mountainous terrain by summer grazing ... The herds come down each winter because the high zones become completely inhospitable and hence agriculture oscillates to the ancient rhythms of the *transumanza*, the annual ascent and descent from mountain pastures. The huge estate thus utilises by its primitiveness and extension otherwise disparate territories and hence extends its economic influence over widely dispersed populations, who are ready to pay rents for the naked earth, for the natural, spontaneous growth of grass in winter, rents which no other sort of agriculture could yield. The primitive structure of this agriculture is organised in an iron ring difficult to break.[5]

From this description it will be clear that the *latifondo* constituted its own true and proper 'system of necessary relations', an economic structure on its own, an original, which cannot be identified with the two models most similar to it which the social sciences have developed, that is, the system of feudal tenure on the one hand and the modern capitalist agricultural enterprise on the other.

With respect to the model of seigneurial tenure worked out by Marc Bloch and W. Kula in two basic works,[6] the *latifondo* differs, in my view, in at least three essential points: (1) a very high direct elasticity in the utilisation of the factors of production in relation to market incentives; (2) an extremely centralised organisation of the labour employed but also very precarious employment of the means of production, both land and labour; (3) relatively high productivity.

With respect to point (1) it is important to underline that the *latifondo* responded to variations in prices in exactly the same way as a capitalist enterprise. The economy of the *latifondo* was stimulated positively by rising prices. As in the capitalist economic model, if the level of activity favours it, the enterprise puts everything into motion. It augments the level of utilisation of the productive forces; it augments its investments; its profits go up. The same thing did not occur in the feudal system, where decisions on investment or the level of social yield either had no relation to the market situation or, as Kula has shown, had a

---

[5] M. Rossi-Doria, 'Struttura e problemi', pp. 7–9.
[6] M. Bloch, *French Rural History. An Essay on its Basic Characteristics*, trs. Janet Sondheimer (Berkeley, California, 1966); W. Kula, *An Economic Theory of the Feudal System, towards a Model of the Polish Economy, 1500–1800*, trs. Lawrence Garner (London, 1976), esp. pp. 41–4, 82 ff.

relationship which was exactly the inverse: investments were decided upon as a consequence of a worsening of the market conditions, since the lords had to compensate for the losses suffered by augmenting global production in order to conserve their proper tenor of life and their proper social position.[7]

In the economy of the *latifondo*, as in capitalist enterprise, production and price were directly related. Ample quotas of unutilised 'free' factors of production were available which could be put to work by a rise in prices. In a way, the *latifondo* reacted more sensitively to changes in markets than the capitalist agriculture because the *latifondo* could mobilise conspicuous reserves of land, labour and capital so quickly. For example, evidence shows that the southern part of Italy reacted more quickly than the northern to medium-term improvements in the price of cereal crops. Land came into cultivation much more quickly in areas of 'backward' *latifondo* agriculture than in the 'advanced' capitalist north.[8] This is not to say that the *latifondo* was more capitalistic than a capitalist enterprise, but only to measure the distance which separates it as a type from the seigneurial reserve and from its own origins and residual features. If that distance is rather large on the level of relations with the outside world, that is, with the national and international markets for goods, it is even greater on the level of internal organisation, that is, of its forms and productive relations. So we arrive at the second point of difference between the

---

[7] The possibility of carrying out such investment was in any case extremely limited. Increase in production could only be achieved by extension, adding new inputs of land and labour to those already employed, but the quantities of factors of production effectively available and easily mobilised were much reduced by the chronic shortage of labour which afflicted the system. The absence of a pool of 'nobody's people', of free labourers in a social environment in which even the beggars had their own corporations and protectors, turned potentially valuable assets and abundant reserves (woods, uncultivated or badly cultivated terrain) into assets whose effective value was zero.

The quantity of labour under feudalism was a variable independent of the level of prices. The relationship between the realised profit and the level of prices was not only inverse but causally the opposite of those relations under capitalism. A rise in prices did not give any increase in social yield. Since the lord's consumption was set by non-economic categories, a general fall in price could lead to an increase in production.

[8] E. Sereni, 'La lotta per la conquista della terra nel Mezzogiorno', *Cronache meridionali*, nos. 1–2, 1956, pp. 10–11.

latifondo and the feudal system of tenure, a point which is yet more important.

At first glance the internal arrangements of the *latifondo* had features in common with the feudal estate. In the *latifondo* the organisation of each territory was divided into two parts. In one of them the proprietor (directly or through one of his employees) carried on economic activity on his own account; the other was subdivided into many tiny plots and farmed by peasants, who paid rent in cash or kind. Table 26 indicates that 38 per cent of the surface area of the Crotonese was farmed under various forms of rental contract. There are two ways to regard such tenures. They could represent a seigneurial relationship between a great feudatory and his tenants adapted to market forces, or, as I think, the dominion of an original form of economic organisation astute enough to conceal beneath the banner of feudalism a very different spirit. I believe that we are looking at something rather like the *camera oscura* in which the images are reversed. All the relations of production on the *latifondo* are the opposite of feudal.

The division of labour and internal space under feudal tenures corresponded to the division between surplus production and the necessary production required to keep the system operating. The surplus was drawn from the farming operations of the proprietor and was consumed (or converted into other consumption goods through the market, such as luxury artisanal products etc.). The terrain farmed by the peasants provided the produce needed for survival because it supplied the needs of the labour force. Each unit meant minimal self-sufficiency for the family holding it. The total extent of all such units was never allowed to fall below the lowest level necessary to keep the labour force from starvation. Any labour surplus to subsistence requirements served the lord's needs by working his domain.

Hence the feudal great estate depended for its survival on the sub-system embodied in the peasant tenants. As Kula has shown, any significant shock to the sub-system reverberated through the whole structure and endangered its survival. Stability in the peasants' family-economy was the keystone of the feudal system of tenure. It limited most severely the evolution of feudal units as economic entities.

On the *latifondo* there was a division of labour and land

between domains farmed directly by the proprietors and those occupied by tiny units held by tenants, but there was no relation between time and territory for subsistence, and time and territory for surplus. It was *all* for production of surplus. Sub-systems did not exist within the economy of the *latifondo*. The great estate remained the unit of production and the concession of tiny plots was so designed as to prevent their turning into the basis for a family-undertaking. Tiny strips of land granted peasants remained just that. None gave rise to the 'signs' which everywhere in the world at all times mark the presence of peasant society: buildings, villages, plantations, little canals, fences, copses etc. Not only were the plots too small but they changed hands too rapidly, the tenures granted by the estate owners were too short and the restrictions on land-use too binding. These features of landlord–peasant relations stupefied observers of the south who came from other regions. Franchetti, writing in the 1870s, has left a vivid account of such relations:

> The relationship between the peasant and the land he holds by paying rent is not continuous and it is difficult for those accustomed to agriculture in other countries or regions to understand. I could not better explain it than by citing the following fact: in many parts of the area the proprietor or the large tenant gives the peasant the right to sow grain but reserves to himself the rights to graze his herds on the stubble between harvest and sowing time. In some places this usage is so customary that it is taken for granted; in others it must be expressly stated in the contract. One can say that the peasant has the right to use the land for part of the year only and, rather than take land for rents, takes rights to sow and harvest a crop ...
>
> The peasant cannot, save in rare cases, augment production by using that which saves him time and effort. He cannot make lasting improvements which are often slow in coming to fruition because the rental period is brief and because he knows that his improvements benefit only the landlord who will, the following year, ask more rent. Rental arrangements last for a year, two, or three at the most, according to the rotation system in use, and, when the time has expired, if the land-holding yields to the proprietor less rent than it might, there are always higher offers from other peasants. The overwhelming majority of proprietors make use of such offers and only in a few places does custom dictate, never observed by all, that the actual tenant may retain the plot by paying the landlord not less than half the highest competitive bid.[9]

---

[9] L. Franchetti, *Le condizioni economiche*, pp. 74–5.

This singular system of agricultural production differed fundamentally from feudal tenure. Under the feudal structure the peasants held their lands on unlimited and ultimately hereditary tenure.[10] The reasons for the difference must be sought not only in the extreme sensitivity of the *latifondo* to market incentives and in its capacity to apply corrections in the volume of productive factors used by suddenly reconverting itself from one type of production to the other according to the oscillations of the prices for cereal or animal products and the level of wages. The total precariousness of the relationship of the little tenant was not due only to the necessity for the *latifondo* to 'keep the field free' from any potential obstacle to its own economic movements in the short period, but also to an element of entrepreneurial policy in the longer term, which really constituted the heart of the latifondist rationality: the necessity to maintain its own labour force in a state of total dependence and total availability. We are dealing here with a nuance which may at first seem difficult to make objective, not least because a rather significant quantum of repression and of 'manipulation' of the labour force is contained in every type of productive organisation, in the capitalist enterprise as well as in feudal tenure. Nevertheless, the particular form of exploitation on the *latifondo* played a fundamental role which helps to explain the curvature of the entire economic and social system.

---

[10] M. Bloch, *French Rural History*, pp. 70–1.
  Here we touch upon a concept which lay at the heart of all medieval thinking about law, and was nowhere more powerful than in its influence on the structure of rural society. Traditionalists to the core, medieval men could be said with slight (very slight) exaggeration to have ordered their lives on the assumption that the only title to permanence was that conferred by long usage. Life was ruled by tradition, by group custom . . .
  One of the most important effects of this extension was that all tenures, whatever their legal status or that of their holders, tended to become hereditary, on a more or less uniform basis. There was no reason for the lords to resist this move, which indeed they assisted by allowing the creation of precedents. It is clear that in the normal way a lord would have no interest in preventing the children of a deceased *colonus* or slave from taking over their father's holding. It would for example be pointless to add such land to the demesne, which depended on tenant labour for its cultivation and could not expand indefinitely without destroying its main source of man-power. Besides, the possession of land without men meant lordship without honour.

The formation of a category of little self-sufficient satellite units would in the long run have undermined the stability and the power of the *latifondisti*. It would have reduced them to simple *rentiers*, deprived of any capacity to intervene directly in the governing of the society. As Sereni observed in his study of the struggles of the peasantry to gain their own land, 'What the peasant share-croppers want is to assert their own stable rights to cultivate the soil of the *latifondo*. Wherever, after bitter battles, the peasants have achieved tenure of longer than three years in spite of tenacious opposition from the owners, they have begun to convert precarious tenancy into permanent holdings by draining soil and planting trees.'[11] The landlord behaved rationally in preventing his peasants from improving the soil. Calculation showed that higher rent or yield would be less significant than loss of political and economic control of the factors of production. The landlords saw clearly that any economic gains to be derived from exploitation and improvement of the land by peasants was strategically less valuable than their control of the peasants themselves. 'The *latifondisti* concede the plots with the explicit understanding that at the end of the contract the ground will be returned in the same primitive state that it was given; they insist on this point to prevent the emergence of any claims to perpetual tenancy.'[12] This insistence reached, in some cases cited by Sereni, the point of anti-economic behaviour. There were *latifondisti* who 'did not hesitate to have their men uproot vines and olive trees which tenants had lovingly planted and cared for on the plots of the *latifondo*.'[13]

The emphasis on this anti-economic component of the behaviour of the *latifondisti* must not, on the other hand, be carried too far. Rather than constituting a normal aspect of the daily management of the enterprise of the *latifondo*, it became one of those 'ultimate presuppositions' which came to light only in moments of acute crisis for the fundamental structures of a system. In spite of its 'barren clay hills, furrowed, miserable and squalid, which sometimes take on the character of a hellish

---

[11] E. Sereni, *Il capitalismo nelle campagne*, p. 171.
[12] *Ibid.*, pp. 171–2.
[13] *Ibid.*, p. 173.

Table 28 *Average cereal production per hectare of surface cultivated in the Crotonese, Calabria, the Mezzogiorno, the country as a whole and in north-central Italy for 1923–8 (in quintals per hectare)*

Crotonese	11.0
Calabria	8.6
Mezzogiorno	9.3
Italy	11.9
North-central Italy	17.2

Source: *Catasto agrario*, 1929

panorama when the burning August sun bakes the soil and not a blade of grass can be seen',[14] the Marchesato of Crotone revealed a notable capacity to utilise human and natural resources. Its grain production per hectare was superior both to the regional and southern-Italian averages by a clear margin and not much below the national average, as Table 28 illustrates.

The large difference between the Crotonese and the north-central average, 11 quintals per hectare to 17, which Table 28 reveals, needs to be noted. Only the most advanced capitalist agriculture in all of Italy, that of the Po Valley, could beat the Crotonese in productivity of cereal crops. In the league table of all agricultural regions in Calabria, measured by production per hectare (see Figure 3, p. 71), the Crotonese came sixth. Only areas like the Plain of Gioia Tauro, the other areas of fertile plains, or the islands of market and fruit gardening around urban centres stood higher. The figure of 229 lire per hectare of taxable yield was equal to mainland Mezzogiorno as a whole, superior to that of central Italy and the islands, and only 13 per cent below that of the whole of Italy, as Table 29 shows.

The figures in the table and the graph suggest strongly that if the *latifondo* was not markedly superior to the other types of cereal-growing farm units, it was not inferior. Its efficiency does not accord with the usual concept of 'feudal' agriculture. The statistics support the argument advanced by Rossi-Doria and by others among the students of the southern-Italian economy that,

[14] F. Milone, *Memoria illustrativa*, p. 5.

Table 29 *Taxable yield per hectare in the Crotonese, central Italy, mainland Mezzogiorno, the islands and Italy as a whole*

	Lire/hectare
Crotonese	229
Mainland Mezzogiorno	230
Central Italy	203
Sicily, Sardinia	192
Italy	265

Source: INEA 1947, *Distribuzione della proprietà*; SVIMEZ, *Statistiche sul Mezzogiorno d'Italia, 1861–1953*, Rome, 1954, pp. 156–7

in a certain sense, the *latifondo* represented a model of technical rationality, an economic form of enterprise which stood at the base of a system of socio-economic relations and territorial arrangements which was peculiarly its own and which was difficult to modify by grades or in single aspects. Given, therefore, certain interrelations among fundamental constituitive elements, it came to be a complex whole based on a precise rationality which discouraged change.

The physical features of the Crotonese themselves discouraged alternative forms of production. After the First World War, returning veterans made a concerted attempt to break the hold of the *latifondo* and to turn themselves into small, self-sufficient peasant proprietors. They occupied the land in a spontaneous wave of peasant unrest and set up their small units. The little farms failed within a few years. There was not enough water, no infrastructure for marketing. They lacked the technical knowhow and the capital necessary for 'a physical reconstruction of the territory'. They were soon in debt and had to sell off what they had painfully acquired. In other words, the things that the peasants lacked made the *latifondo* a rational arrangement of the productive process.

Given a certain territorial structure, the *latifondo* represented an obligatory economic form and vice versa. It is in the 'systemic' character of the *latifondo* that its strength, its capacity for reconstitution and self-regulation must be specifically located, a strength which prompted some observers 'to swear by the

Table 30 *Yield on agricultural property by size*

Size	Lire/hectare
Up to 50 hectares	308
50 to 300 hectares	195
300 to 500 hectares	211
500 to 1,000 hectares	221
Over 1,000 hectares	231

Source: INEA 1947, *Distribuzione della proprietà*

indestructability of the *latifondo* and to condemn as utopian any attempt to transform it'.[15]

As early as the eighteenth century the physiocrat Quesnay had argued that grain-growing demanded both grand scale and managerial centralisation: 'Territory destined to be sown with grain ought to be unified in tenancies as large as possible, administered by rich farmers. There will then be lower costs for maintenance and repair of buildings as well as lower costs of production. Returns on large holdings will be correspondingly greater than on small ones.'[16] Quesnay's observation would appear to be supported by the evidence. The greater the concentration of ownership the higher the return. Table 30 makes this clear. If the very small number of market gardens and coastal farmers with units of less than 50 hectares is excluded, bigger meant more profitable. The estates of more than 1,000 hectares make up about 50 per cent of all taxable income and register the highest yield per hectare.

Such figures must make it clear that the *latifondo* had an economic *raison d'être*. It may have been primitive and crude but it had its inner logic, a logic which has nothing to do with the disorganisation, irrationality and 'historical' character of the feudal estate, of the survival of past modes of production, of backwardness as such. I believe that the weak points of the

---

[15] C. Barbagallo, *La questione meridionale* (Milan, 1948), p. 115.
[16] Karl Kautsky, *La question agraire*, trs. Edgard Milhaud and Camille Polack (Paris, 1900), p. 197.

latifondo were not its economic performance in the short or medium term but other elements of its social and economic make-up.

In looking for the reasons which made up the specificity of the *latifondo* with respect to the feudal enterprise, one must be careful to avoid falling into the trap of making the capitalistic aspects too evident. It is certainly possible to identify many aspects of the modern capitalist enterprise in the *latifondo* and, in the previous pages, I have underlined many of the most important, but one must not forget that, in a typical or ideal classification of the forms of economic enterprise, the distance which separates the *latifondo* from the undertaking governed by the relations of capitalist production is somewhat less than that which separates it from the logic of the feudal system. In this regard, Kautsky has observed that the *latifondo* represented 'the first form of large-scale agricultural capitalism'.[17]

At the same time we have to bear in mind a very elementary objection and one which, precisely because it is so elementary, runs the risk of being overlooked: if the *latifondo* conformed to the structures of a capitalist enterprise in all its essential forms, how can one explain its disappearance within the course of a few years? From the beginning of the 1940s to the beginning of the 1950s, in fact, a structure of production which had succeeded in giving life to a precise and indentifiable mode of resource utilisation over the course of a long secular evolution and had created a specific society and economic order disappeared practically without trace. If it had been a fully capitalist form of production, it ought to have had the strength to adapt and transform itself to the new order brought about by the war-time crisis.

This has been the single most difficult problem of my research. It was clear that the *latifondo* was completely tied to the market. Market prices performed a crucial role in its operation. One has only to think of the part played by protective tariffs on grain in the history of Italy over the half-century after unification. Nor can one ignore the agreement hammered out between the agrarians and industrialists of the north to give tariff protection to nascent

[17] *Ibid.*, p. 231.

northern capitalism and to southern cereals to form an idea of how crucial was the part played by southern estate owners in the political economy of Italy between 1861 and 1950. Labour was acquired through the market. We have seen how the estate owners discouraged any attempt to 'throttle' the labour market by long leases, free use of the soil and so on. It seemed to me essential to try to make clear how the *latifondo* differed from a capitalist agriculture, if I was to make precise the functioning of the institution.

Here are, I believe, the main differences, concentrated in two sectors: (a) in the cycle of *reproduction* of the individual enterprise and the entire system; (b) in the very 'static' structure of the single *latifondo*.

Let us begin with the first point. Under capitalism the pressure of the competitive struggle and the 'animal spirit' of accumulation proper to the bourgeoisie work together to ensure that the main part of the surplus generated gets re-invested. In the *latifondo*, too, the major part of profits obtained by the exploitation of wage labour re-entered the productive cycle, but the manner in which this re-investment took place was utterly different. Capitalism employs its profits to expand plant and machinery and hence reduces the amount of labour. Economic progress is thus intensive, qualitative. For reasons both economic and cultural, the owners of great estates tended instead to direct their own re-investments along the same lines as the original investment: they tended to buy more land. In this case economic progress was clearly quantitative and the reproduction of the system was purely extensive.

What were the reasons that prevented the *latifondo* owners from investing their profits in labour-saving devices? In effect their very existence as a 'status group' in the Weberian sense prevented them, and that in two very important respects: (1) their particular position of dominance in the labour market; (2) 'their particular culture and their effective claim to social esteem founded on a style of life' which originated in the possession and free disposition over the land, the most prestigious of all signs of social status.[18]

---

[18] 'Money and entrepreneurial position are not in themselves status qualifications, although they may lead to them ... Commercial classes arise in a market-oriented economy but status groups arise within the framework of

The question of control over the labour market occupies a central position in our problem. The owners of the *latifondi* in the Crotonese controlled that market absolutely. Since they had a monopoly of all other means of production as well, they approached something like total control over demand for labour. Absolute market power of that kind soon brings what economists recognise as 'political influences' into the operation of the economic balance between supply and demand. Economic and political power merge.

This confluence of economic and political power is not simply a formal problem, as it might appear at first glance. If Weber was correct in arguing that the quality of the possible sources of supply in the market represented the condition common to the destiny of all the individuals who made it up, in that sense a class situation was essentially a market situation. That reality was the deepest 'sense' of the economic, social and civil life typical of the *latifondo*. The peculiar characteristics of the *latifondo* can be traced back to the autocratic nature of the relationship between proprietor and labourer. Total control of the labour market guaranteed the owners a consistent level of extra profit, a kind of 'differential yield' which was generated by the absurd, macabre conditions in which peasants fought for work. As Rossi-Doria saw clearly,

... the fact is that the landed property under the present system of the economy yields greater returns than any other system could. The rents paid and the shares required in tenancy or share-cropping have nothing whatever to do with any conceivable capitalized yield from the plot of land ... they represent not what would be left over after having compensated labour and paid for capital at normal rates of interest but what landless peasants in despair are prepared to offer. They are competitive yields.[19]

Hence transformation of the *latifondo* into anything like capitalist agriculture was impossible. Labour had to be kept in conditions of constant struggle, insecurity and dependence in order to assure the owners that peculiar market set-up which made the *latifondo* profitable. There could be no 'creative destruction', in

organisations which satisfy their wants through monopolistic liturgies or in feudal or in *ständisch* patrimonial fashion.' Max Weber, *Economy and Society*, vol. I, pp. 305–6.

[19] M. Rossi-Doria, 'Struttura e problemi', p. 30.

the Schumpeterian sense, by which a firm renews its plant and machinery, reviews and improves its methods or seeks new markets. It was not only the roots in the market of their class power which prevented that conversion, but also their particular position of dominion over extra-economic relations which expressed itself in a very marked physiognomy of status.

The sparking off of a process of capital accumulation would have constrained the *latifondisti* to become something 'other than themselves', to abandon a style of life and cultural trappings which were for them no less indispensable than pure and simple economic power. In an economic environment in which the process of subordination of 'Madame la Terre' to 'Monsieur le Capital' neither had taken place nor gave much hope that it would, the 'honour of their status' as *latifondisti* rested on a monopoly of the one most important material good, the soil. The landed monopoly was the measure of the well-being of the *latifondisti*, distinguished his status and his conduct in every field. It assured him the free time necessary to dedicate himself to the pleasing entertainments of society and to the aristocratic 'duties' demanded of him by the world of Naples, the capital of the Mezzogiorno.

The universe of the *latifondo* presents, therefore, a peculiar interlocking of the relationship of 'class' to that of 'status'. This does not conflict with the fundamental Weberian assertion that these two forms of the distribution of power oppose each other, but instead provides an explanation for the tendency of the *latifondo* to reproduce itself not qualitatively by improvements but quantitatively by extension.

The second fundamental element of differentiation between the *latifondo* and a capitalist enterprise may be traced, as we have seen, in the 'static' structures of the *latifondo* itself. It lacked that very diadem of peasant mini-holdings which we have also seen made a crucial difference between the *latifondo* and feudal tenure. The difference between the small holdings which surround the capitalist enterprise and those around the feudal estate is that, in the former case, the holdings are semi-autonomous and tied to the great estate by relations of salaried labour, whereas under feudal relations the peasant holding was self-sufficient, the necessary products had to be made within the peasant sector, and the relationship with seigneurial reserve based itself on obligatory and free labour under the regime of the *corvée*.

The existence of the modern capitalist enterprise in agriculture has been strictly tied to the existence of a series of small satellite holdings which furnished the labour force. By contrast to industry where the process of concentration proceeded without economic, political or natural obstacles and led to a progressive tendency to eliminate the little enterprise, relations in agriculture have been characterised both by concentration and by parcellisation. As Kautsky put it in the preface to the French edition of *Die Agrarfrage*,

> When I began this research on the agrarian question, I thought that ... the peasant enterprise was threatened on the one side by disintegration and on the other by the great estate, and for that reason agriculture would follow the same evolutionary path, if under different forms, as industry: proletarianisation at one pole and progress toward the great capitalist enterprise at the other ... Against my expectations, I found that we cannot expect to see in agriculture the disappearance of either great or small holding, and that we indeed find a tendency towards proletarianisation, which is everywhere true, but also at the other pole a constant oscillation between the progress of the small holding and that of the large ...[20]

The reasons for this basic peculiarity of the structure and dynamic evolution of modern capitalist agriculture coincides with its limits, analysed in Section VI of *La question agraire*. These limits to concentration are, in the first place, *physical*, since the most important means of production, the land, has a fixed extension which cannot be modified at will. It is simply impossible to concentrate all production in a particular sector in one plant as is often done in industry.

The limits to concentration are, secondly, *political*. Given the limited amount of soil, expansion of a great estate takes place by expropriating the small holdings. Throwing peasants off the land on too great a scale appeared dangerous to the men of government and to political economists, who frequently tried to discourage it.

Finally, the limits to concentration are economic, since in many, not trivial, aspects of production, the little unit has proved

---

[20] K. Kautsky, *La question agraire*, p. iii.

to be technically superior to the big one. But the most basic economic limit must be sought, still according to Kautsky, in another factor, and that is in the inability of the great estate to generate within itself, and to conserve, its own salaried labour force, and, as a consequence, to be forced to use a category of small peasants who are not autonomous but who offer the needed labour. Hence, Kautsky argued,

> It is the proprietors (or tenants) in the small units who in the countryside are better able to raise large numbers of sons suited to farm work; they furnish a labour force big enough to meet the needs of the small unit but also a surplus, be it because as small tenants they cannot be entirely occupied on their own holdings and hence themselves go out as day labourers on the large holding, or because, as all peasants tend to do, they produce families much too large to find full employment in the domestic economy, and in the person of sons supply that surplus of workers which finds employment as servants or day labourers on the big estates.[21]

Concentration of the means of production and accumulation of capital in agriculture cannot pass a certain point determined by the proportion between the quantity of land and labour needed by the great estate and the number of peasant farms operating semi-autonomously within the orbit of the great unit. As Kautsky saw it,

> The sources of production of new labour diminish as soon as the great estate expands and supplants the little units. By absorbing peasant holdings, the great estate expands its territory but diminishes the number of persons available to cultivate it. That fact alone brings it about that in spite of its technical superiority the great estate can never dominate an area completely ... Where the little units have lost too much terrain, the great estate becomes ever less profitable and begins to decay ... In many cases the absence of labour is certainly the cause of the retreat of the great estate to the advantage of the tiny unit, be it in the sense that the great estate owner or rich tenant breaks up part of his holding to sell to petty proprietors or to rent out little pieces of terrain to small cultivators, or be it in the sense that entire great estates are sold or put up for auction and then divided into little properties ... So like the process by which the great estate eliminates the peasant small holding, the reverse process finds its own natural limits. To the extent that the number of little properties begins to grow on the flanks of the great estates, so the number of labourers at the disposition of the estate

---

[21] *Ibid.*, p. 242.

Table 31 *Percentage of the population of the Crotonese in small villages or isolated habitations to the total population*

1861	1881	1901	1911	1921	1931	1938	1951
13.4	12.2	10.7	9.2	11.3	10.1	6.6	6.1

Source: ISTAT, *Censimenti della popolazione*

owners increases. The vitality of the great estate returns as it takes advantage of its superiority over the small all over again ...[22]

This description of the 'laws of motion' of capitalist agriculture helps us to understand better the original elements of the agricultural enterprise which underlay the *latifondo*. In it there was, in fact, no tendency whatever toward parcellisation of the soil, and the large undertaking based on wage labour remained the exclusive protagonist of production at every stage of the economic cycle, short, medium or long. The small autonomous or semi-autonomous peasant farm tended indeed to disappear completely, leaving in its place an absolute concentration of labour and land.

The absence in the *latifondo* of the pendular movement between concentration and parcellisation of economic activity cannot be directly documented by means of the existing agrarian statistics because of the lack of statistical 'fit' of the existing series and because of the very long period which passed between the two principal agricultural censuses in Italy, those of 1930 and 1961. I have other indirect evidence drawn from settlement patterns revealed by the population censuses which, of course, occurred more frequently. The loss in directness is, I think, compensated by the gain in precision, for, as I have argued, peasant settlement, peasant farm and peasant family make up a triad of interlocking structures. Hence, where there are many small holders, there will be many habitations and vice versa.

Table 31 shows that there is no trace of oscillation in settlement patterns over the 90 years covered. The slight upward movement in the figures between 1911 and 1921 reflects the post-war

[22] *Ibid.*, pp. 242–3.

struggle for the soil and the occupation of lands by peasants, a tendency soon reversed. If anything, the figures suggest that the process of concentration of ownership by the great estate owners continued steadily until 1951.

Family farm and the market for labour

It is now necessary to confront a crucial problem in the analysis. In the previous section, I argued that the capitalist enterprise could not by itself furnish enough labour to work its lands and had to have recourse to day labour supplied by small, semi-autonomous peasant proprietorships. The *latifondo*, it would appear from the above analysis, seems not to have suffered from this internal contradiction. It had the possibility of employing labour offered under conditions of great advantage by landless workers. It exploited a 'pure' supply of labour uncontaminated by other economic categories.

The problem is this: why is it that great capitalist estates failed to have at their disposition large numbers of rural proletarians? By means of what mechanism could the great *latifondo* succeed in creating and, above all, of *conserving* a class of 'pure' agricultural proletarians whose presence in the countryside constitutes an exception?

The answer to the first question demands a brief analysis of the ruling relationships between the system of family farm described in the first chapter, with its structures of social integration, and the supply of labour in agriculture. I shall devote this section to that problem. The main part of the chapter will be dedicated to an answer to the second question, an answer which coincides in practice with the study of the particular form of socio-cultural integration which made the *latifondo* what it was.

The point of departure for the analysis is constituted by a characteristic peculiarity of the labour market in capitalist agriculture where great estates predominate: the chronic scarcity of labour. Shortage of labour is a limit which industry has historically rarely encountered. The ruin of the little autonomous peasant producers and of urban artisan activity gave an exclusive advantage to industry, ensuring for a long time a regular and 'limitless' supply of proletarian labour.

This flux of manual labour, added to the proportion of the labouring classes made surplus by technical progress in the process of production, allowed the establishment of a mechanism of self-regulation typical of the urban labour market: the industrial reserve army. Both Marx and Polanyi have emphasised that the creation of this urban labour market was no idyllic process in which the forces of light and progress peacefully conquered social areas both backward and moribund to the greater good of mankind and in the name of the 'rational' logic of the laws of supply and demand for goods. In reality the transformation involved one of the most violent catastrophes in the history of humanity. It brought the destruction of entire pre-industrial civilisations and the violent acculturation of the forces of production thus 'liberated' from traditional chains.

For our purposes, there is only one aspect of this vast spectacle we need to consider: the irreversibility of the transfer of population from the country to the cities. Two elements combined to reinforce the cleavage between urban and rural labour markets. In the countryside, the social structure which had survived the cyclonic changes of mercantile capitalism became much more rigid while, in the towns, a new generation of urban workers became socialised under town conditions and lost rural roots and skills. There was no communication between the two markets for labour or, perhaps more precisely, there was a one-way communication formed by the steady trickle of labour from farm to factory. As Kautsky observed, 'He who is born in town or goes there in his youth is lost to agriculture, which in the present circumstances cannot meet its need for labour by enticing labour back onto the land from the industrial proletariat.'[23] Urban industry can produce and conserve the wage labour that it needs, thanks to the industrial reserve army and to the presence of specific mechanisms of socio-cultural integration. The great agrarian capitalist estate cannot. But what is the content of the mechanism of socio-cultural integration by which the new urban generation is socialised? In what does the rigidity of the rural response lie? What traditional social structures prevent the formation of a stable rural proletariat?

[23] *Ibid.*, p. 237.

The explanation of these phenomena may be found, I think, in the fact that rural society organises itself in families which are also productive units and in productive units which are also families. Economic production is embedded in a web of family relationships which constitutes the exclusive, normative reference point for individual behaviour. No ways of life, means of production nor social action are permitted which differ from those proper to the system of family-undertakings, where the head of the family is entrepreneur and the members the employees.

The 'laws' of the means of familial production become much more coercive when the forces of the market threaten it. These laws prevent the formation of a stable proletariat in the countryside. Hence the great agrarian capitalist enterprise can never dispose of a reserve army of production which is permanent and proletarian. It is for these reasons that it faces chronic scarcity of labour. Recourse to the surplus labour generated on the little peasant holdings becomes a vital necessity for it, and explains the categoric assertion of Kautsky that both large and small holdings are necessarily present in capitalist agriculture.

The enormous advantage acquired by urban industry has consisted precisely in its ability to give place to a system of integration of the labour force completely independent of the family-undertaking. It gives workers personal liberty and freedom of movement. The existence of an apparatus of sociocultural integration founded on social class and on working-class culture, instead of on family and kinship, certainly bears its not inconsiderable charge of alienation and suffering, but, with respect to the very bottom strata of the rural population, it represents a real step forward. Between the rural serving wench, the illegitimate son, the 'man from nowhere', the unmarried in the rural social order, on the one side, and the factory worker on the other there is an abyss. It is not so much the material conditions of life which distinguish the two worlds, for often in terms of wretchedness there is not much to choose between them, but in their position within the wider social ambit. Kautsky saw it perfectly at the turn of the century:

> The worker has the chance to make a home for himself without necessarily becoming independent as a labourer, and we know that he

makes good use of this possibility, increasing thus the flow of salaried proletariat in the process of becoming a class apart . . .

In the cities salaried workers enjoy greater liberty and more civil conditions of life . . . To have one's own house means not just having the means to marry and rear a family but also to become active as a citizen, to move outside the area of labour, to meet people who share the same ideas and to conquer for oneself better living conditions, with the possibility of organising and participating in the life of the community and of the state . . . Workers who have nothing, and particularly the unmarried among them, are the ones who most easily abandon the countryside . . .[24]

We can now confront the second question posed at the beginning of the section, that is, the 'production and conservation' of the labour force on the *latifondo*. Once again we run into the paradox that the *latifondo* seems to be more capitalistic than capitalist agriculture, since it seems able to do without the supply of labour produced and provided by the mini-units of satellite peasant undertakings and hence the entire system of the family farm. The social structure of the Crotonese before 1950 seemed to have realised the impossible, presenting almost no trace of what sociologists have regarded as the basic unit of peasant society, that is, the family farm.[25]

As I have repeated several times, the society of the *latifondo* was a class society in its purest form. It was based on a stratification brought about by the position of individuals in the market; that is to say there existed in the Crotonese a very numerous category of people possessing and selling in the market place only one type of merchandise, their own labour. This is, in effect, the classical Marxist definition of the proletariat.

What, then, were the mechanisms of production and conservation of this class? What types of integration operated on the *latifondo* in place of the norms of the peasant family-undertaking which not only secured a stable supply of labour but 'held the whole system together'?

My central argument is that the *latifondo* in the Crotonese was able to succeed in perpetuating and strengthening itself thanks to

---

[24] *Ibid.*, pp. 237 and 291–3.
[25] P. A. Sorokin, C. C. Zimmerman and C. J. Galpin (eds.), *A Systematic Source Book in Rural Sociology* (New York, 1961); A. V. Chayanov, *The Theory of the Peasant Economy* (Glencoe, Illinois, 1966).

a form of repressive integration of the labour force sustained essentially by two elements: the autocracy of the great proprietors and a permanent disequilibrium within the labour market. The reciprocal interaction of these two elements had the effect of consolidating them, thus allowing the whole system to expand well beyond its own proper bases.

Autocracy was the essential feature of the *latifondo*. From the sociological point of view, autocracy represented the differential element which distinguished it from capitalist agriculture and made the entire latifondist society different from the great majority of all other agricultural production systems. The autocracy had its roots, on the one hand, in the particular situation of constraint on the labour force typical of latifondist relationships of production and generated by the 'double monopoly' of the proprietors both of the means of production and the means of coercion; and, on the other, in the permanent state of overpopulation which created the unique supply of labour and contributed to the total subordination of the labourers. Yet such overpopulation was simultaneously an effect of autocracy, since it grew out of a situation, as we shall see, which initially put the great proprietors at a genuine disadvantage and which they needed force to reverse.

In the next section I shall describe the contents of autocracy under the profile of internal control over the labour force and external organisation of production. In the succeeding section I shall go on to analyse the particular structure of the labour market in the *latifondo* and its relationship to the autocratic power of the proprietors.

Autocracy

The administration of a *latifondo* was the first problem. An estate covered a vast territory, larger even than the figures I cited at the beginning of the chapter. Those referred only to the huge holdings in the Marchesato itself. In addition to the 100,000 hectares in the plains of the Marchesato, the great barons owned sprawling pasturage and woodland in the mountains of the Sila and hence the mountain economy got locked into the iron ring of *latifondo* relationships. The barons had a monopoly of the eastern slopes of the Sila, those facing the Ionian sea, and a substantial portion of the mountain meadows in the extraordinarily high plain of the Sila. Take as an example San Giovanni in Fiore, the little mountain town made famous by the thirteenth-century visionary, the Abbot Joachim of Fiore. San Giovanni is the only community in the area whose entire territory is between 1,000 and 1,500 metres above sea level. It is about 80 kilometres by road from Crotone. If we look at the ownership of land, we see not only the same crushing inequalities of wealth and poverty but the same names we have seen in the plains. Five proprietors held territories of more than 1,000 hectares within the community's boundaries, two of which exceeded 2,000 hectares. The Zurlo brothers, in addition to the 1,414 hectares situated in the foothill community of Scandale and other possessions all over the plain, owned 465 hectares on the slopes of Monte Nero. In other parts of the high Sila, the story was the same. Giulio Berlingieri, besides his immense holdings in the Marchesato and the foothills known as the 'pre-Sila', possessed a further 1,500 hectares above Lake Arvo, that is, in the highest part of the Sila massif.

The lives of some 200,000 persons, living in an area of about 2,500 square kilometres, equal to roughly 20 per cent of the whole surface of Calabria, came to depend on the decisions of seven or eight great land-owners. The management of an enterprise so enormous threw up problems quite unknown in other types of agriculture. Think, for example, of the problems posed by the annual cattle drive, the *transumanza*, and the jurisdictions of the local communities over which the cattle wandered, or the problems of security posed by holdings sprinkled over territory larger than most English counties and over holdings separated from each other by as much as 100 kilometres. Think of the consequence for employment of a decision to reconvert 500 or 1,000 hectares from grain to pasturage, especially if the 1,000 hectares were in one or two communities. Finally, think of the problem of order posed by a landless labouring class, starving, numerous, and in perpetual ferment, or the wasps' nests of litigation arising from the more or less fraudulent origins of a large part of the latifondist holdings and dragged on as hereditary lawsuits even to the present day.

The solution arrived at by the barons of the Crotonese in the face of this enormous mass of problems and conflicts thrown up by the sheer scale of their property and by their monopoly of the means of production was to add the monopoly of the means of coercion and administration. Especially after the unification of Italy, the proprietors exploited a sort of delegated authority consigned to them by the rickety new state to get control of law and order and to operate the civil and juridical administration. In that 20 per cent of Calabria which fell under their sway, the barons of the Crotonese were, for all practical purposes, the state.

These state functions were carried out using either the proper organs of the state or by private violence. In the areas of local autonomy, less important in the array of public power, the barons governed by interfering personally or by using their agents. 'The great agrarian proprietors are the visible and invisible masters of local politics. They rarely participate in person ... At the head of administration they put their people, almost always some of their lawyers, who regularly do the bidding of their masters.'[26] In more delicate sectors or more prestigious aspects of the state service, in the courts and, above all, in the prefectures and sub-prefectures, the baronial monopoly of office tended to become more overt. The proprietors themselves, or their sons, nephews, relatives or close friends, tended to hold the key posts.

The almost limitless exercise of the powers of justice and administration not only constituted an effective guarantee of security of property and liberty of action for the proprietors and entrepreneurs of the entire zone but put into their hands a fearful instrument of economic power. Thanks to it, the barons consolidated their power of command, preventing the emergence of new groups or new forces which would inevitably have established a dangerous pluralism of powers. The rigidity of their dominion allowed no space for the rise either of a petty bourgeoisie, whose function would have been to mediate a consensus, or of an indigenous commercial and industrial bourgeoisie. On the eve of the Second World War the society of the *latifondo* presented itself incredibly starkly. A rigid class structure polarised class against class, allowing no room for mediation or alliance of any kind.

[26] L. Repaci, 'Baroni controluce', p. 1238.

In such a situation, all outlets for peaceful resolution of conflicts were closed. A *bracciante* who had been wronged by a member of the latifondist administration had nobody to turn to. The typical solution of the Plain of Gioia Tauro, that is, the creation of elementary self-policing on the basis of the mafia and capable of striking back at the proprietors or at least forcing them to mediation, was impeded by the absence of even a minimal polycentrism within the economic and social structure on which to build some sort of politics of alliance. The outlet through individual rebellion or banditry was also difficult because the barons monopolised both public and private means of violence. The outlet valve for a good part of the discontent generated by the ferocity of social conflict within the latifondist society was in fact the very repressive apparatus at the service of the proprietors which carried out functions of control and repression parallel to the state organs. Where the violent and rebellious young elsewhere became bandits or *mafiosi*, in the Crotonese an important part became paid hirelings of the barons.

The private police were a very important instrument of their power throughout the territory. Not only did they succeed in providing for law and order within the estate, imposing on the labouring masses of peasants any order of their masters, threatening with harsh sanctions any transgression and assuring the complete security of persons and property on the *latifondo*, but they tended to assume that monopoly of force in the countryside at large which normally constitutes one of the distinguishing features of the modern state.

The armed guards in the pay of the proprietors tended therefore to intervene in all incidents of private conflict which fell within their jurisdiction and not just those inherent in safeguarding the baron's rights and properties. Even if the vastness of their authority was similar to that exercised by the mafia – they intervened in economic transactions, in 'horizontal' conflicts between individuals and the like – the private police of the *latifondo* remained fundamentally different from the mafia. The private police were, and always remained, dependent employees, simply executors of orders from above, without their own authority or even delegation of powers. The peasant population hated and despised them. They were just another manifestation, like the carabinieri and other tools of the state, of public violence against them. In pre-war popular Calabrian poems and songs, there are frequent references to, and laments about, the *caporali* (the guardians of the *latifondo*) as incarnations of patriarchal tyranny.[27]

In spite of exceptional moments of turbulence, the solid control of this private repressive bureaucracy along with the control of the administrative and coercive organs of the state assured the owners of the *latifondo* complete dominion over the class which sold its labour in the Crotonese. They were thus able to perpetuate a social and productive system built exclusively on repression of the manual worker.

We come now to an analysis of the second dimension of the autocratic control of the labour force in the *latifondo*, that internal to relations of production within the enterprise. The repressive apparatus found in each latifondist holding not only carried out functions which guaranteed politically the existing order of production but entered into the very process of production itself. Repression was an essential part both of the hierarchy and of the division of labour within the enterprise. Since it coincided with a good part of the organisation of labour on the *latifondo*, it was in Marxist terms both a 'productive force' and a 'relationship of production'. The armed guards were part of the overheads. They had fixed employment on fixed wages. Their task was to intervene in the production process both as supervisors and as coercive directors of the casual labour. Such employees on fixed wages were preferably not recruited from the local population. Their efficiency grew in proportion to their lack of ties with the population they controlled. They also had certain work to do.

The greater part of the salaried employees are drawn from the hills and mountains above the Crotonese . . . In general they are employed in the custody of the cattle; they are pastors, cowherds, swineherds. There are, however, some tasks preferably assigned to peasants from the locality, such as care of the work horses and oxen. Within the farm as such we can distinguish two groups of persons on fixed salaries, one which takes part in the cereal cultivation, and the other which works in the pasturage and

[27] It was only after the disappearance of the *latifondo* in the 1950s and 1960s that there was any verifiable stirring of independent activity among the persons on fixed wages. The rise of a mafia in the Crotonese, which took place after the war, drew its recruits almost exclusively from former fixed-wage earners of the *latifondo*, or from ex-tenants of the barons.

animal husbandry. To the first group belong the *massaro* or steward, the *bovaro* or drover, the muleteer, the guard and possibly others ... The steward has the job of watching the peasantry and nothing more ... He looks after the smooth running of the work and the well-being of the livestock. In the morning he sends the peasants to the fields; during the harvest he organises the nightly guard on the threshing floor ... To the second group of fixed salaried employees ... belong the pastors, the cowherds and their respective *caporali* ... The *caporali* of the sheep or cows are supposed to watch shepherd and cowherd to make sure that the herds are properly taken to pasture ... The job of the *caporale* is extremely delicate. It is a job of trust and skill ... The *caporale* has the right to take disciplinary measures on his own dependent employees.[28]

Such salaried employees, armed and on horseback, accompanied the annual cattle drive in the spring from the lowlands to the high pasture in the Sila. They watched the shepherds and kept wolves away. This particular category of employee made up one of the largest entries in the books of the enterprise. The annual expenditure on fixed salaries of a typical *latifondo* would easily equal the total wages paid to day labourers, who were four times more numerous. According to the official figures worked out in Table 27 (p. 129), there were in the Crotonese in 1936, 1,531 persons on fixed salaries as opposed to 6,841 day labourers or *braccianti*. The permanently employed made up 11.2 per cent of the total agricultural labour force.

The existence of a costly apparatus of repression of this type – and it is well to repeat the point – constituted an absolutely fundamental element in the operation of the *latifondo*. It created a permanent pressure on the *braccianti* and permitted the extraction of a great quantity of surplus. That which in the modern forms of capitalist industry is incorporated into the technology of assembly line and work discipline and in the feudal system remained substantively external to the productive process (in that it had its machinery in the peasant himself) became in the *latifondo* a material and visible factor in production itself.

The authoritarian organisation of labour on the *latifondo* had the additional advantage of fitting perfectly the character of labour needed for production. Grain culture does not need complex technical operations like pruning or grafting, activities

---

[28] G. Brasacchio, *Nuovi orizzonti dell'agricoltura crotonese* (Catanzaro, 1950), pp. 132–4.

which give rise to specialisation and skill among rural workers and hence to a consequent stratification among the work force itself. Grain crops need a great deal of unskilled labour for very short times of the year. The labour force was expected to supply a certain quantum of 'work' rather than 'labour' in the strict sense, and the difference is important. Hard work can be extracted by force or threat, driving people to their physical limits, while skilled labour cannot be. The economic efficiency of the *latifondo* came to depend on the absolute observance of the hierarchy of prestige and power, on prompt execution of work which was hard but simple and which at the most demanded simple cooperation. The reasons for the autocratic bone structure of the *latifondo* and its relations of production are, therefore, not to be sought in some sort of 'survival' of feudalism or in the 'ideology' pure and simple of the proprietors, but in an intricate whole composed of economic rationality and social system which makes up the originality of the *latifondo* as a socio-economic entity in comparison with other forms of social and economic organisation identified and defined by social science. A latifondist holding was *necessarily* an autocratic enterprise, irrespective of the numbers employed or the absenteeism of the proprietor. The organisation of the *latifondo* can only be likened to that of a military unit in which the high command retains the exclusive privilege of taking decisions on every aspect of the existence of the soldiers and where power can only be delegated within very strict limits.

Autocracy characterised not only the relationship between the proletariat and the armed employees who guarded and controlled them but also the relations between workers and the managerial figures on the *latifondo*. In the Crotonese of the 1940s the proprietors rarely occupied themselves with the running of their enterprises, not least because few resided regularly in the area. Direction of the operations of production was generally entrusted to an administrator or to a local agricultural entrepreneur, who was known in the local jargon as an *industriante*. It is important to get the precise character of the *industriante* into our analysis. In the first place, this is not a case of the capitalist split between owner and manager so much discussed in recent American writing. Nor was the *industriante* the Calabrian equivalent of the Sicilian *gabellotti*, the ruthless and aggressive middlemen of Sicilian agriculture, who by cunning and fraud and *mafioso* violence came to supplant the Sicilian great lords. The barons of the Crotonese never lost their roots in their native soil, and that not least because of their own origins in a recent past.

The great barons of the Crotonese had, in general, themselves been administrators and tenants of feudal holdings. Their ancestors had certainly not been on the Crusades. It is enough to consult the list of feudal holdings in Calabria in 1500 to see that.[29] Not one of the barons of the Crotonese possessed a thing at that time. Their rise to power took place during the break-up of the feudal and ecclesiastical *ancien régime* which took place between 1750 and 1850. In those hundred years the face of Calabria changed and gave rise through various steps to the bourgeois latifondist set-up of the modern Mezzogiorno.[30]

The *latifondisti* of the Crotonese maintained to the last the strictest control over all the intermediate personnel of their estates. By a series of shrewd managerial techniques they prevented the slightest development of autonomy. The administrator (or the 'factor' who was in charge of the personnel) was frequently rotated from one holding to another. Strategic decisions such as how much and what to plant, how much and at what price to sell, how much reserve to deploy and when remained the exclusive prerogative of the proprietor.

The typical administrator was, in any case, not an expert specialised in farm management but simply a labourer who had been in his master's service for many years and who had distinguished himself by his respectful demeanour, by his acquaintance with local usage and, above all, by his devotion to the employer. His fundamental job was simply to control production under orders from the proprietor. His sphere of action was rigorously limited. His power over finances was confined to small transactions and payment of wages.

From the proprietor's point of view, his administrators were simply dependants like anybody else, even if they received a high (but not very high) salary and enjoyed certain privileges not conceded to the others. From the point of view of the *braccianti*,

---

[29] G. Galasso, *Economia e società nella Calabria del '500* (Milan, 1976).
[30] A. Placanica, *Cassa sacra e beni della Chiesa nella Calabria del '700* (Naples, 1969).

the administrator was the man who enjoyed the boss's confidence, and the one authorised to deal directly with them. His daily activities consisted in control of day labourers either directly by inspecting their places of work himself, or indirectly through his *caporali*, stewards and guards.

When, therefore, at the beginning of the twentieth century the *industriante* class began to emerge, it was into a very restricted economic and social space. The *industrianti* tended to rent pieces of land 'usually of 250 to 300 hectares but sometimes up to 1,000, which they would organise and stock for their own accounts'.[31] This class grew until by the 1940s it controlled over half of the latifondist holdings of the great Crotonese estates, but its role was always subaltern both in the relations of production and in the social hierarchy. It mediated and provided social connections but lacked autonomy or any innovative charge in the face of baronial power.

It is important, too, not to confuse the *industriante* with the figure of the *Pächter* or tenant to whom Marx assigns a vital role in the emergence of capitalist farming in England. In *Das Kapital*, Marx devotes chapter 24 to an attack on the myth of 'primary accumulation of capital', and part IV defines the tenant as the person 'who applied himself to the expansion of his own capital through employing wage workers and who handed over part of the surplus product, whether in money or in kind, to the landlord, as rent ...'.[32] In purely formal terms the *industriante* seems to fulfil precisely the functions described by Marx but, in practice, he was, as we shall see, prevented from doing so. Nor was the *industriante* like the *gabellotto* in Sicily, who by means of mafia techniques extorted surplus product by keeping rents and wages low and usurping the liberty to run his tenancy as he saw fit. The crucial difference in the case of the *industriante* was his dependence on the landlord. Whereas the English tenant had achieved the freedom to manoeuvre granted him by long leases (99 years) at fixed rents in times of inflation and could make his

---

[31] INEA, *Rapporti tra proprietà*, p. 79.
[32] Karl Marx, *Capital*, translated from the 4th German edition by E. and C. Paul (London, 1972).

own decisions about crop and rotation, the *industriante* of the Crotonese never succeeded in imposing the two fundamental preconditions of capitalist agriculture on the landlords: stability of tenancy and liberty of action. The tenancy or rental agreement of an *industriante* in the Marchesato normally lasted for six years at the most and was not protected by any customary right of renewal on the part of the lessee. In addition, either the proprietor or customary usage, not the *industriante*, determined whether payment would be in cash or kind, which, of course, damaged the *industriante* by restricting his ability to switch as market forces demanded.

The most important restriction on the *industriante* was the obligatory crop rotation on a six-year cycle: fallow, grain for two years, pasturage for three. This obligation effectively prevented structural change in the latifondist economy and forced the *industriante* to use the methods favoured by the barons, that is, to exploit the only variable source of surplus: the wages of the *braccianti*. The lease called *a tutt'uso*, which was widely diffused in areas where capitalist agriculture had established itself and which permitted the lessee to choose whatever combination of crop seemed to him most advantageous, never had much force in the Crotonese.

As in the case of the little tenant of a fraction of land, so the large tenant was expected to leave the holding in precisely the state he had found it. This was not just to ensure the obvious requirement that the tenant not diminish the value of land, livestock or other equipment, but above all to prevent any improvements in terms of investment or modification of systems of cultivation which might have ended by modifying the sequence of the latifondist phenomenon, its monoculture, its extension and its autocracy.

The fundamental fact that the large tenant was placed in an inferior position to the baron brought it about that the speculative sides of his position became more pronounced than the entrepreneurial and augmented all the worst features of the system itself. The *industriante* merely exacerbated the bad features and brought no compensatory good ones. The available research and official enquiries underline that the *industrianti* exploited land

and labour savagely. They increased the precariousness and nomadic quality of production and they accentuated the physical ruin of the terrain.[33]

Immigration and the labour market

The second pillar of the latifondist system and its social and economic integration was the permanent disequilibrium in the labour market. There was always a large surplus of supply over demand to the advantage of the proprietors. This made the day-labouring classes subordinate and stable. The visible constraint of physical force and intimidation ran parallel to the invisible and more impersonal constraints operating through the labour market. The existence of a labour market of an entirely capitalist type in which the commodity, 'labour', was bought and sold under conditions of perfect mobility and formal liberty, made up an essential part of the latifondist structure. It was thus very different from systems of productive organisation described by Barrington Moore as 'labor repressive forms of capitalist agriculture' in which the control of the labour force involved exclusively political means. There is no parallel here to the case cited by Moore where American negro slavery was 'a decisive adjunct to capitalist development'.[34] Workers on the *latifondo* were moved by stimuli from the market and the goad of hunger. The stability of the system was increased by that fact. Competition for jobs kept salaries low. Competition was so severe that workers accepted the hardest of working conditions imposed by the authoritarian organisation of the *latifondo*. The social subordination of the day labourer on the estate itself simply reflected the parallel relationship of the market between employer and employee and, of course, reinforced it.

This overabundance of labour supply in the *latifondo* needs to be looked at a little more closely, since it seems to contradict evidence drawn from official sources, from population censuses and the various INEA enquiries about types of economic activity. All these official bodies agree in designating the Crotonese as an

---

[33] G. Brasacchio, *Nuovi orizzonti*, pp. 141–2; J. Meyriat, *La Calabria*, pp. 145–6.
[34] Barrington Moore, *The Social Origins*, pp. 495–6.

Table 32 *Density of the supply of labour per each square kilometre cultivated by farming units employing paid persons in the Crotonese, in Calabria and in the Mezzogiorno*

	Paid labour force * (a)	Sq km of surface (b)	Density per sq km (a:b)
Crotonese	8,372	378.73	22
Calabria	164,513	1,551.06	106
Mezzogiorno	1,026,665	8,076.85	127

Sources: *Censimento della popolazione*, 1936; INEA 1949, *Tipi di impresa nell'agricoltura italiana*
* The figures reported in column (a) include two of the three fundamental categories of persons employed in agriculture, that is, employed (workers on fixed salaries or labourers on annual contract) and the underemployed (casual labourers of every type). Emigrants were not recorded among the employed persons, but this alters the result very little since emigration had virtually ceased by 1936.

area which suffered from a potential scarcity of labour rather than excessive supply. In Table 32 I have put together the figures for the density of labour force per square kilometre cultivated by enterprises using paid labour for the Crotonese, for Calabria and for the Mezzogiorno as a whole.

The figures reveal clearly that, as is well known, the Italian south and Calabria both suffered from a marked oversupply of labour while the Crotonese seems to have had about one fifth of the Calabrian level. It is true that the great estates of the Crotonese were not very labour intensive and needed less labour. In spite of that, there was a very marked difference between the labour market of the Crotonese and other areas. In Table 33 I have tried to put together supply and demand figures for the three areas.

Table 33 shows that the Crotonese had an excess of labour much smaller than the region or the south as a whole. The figures probably underestimate the entire volume of demand for labour in each area. Another set of calculations which was made by R.E. Dickinson in the 1950s arrived at an overall surplus of labour for the entire south, and calculated that the Crotonese was one of the

Table 33 *Relation of demand to supply of labour for every square kilometre cultivated by farming units employing paid labour in the Crotonese, Calabria and the Mezzogiorno*

	Supply of labour per sq km	Demand for labour per sq km *	Excess of supply over demand
Crotonese	23	18	22%
Calabria	106	28	74%
Mezzogiorno	127	43	66%

* Calculated by using the coefficients worked out by the *Inchiesta parlamentare sulla disoccupazione in Italia*, Rome, 1954, vol. I, tome 2, which worked out the number of days of labour necessary for the cultivation of a hectare of terrain in the different 'homogenous zones' of Italian agriculture.

few areas on the mainland where demand actually exceeded supply. Figure 4 reports Dickinson's findings.

The key point to remember is how irregular demand was in the Crotonese. Cereal monoculture demanded for certain operations and for certain times of year a number of workers four times greater than the annual average. Hence for roughly a third of the year the supply of labour available within the Crotonese was drastically insufficient. If we were to make a graph of the working days of the typical day labourer of the Marchesato, we could easily see a gross disequilibrium. In the months of June, July, August, September and October, this area enjoyed conditions of almost full employment for local labourers. For the other 150 days, roughly from December to 30 April, there were conditions of unemployment almost equally total.

It follows that from the employer's point of view there was a serious labour shortage at precisely the times he most needed to have it. From the labourer's point of view, the problem was to cope with the long winter period of unemployment. This insufficiency of the supply of labour must also be placed in the context of the relatively thin settlement of the Crotonese. With 92 inhabitants per square kilometre, the Marchesato ranked among the lowest in density of population of all plains or hill areas. Then

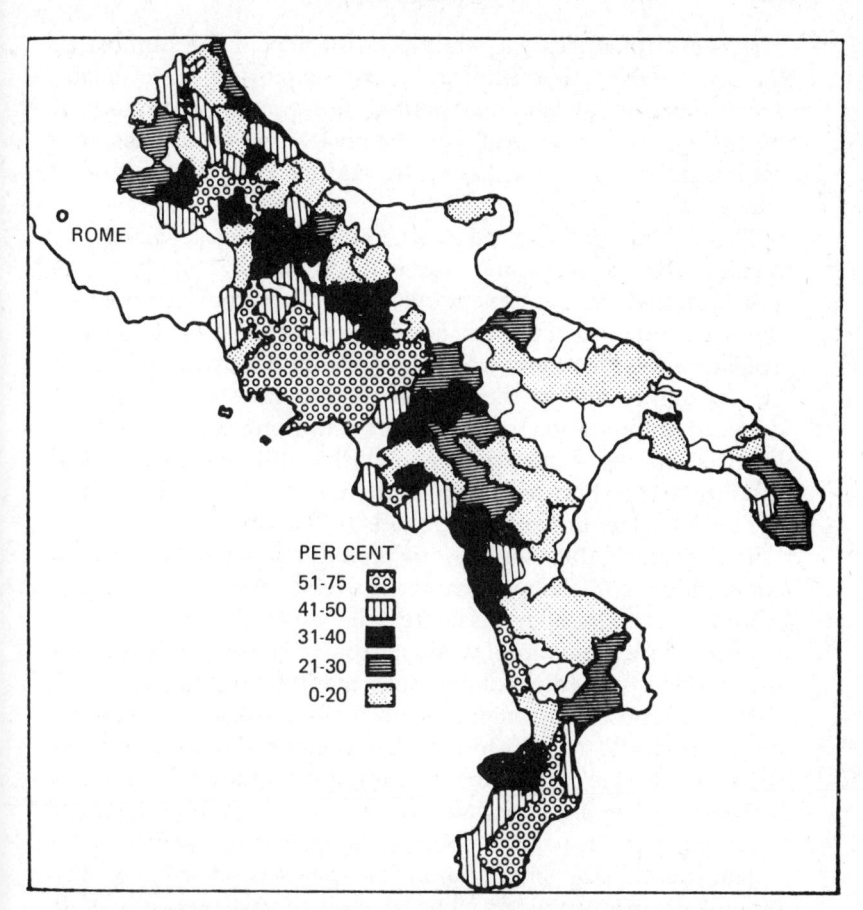

Fig. 4 Underemployed labour expressed as a percentage of the total number of employed persons in each zone of the Italian south (Whitened zones on the chart are those characterised by an excess of demand over supply)

Source: R. E. Dickinson, *The Population Problem of Southern Italy. An Essay in Social Geography*, Syracuse, NY, 1955, p. 81

there was the very structure of cultivation itself. As we have seen, it was a purely extensive system. The harvest gathered was a function of the territory cultivated. If the surface area owned by a proprietor was much greater than he could cultivate with the available labour force (in general, extension of production at a given level of prices was simply a function of the number of hands available), he could leave a part as pasture. In principle, the number of day labourers limited the agricultural production of the *latifondo* and it would not be misleading to say that, in a certain sense, for the great estate the supply of labour was always scarce.

The central problem now becomes one of reconciling the results of the surveys and studies just cited and the previous assertion that the permanent oversupply of labour accentuated the subordination of the day labourer to the great estate owner. The answer is that there was large-scale immigration to the area big enough to reverse the normal relation between supply and demand. Immigration had two aspects: the long-term movement into the Crotonese of the peoples of the high Sila and the foothills; the other, the short-term immigration which responded to the demand for labour for short periods of the year.

The effect of the two types of immigration was to increase competition in the labour market between sellers and reduce it among buyers. In moments of great demand for labour, seasonal migration prevented local workers from exercising influence on the market by the threat of unemployment, thanks to the greater competitiveness of the migrants (normally younger, more robust and more docile than the locals). At moments of weaker demand the steady trickle of permanent immigration added to the natural increase of the local population and made the employment situation of the resident labourers yet again more grave.

The permanent immigration of the second half of the nineteenth century was a phenomenon of vast proportions. It had links with the very origin of the modern *latifondo* in the bosom of the older productive and proprietorial order of feudalism. The 'primary accumulation' of the *latifondo* in the Crotonese sprang fundamentally from a process of concentration of ownership of land plus an overturning of the relationship between mountain and plain which caused a violent crisis of settlement among the ancient mountain people of northern Calabria. Between the end of the eighteenth century and about 1850, three quarters of the holdings in the Sila and in the Marchesato changed hands. From usurpation of the commons, from the disintegration of feudalism and the sale of ecclesiastical holdings there emerged a new economic and social system which had its centre in the plains and along the coastal hills and no longer in the mountains.

The economic and social structures of the communities of the villages of the Sila were literally broken up by the fraudulent enclosures of the new proprietors (called the 'defences'). They prevented the pasturage of the village herds and restricted the communal area available to grow rye, potatoes and the like. They forbad the use of the forests and forest products sanctioned by customs of great antiquity and considered as the common heritage of all village dwellers. The woodmen, semi-nomadic shepherds, itinerant cultivators, the charcoal burners, that whole range of 'dwellers in the woods', described by Bloch as the typical elements of the social landscape of the European forest, were suddenly tipped onto the slopes of the hills and poured down to the outskirts of towns like Crotone, Cutro, Melissa and Strongoli, camping on the edges of town and swelling the population of the Marchesato already sweltering in the cauldron of labouring misery.

After a long period of stagnation, the population of the Crotonese began to rise. The statistics collected by the new unitary state show a growth between 1861 and 1901 of 41 per cent, with average rates of growth per decade reaching 16 per cent, or 4 to 5 per cent per year on occasion. Another indicator of the intensity of this shift of population can be found in the two figures provided by the census of those years, population resident versus population merely present. In the 1860s and 1870s there were always some 10 per cent more present than resident and in some communities as much as 15 per cent or 20 per cent at certain times.

The flood of proletarianised mountaineers and shepherds onto the labour market of the Crotonese was, in the early years after unification, a consequence of 'expulsion' or 'push factors'. The cereal production of the Marchesato was in decline or at least stagnant and, from the unification until the late 1880s suffered from the world-wide fall in prices for cereal crops which the so-called 'great depression' ushered in after 1873. It was only after 1887 with the beginning of protection for domestic cereal production that the situation changed. Now the presence of a mass of labour on the market contributed to an expansion of area under crop. The new estates grew rapidly and the emphasis shifted from livestock to seed crops. Now 'pull factors' began to work on the miserable populations still clinging to their older styles of life in the high mountains.

By the early years of the twentieth century the population of the Crotonese was sufficiently large to provide a platform to sustain a certain limited level of productive activity. The flood of labour generated by the 'primary accumulation' of the *latifondo* system had permitted the growth of a network of huge estates in a semi-populated zone, without infrastructure and isolated from the rest of Calabria and the world. The Crotonese would probably have remained in this curious equilibrium if the second phenomenon, temporary migration from other zones of the Italian south, had not appeared. It was the new source of labour which allowed the system to make a qualitative leap to a scale of operation unimaginable before. The morphology of the *latifondo* reached its maturity and remained in practice in that shape up to the moment of its disappearance during the crisis of the years 1943 to 1950.

The first great investigation of the phenomenon of internal migration took place in the early years of the twentieth century. It found that in 1905 the province of Catanzaro, of which the Marchesato di Crotone is by the far the most important part, was the site of a seasonal migration which involved in its various phases a small reserve army of some 16,000 labourers.[35] The total male agricultural labour force of the province in 1901 had amounted to slightly less than 100,000, of whom roughly half were rural daily labourers, *giornalieri di campagna*. Hence 16,000 already represented something close to a third of all daily-wage labour in the province. If from the figure for periodic migrants we subtract the numbers of internal emigrants, we get the net total of migration into the province either from other zones of the province itself or from other regions. The sum of 10,695 is really quite remarkable and stands comparison with such movements on a national scale. Only the provinces of Foggia in the south and

[35] Ministero di Agricoltura, Industria e Commercio, *Le correnti di migrazione interna in Italia durante il 1905* (Rome, 1907), pp. 35–7.

Novara in the north had totals for seasonal migration higher than that of Catanzaro.[36] Such statistics reveal that the Crotonese of the first decades of the twentieth century, and indeed of the following decades, as confirmed by statistics on internal migration of the 1920s, was one of the most unbalanced of agrarian labour markets from the point of view of supply and demand.[37] According to the statistics of the census of 1901, the Marchesato had forty-seven thousand people, eight thousand of whom were pure daily labourers. In the summer and autumn of each year there was added to that total roughly the same number of persons who came from other areas, either of the province of Catanzaro or farther afield from the provinces of Cosenza, Reggio or even Lecce.

Seasonal labour had a double function in the political economy of the *latifondo*. First, it brought the system into a temporary equilibrium, filling the gap between supply and demand. Seasonal migration prevented locals 'from going mad' about wage demands, especially in the crucial period of reaping when on occasions of real shortage daily wages might shoot up to six or seven times normal levels. The flood of seasonal workers discouraged any form of collective association and left the owners in their autocracy as the sole controllers of all the productive and vertical social relations. Secondly, as the migrants became regularised and reliable with the passage of time, the quantitative growth of the *latifondo* could begin all over again. Between the two wars the system reached its greatest spread.

If the migratory labour force played the role of sustaining the autocratic social, economic and political order of the *latifondo* from without, that autocracy in its turn reacted by increasing and organising the migration. One of the most important functions of the bureaucracy of repression which controlled every estate in the region was the recruitment of seasonal labour. There existed a whole network of 'foreign correspondents' sprinkled through the peasant villages of the interior of Calabria, in the overpopulated areas of the western coast and even in the regions of Apulia where small peasant proprietorships predominated. These cor-

[36] *Ibid.*, pp. 35–7.
[37] Commissariato Generale per le Migrazioni Interne, *Le migrazioni interne in Italia nell'anno 1927* (Rome, 1928 and annually thereafter until 1940).

respondents also came to be called *caporali* although they were rarely directly employed by the great estates. They tended to be labourers working for themselves in agriculture, or small builders or small master-craftsmen, persons who controlled a small local clientele. Occasionally, a proper *caporale* employed by the estate would be sent out as a travelling recruiting officer to enrol squads for the coming season.

The *caporali* undertook to provide a fixed number of labourers with precise characteristics – skill, strength, socialisation within the work force and docility – for a certain period of the year. Frequently the *caporale* worked out the contract, stipulating the number of hours to be worked, wages and other conditions of work. The *caporale* assumed the responsibility for the conduct of his men, for resolution of squabbles and any incidental acts of insubordination by members of his squad during the summer sojourn at the estate. It was the *caporale* who paid out the *caparra* or deposit, that is, the advance on future wages. The need for a substantial quota of 'secure' labour during the crucial periods of the year was so great that the wage advances were often made a year ahead.

In the struggle for survival in the market for human labour, the superiority of the migrants was crushing. They were younger, healthier and more resistant to hard work than the locals. They were not weakened by malaria and chronic malnutrition. In a competition based essentially on biological criteria such as that on the *latifondo*, the health of the migrants was enough to put the local labour force in constant danger. If, for example, the flood of migrants exceeded the immediate local needs, it was the resident *braccianti* who would be released or forced to look for work elsewhere. The summer months in the Crotonese saw much coming and going. To make matters worse, the supply of local labour was not evenly distributed among the various communal markets for labour. This tended to happen because not all the various zones of the Marchesato were perfectly in phase, a tendency which the proprietors, for obvious reasons, chose to accentuate rather than to level out. The owners' ability to import seasonal labour brought about a further weakening of the bargaining power of local labourers, who now had to hurry from place to place as demand dictated. In those villages where scarcity of labour was chronic, the owners brought in seasonal workers to keep wages down. Where supply and demand were better balanced, the owners used seasonal workers to keep the locals off the rolls. Even in communities where there was permanent surplus, the owners tended to bring in seasonal workers to increase the outward flow of locals.

It seems pretty clear that the intermittent quality of work and the consequent coming and going of local workers annulled any advantage they might have derived from the high levels of employment during the busy season. The constant flux prevented that coagulation of common interest and understanding, the prerequisite of union activity. The formation of understandings or accords or associations tending to monopolise the sale of labour was further impeded by the cultural cleavage between the two circuits of labour. This cleavage expressed itself in the dichotomy between the particular character of seasonal labour and the universal character of local labour with respect to the administration of the *latifondo*. Contrary to what an analysis of the social order in terms of 'paternalism', 'clientelism', 'feudalism' or 'semi-feudalism' might lead one to expect, the relations between the estate and its local labour force had a rigorously impersonal and abstract character.

At Isola di Capo Rizzuto, the village of the *latifondo par excellence*, nobody ever saw Baron Barracco. He lived for only a few days each year at Isola, never went out of his house and knew none of his tenants. He demanded the most rigid observance of hierarchy in his administration ... Every corner of earth, every object, bore the seal of the baron. He was in effect always present in the village even if he was there in person for only a few days.[38]

The owners of the *latifondo* were regarded by the peasants as a kind of natural catastrophe, 'sent by heaven along with clay soil and bad weather'.[39] All labourers were equal in the sight of the baron, indistinguishable quantities of an abstract commodity called labour, interchangeable, consumed, discarded and replaced by other equally abstract units. The relation baron–*bracciante* lacked even the mask of a relationship of personal

[38] J. Meyriat, *La Calabria*, p. 145.
[39] G. Brasacchio, *Nuovi orizzonti*, p. 147.

dependence or subjection, not least because the two parties never saw each other. 'It is easier to talk to God than the Baron Barracco', an old labourer remarked to Giovanni Russo.[40] 'In such an atmosphere', wrote Brasacchio, 'the proprietor lives uprooted from society; some are literally invisible.'[41] The owner of a *latifondo* was neither a feudal lord nor a modern boss with a network of clients. The substance of his relations with his dependants was neither seigneurial nor the unequal exchange of service which makes up the essence of clientelism. It was naked authoritarianism. 'Loyalty' toward one's feudal lord or 'submission' to the boss have a common matrix in the law of redistribution, which imposes on him who stands above certain duties to those below in the organisation of life and of 'service'. Even tenuous reciprocity was utterly lacking in the relationship of abstract, absolute, impersonal subordination which tied labourer to *latifondista*. He 'gave nothing' in exchange for his evident position of power. He diverted nothing from his huge surplus for the ordinary needs of the community, that minimal paternalist charity which serves to justify in some measure the existence, and to augment the prestige, of that status group whose members aspire to be leaders before they want to be employers: defence against external threat, resolution of conflicts and patriarchal redistribution of resources, charitable donations, religious building and good works. 'From the houses of the *signori*', a *bracciante* of the Crotonese told Nitti, 'not even smoke comes out'.[42] As Repaci put it, 'a terrifying invincible avarice' seemed to be the most salient feature of the public behaviour of the barons of the Marchesato.[43]

The seasonal labour circuit was, on the other hand, immersed in the particular, an intricate network of ties of friendship, kinship, local relations, which prevented the evolution of any tendency to conflict on a class basis. The sector of seasonal labour was the only area of activity on the *latifondo* where one can detect elements of instrumentalised human relations not directly tied to the market. Those on fixed wages on the *latifondo* maintained and

[40] G. Russo, *Baroni e contadini* (Bari, 1979), p. 53.
[41] G. Brasacchio, *Nuovi orizzonti*, p. 147.
[42] F. S. Nitti, *Inchiesta sulle condizioni*, p. 43.
[43] L. Repaci, 'Baroni controluce', p. 1239.

enlarged their ties with their villages of origin, helping to get friends, kith and kin called for summer work. The *caporale* tended to be the centre of a group of brothers, cousins, adopted kinsmen and neighbours. Here the dependency and subordination contained in the autocratic relationships were tinged by clientelism and paternalism. Conflict with the native workers of the village assumed the character of 'ethnic' conflict. One could say, then, that no class of seasonal workers existed. Each squad of workers was jealous of the others for a thousand and one reasons, ranging from differences of geographical origin and trade to differences in relations with the local administration of the estate.

The seasonal workers lacked the disposition for union activity or class struggle. Their character as temporary and migratory workers militated against solidarity. The seasonal worker was generally young, unmarried, or recently married. The prevailing age group was that between 18 and 30. Summer work meant merely a useful extra source of income to put on one side for getting married or for savings for the various eventualities of life. The wages received had little to do with the workers' biological survival. That was guaranteed by their other activities at home. All that discouraged any tendency to fight for more or for better conditions on the great estate. When he had earned as much as possible by working as hard as possible, the seasonal worker went home where he at once found himself reabsorbed into a society and culture radically different to that of the area dominated by the *latifondo*.

Labourers, emigration and class struggle

The corner stone of the *latifondo* was, therefore, a labour force obedient, numerous and cheap. Without it the *latifondo* could not have existed as a 'type' of productive organisation qualitatively distinct from any other. It could never have achieved that extraordinary elasticity in confronting the market for goods which allowed it to survive alongside forms of production much more advanced. The failing of any one of those three characteristics of the labour force would have endangered the integrity of the entire system. The great achievement of the *latifondisti* lay in creating an economic and political set of devices capable of producing a labour force which was, as I have said, obedient, numerous and cheap.

Class struggle and emigration struck at all three of these features, and hence endangered both the basic mechanisms on which the *latifondo* depended: autocracy and disequilibrium in the labour market. Their effect could not promote rationalisation or modernisation but only a wasting away of the essential substance. Any mention whatever of 'flight' of labour from the estate struck the system in its crucial articulation. It was therefore always necessary to maintain workers both in a subordinate and a flexible state. Emigration, in fact, had the effect of thinning that supply of local casual labour which represented the basis of the entire operation. The decisive circuit of the *latifondo* – and it is well to repeat it again – was provided by the resident population of casual day labourers, for they alone – through the organised immigration of seasonal workers – were in a position to overturn the relationships of the market which formed the basis of latifondist power. Class struggle struck directly at autocracy. What emigration did on the economic plane, class conflict tended to do on the political.

As long as these two 'non-dialectical contradictions' remained latent or manifested themselves in restricted forms, the system continued to survive. At the moment that either came to the surface in a complete or prolonged form, the system faced a crisis. Class struggle and emigration operated on different levels. They constituted two radically different alternative reactions to the *latifondo*. They tended to exclude each other. When there was the one, there was less or none of the other. Besides, there existed a not unimportant hierarchy between them. They differed a great deal in their feasibility. Both could, in theory, have brought about the collapse of the system, but, for reasons which I shall develop below, mass emigration was never a real possibility, odd as that may sound given the appalling conditions of life for the overwhelming majority of the residents of the Marchesato. Mass emigration by *braccianti* constituted a 'theoretical', not an actual, contradiction in the system.

It takes very little imagination to see that, with conditions as they were in the Crotonese, the costs of class struggle were much higher than those of emigration. Collective rebellion might lead

Table 34 *Annual average emigration from the 'latifondo', from the peasant community of the Cosentino, from Calabria and from the Mezzogiorno from 1884 to 1915*

Area	Emigration per 1,000 inhabitants
Cutro/Isola di Capo Rizzuto (Crotonese)	7
Figline Vegliaturo/ Piane Crati (Cosentino)	41
Calabria	18
Mezzogiorno	11

Source: Ministero di Agricoltura, Industria e Commercio, Direzione Generale della Statistica, *Statistica dell'emigrazione italiana all'estero, 1884–1915*

to direct repression or 'artificial unemployment', both weapons easily to hand in the barons' arsenal. Hence common sense suggests that mass emigration should have involved more people. In ordinary speech (but also in scientific terms, though less consciously) emigration and misery were always associated, and misery was the lot of the *braccianti* of the Crotonese. Yet the paradox is that no such response took place. A quick glance at the official statistics in Table 34 for the period 1884–1915 shows how wrong the easy association of long-distance emigration and misery is. The two most wretched and oppressed communities of the Crotonese, indeed of all Calabria, were Cutro and Isola di Capo Rizzuto. These two villages had a rate of emigration well below the national or regional averages and a fraction of that in the peasant communities of the Cosentino. Remember too that these were the peak years of Italian migration to North America. Over a million Italians entered the United States in the year 1917 alone. During the first decade of statistical enquiry, 1876 to 1886, there was no emigration registered in the Crotonese against a rate of 10 per 1,000 in the Cosentino. Only at the beginning of the twentieth century did the communities of the *latifondo* begin to reach that level.

The reasons for such 'strange' behaviour have to be sought in the organisational structure of the society, that is, within the autocratic regime itself. Seen 'from below' the Crotonese was a regime of subordination and total impoverishment of the labouring class. Analysis reveals that the reasons for the low level of emigration are to be found in the chief features of the labouring class itself and that class struggle and not emigration became the main outlet of protest against oppression.

There were four important obstacles to emigration, factors which from a different point of view provided the 'push' towards class struggle: (a) destitution; (b) the weakness of relations of family, kinship and traditional friendships; (c) weak entrepreneurial individualism; (d) intense sociality. These four factors provide a structural profile of the social order of the labourers in the Crotonese and become more comprehensible when placed in comparison with the other two areas analysed in this work and with information drawn from the region in general.

The most important characteristic of the labouring class of the *latifondo* was its terrifying, unspeakable wretchedness. From the letters and documents, the official statistics and enquiries I have looked at for this study, there emerges an impression of appalling misery. I was strongly reminded of the picture painted by Engels in his early work on the condition of the working classes in England at the beginning of the industrial revolution. The *braccianti* of the *latifondo* were always delicately poised on the knife-edge of survival. In bad years they starved to death or died of malaria. They were degraded physically and deprived of culture. Whole pages of *The Situation of the Working Class in England* of 1845 could be used to describe their plight if the geographical references were changed. Pure survival was at risk and the struggle just to keep alive distinguished the peasants of the Marchesato from the peasants of the Cosentino and from practically all the other groups of the poor in Calabria or the Italian south after the 1840s. If one could construct a sort of Malthusian graph of the limits of biological survival for a population, the peasants of the Cosentino would be way above the base line. Poor peasants and labourers in Calabria and elsewhere would be just above it, while the labourers of the Crotonese would be continuously on or just below it.

The annual income of a labourer's family in the Crotonese in

1947 was about 100,000 lire,[44] half that of a poor Calabrian peasant family, a third of that of an agricultural labourer in the north of Italy, and only a quarter of that of a peasant family in the Cosentino.[45] If we divide the global sum by five or six, the average size of a family in that area, we arrive at an annual income per head well below the sum of money needed to assure survival. It amounted in the years 1947–50 to roughly 30,000 lire per head (roughly £30). The papers of the parliamentary commission on poverty in Italy of the 1950s contain figures on average daily food consumption of poor families in various regions of Italy. The figures for the Crotonese, even in the dry language of official documents, were bad enough 'to render any further comment superfluous'. More than 80 per cent of the diet of a labourer in the Crotonese consisted of low-protein foods, compared to 57 per cent of that for the typical poor southern-Italian family, 45 per cent the average poor family in Italy as a whole and 38 per cent the north-Italian poor family (see Table 35).

Such figures are calculated by dividing the annual estimated consumption by 365, but that itself was problematic in the Crotonese. Not a little of its wretchedness was caused by the wide swings in levels of consumption during the year. The labourer in the Crotonese differed from other poor peasants too in his dependence on the shop and the market for his articles of consumption, just as he was dependent on the labour market for his wages.[46] Hence he consumed what his employment permitted. The general physical weakness of the population made it susceptible to disease. Gissing in his travels was appalled by what he saw at Cotrone (as it was then called):

> The common type of face at Cotrone is coarse and bumpkinish; ruder, it seemed to me, than faces seen at any point of my journey hitherto. A photographer had hung out a lot of portraits, and it was a hideous exhibition; some of the visages attained an incredible degree of vulgar ugliness. This in the town which still bears the name of Croton. The people are all more or less unhealthy; one meets peasants horribly disfigured with life-long malaria.[47]

[44] Roughly £100 at the official rate of exchange then (Translator).
[45] *Atti della Commissione Parlamentare di Inchiesta sulla Miseria* (Rome, 1957), vol. II.
[46] G. Brasacchio, *Nuovi orizzonti*, pp. 125 and 233.
[47] G. Gissing, *By the Ionian Sea*, p. 71.

Table 35 Daily consumption by type of nutriment for poor families in the Crotonese, in the south of Italy, in Italy as a whole and in the north

Type of food	Crotonese no.	Crotonese %	Poor families in the South no.	South %	Italy no.	Italy %	North no.	North %
			(quantities in grams)					
Bread + flour	667	59.2	342	36.4	325	29.1	297	23.5
Soup + pasta materials	167	14.8	164	17.5	155	13.9	164	13.0
Dried vegetables	100	8.9	29	3.1	22	2.0	16	1.3
Total of poor foods	934	82.9	535	57.0	502	45.0	477	37.8
Meat	8	0.7	9	1.0	31	2.8	49	3.9
Cheese	2	0.2	4	0.4	12	1.1	18	1.4
Fish	—	—	16	1.7	17	1.5	17	1.3
Milk + eggs	—	—	63	6.7	154	13.8	249	19.8
Total of rich foods	10	0.9	92	9.8	214	19.2	333	26.4
Potatoes, vegetables, fruits	80	7.1	243	26.0	301	27.0	330	26.1
Fats	84	7.5	35	3.7	41	3.6	46	3.6
Sugar, coffee, etc.	18	1.6	33	3.5	58	5.2	76	6.1
Total of other foods	182	16.2	311	33.2	400	35.8	452	35.8
Total of all foods	1,126	100	938	100	1,116	100	1,262	100

Source: *Inchiesta parlamentare sulla miseria*, Rome, 1957, vol. II, tome 3, and for the Crotonese, Brasacchio, *Nuovi orizzonti*, pp. 220–1

During the 1930s and 1940s there were still recorded cases of pellagra and deaths from scurvy. Tuberculosis, typhoid and infectious diseases of every sort ravaged the area with much higher frequency than elsewhere. According to official statistics, during the five years between 1945 and 1950, the province of Catanzaro (which for our purposes equals the Crotonese) yielded two thirds of all the cases of malaria in the entire region, at a rate of roughly 30,000 victims out of a population of 46,000.[48] A little imagination will suggest what these numbers mean in human suffering and degradation.[49] As late as 1953, three years after the land reform had destroyed the *latifondo*, the enquiry on poverty found that at Cutro 'the population suffers from a general weakness of physique so great that the percentage of those rejected as unfit for national service is among the highest of all the communities in Italy'.[50]

Malaria and misery shaped the physical appearance of the population of the *latifondo* in the Crotonese. Even today they look different from the inhabitants of the other Calabrian regions. A person of ordinary height standing in the streets of Crotone sees himself surrounded by a dwarfed population. The average height of the inhabitants of the zone is 10 centimetres less than the regional average. All the accounts of travellers like Gissing and of official enquiries of various sorts contain the same descriptions of the people: small, dark, frail, chronically ill. As Brasacchio wrote:

> The *bracciante* of the Crotonese displays the physical characteristics which reflect the area in which he lives ... agile and lean, the heavily lined face even of the youngest denounces the terrible struggle for survival. The pallor characteristic of malaria is hidden beneath the deep brown skin burnt by the summer suns, which gives to the face a curious olive colour. Women after the age of thirty are already in a full state of degeneration physically.[51]

The difference between the *bracciante* and the peasants of the other regions of Calabria was marked. After Gissing had spent several months in Crotone, himself dangerously ill, he at last took the train which bore him out of the area. As he describes it,

> At one of the many way stations entered a traveller whom I could not

---

[48] *Atti della Commissione Parlamentare*, vol. II, tome, 3, p. 56.
[49] F. S. Nitti, *Inchiesta sulle condizioni*, pp. 89–90.
[50] *Atti della Commissione Parlamentare*, vol. III, p. 317.
[51] G. Brasacchio, *Nuovi orizzonti*, p. 127.

numbers per 1,000

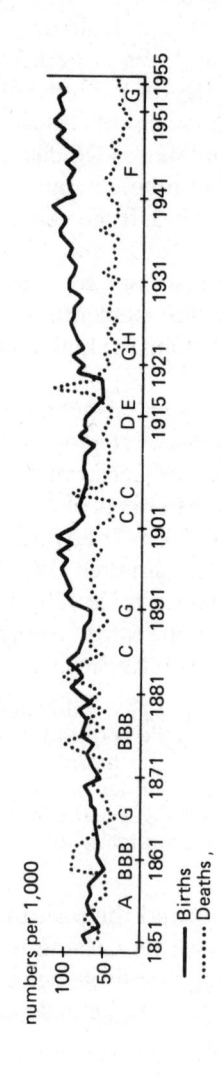

Fig. 5 Fertility and mortality in the *comune* of Melissa from 1851 to 1955

The signs at the base indicate:

A   epidemic of cholera
B   outbreak of smallpox
C   epidemic of diphtheria
D   'Spanish' influenza
E   beginning of communal distribution of quinine
F   beginning of DDT spraying
G   distribution of land to the peasants
H   the first mechanical threshers

Source: M. S. Mercurio-Amoruso, 'Inchiesta economica su Melissa', *Quaderni di geografia umana per la Sicilia e la Calabria*, vol. III, 1958

regard but with astonishment. He was a man at once plump and muscular, his sturdy limbs well exhibited in a shooting costume. On his face glowed the richest hue of health; his eyes glistened merrily. With him he carried a basket which, as soon as he was settled, gave forth an abundant meal. The gusto of his eating, the satisfaction with which he eyed his glass of red wine, excited my appetite. But who was he? Not, I could see, a tourist. Yet how account for this health and vigour in a native of the district? ... At once I understood. This jovial, ruddy-cheeked personage was a man of the hills. At Catanzaro I should see others like him ... [52]

In view of the general physical weakness of the population, it is not surprising that the mortality rate on the *latifondo* was particularly high. In Figure 5 I have portrayed the course of births and deaths in an important community of the Crotonese between 1851 and 1951 to 1955.

In Melissa only at the beginning of the 1920s did live births begin to establish a permanent superiority over the rate of deaths. For most of the preceding period the two figures criss-crossed each other and in one period deaths exceeded births for three successive years. For the entire decade and a half between 1861 and 1875 there was no natural increase of the population at all, since for every sixty births per year there were just about 60 deaths. Until the end of the Second World War, when malaria fell sharply under the great DDT spraying programme begun by the British and American armies, and until the widespread distribution of antibiotics in the years after the war, the mortality rate was always much higher than the already high rate in Calabria at 37 per 1,000 in 1861, still at 20 per 1,000 in the 1920s and in some years at 45 to 50 per 1,000.

In a modern society the mortality rate affects a class of the population, the old, whose disappearance causes least disturbance to the economic and social functioning of the community, at least as long as that rate does not rise to levels which affect life expectancy or fall to levels at which the old become too much of a burden. In the *latifondo*, the reverse happened. The rate of mortality was kept up by the death of the very young, especially the new born. Toward the end of the 1930s, infant mortality in

---

[52] G. Gissing, *By the Ionian Sea*, pp. 104–5.

some of the communes of the Marchesato had reached 30 per hundred. At Melissa, as Mercurio-Amoruso writes,

> infant mortality was until 1900 very, very high – mainly because of intestinal infections during the summer – and in the second half of the last century in about ten years exceeded 50 per cent of all deaths. After 1900 the rate tended to fall. Between 1921 and 1940 it was equal to 44.1 per cent of all deaths . . . But in reality a sharp fall in the rate of deaths of children between 3 and 6 years old, which began about 1910, masked the rise of mortality rates among the very young, especially those in the first year of life, which again reached very high totals . . . it is now as it was 100 years ago.[53]

Mortality in other, not infant, age groups remained higher than regional or national averages. For every 100 deaths in the Crotonese 15 befell persons between the ages of 20 and 40, compared to 7 to 8 for Calabria and 6 to 7 for Italy as a whole. The death of young people in the fully productive ages struck the sentiments of the population more sharply than the death of infants and was the cause of the high number of widows and orphans in the population. The highest rates of mortality were those in the age groups 50 to 70, and an 80-year-old was a rarity. In the socio-cultural panorama of the Crotonese, a traditional figure of the peasant community was missing: the grandfather, the patriarch, the wise old man, 'who knows', who has experience of life, who gives counsel. At Cutro and Isola di Capo Rizzuto in 1951 the census found that only 6 per cent of the population were over 60, compared to 9.9 per cent for Calabria, 10.7 per cent for the Mezzogiorno and 12.2 per cent for Italy as a whole. Persons over 70 made up about 40 per cent of deaths in the rest of Italy during the 1940s but in the Crotonese only 25 per cent.[54]

The consequences of all these demographic factors is reflected in the figures for life expectancy. Average life expectancy in the Crotonese hovered about 32 years during the 1930s compared to 54 for the Mezzogiorno and Italy. In Figure 6 the figures for Melissa are set out, and it will be seen that the 1930s already

---

[53] M. S. Mercurio-Amoruso, 'Inchiesta economica su Melissa', *Quaderni di geografia umana per la Sicilia e la Calabria*, vol. II, 1958, p. 68.

[54] The figures are drawn from the official population surveys and from the volume by SVIMEZ, *Statistiche sul Mezzogiorno d'Italia, 1861–1953* (Rome, 1954).

50 YEARS

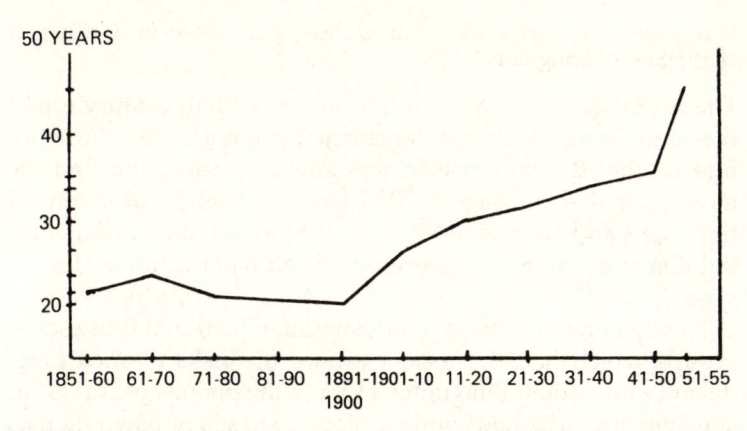

Fig. 6 Average life expectancy in the *comune* of Melissa from 1861 to 1955

Source: Mercurio-Amoruso, 'Inchiesta economica su Melissa'

marked a great improvement on the late nineteenth century, when average life expectancy was scarcely more than 20 years.

It would not be very useful to expand further on other aspects of life among the day labourers in the Crotonese. It is easy to imagine what sort of habitation and in what sort of villages such people had to live. During the 1950s the majority of the centres in the Crotonese had neither paved streets nor sewers. Some had no water and most had no electricity. Almost all homes lacked kitchens or any sort of plumbing. Most had two rooms or so in which five to ten people lived. Forty per cent of the population were still illiterate.

The most important point here, beyond recording the human misery behind all these figure, is to note what effect such wretchedness had on the chances of emigration. The moment one puts the two phenomena together it becomes clear that there is a level of misery below which emigration was simply impossible. A population like that of the Crotonese had neither the physical nor economic resources to consider the hazards of long-distance emigration which opened up in the late nineteenth century. As early as the 1880s, Jacini noted in his enquiry that

the true idea which agitates the mind of the emigrants is to go in search of their fortunes. But it is not the poorest of the poor who go, for the poor cannot raise the money for the passage, but those who already have a little something put aside ... it is these who make up the largest contingent of emigrants ...[55]

The investigation by Nitti in the early twentieth century found the same thing. 'Many peasants who have not gone to America told us that the only reason was that they could not find the money for their passage ...[56] "I have not emigrated because I have sons and no money."[57] ... "One has got to go to America, but I have not gone there because I never had the money for the voyage" ...'[58]

The dynamics of this type of emigration favoured those social groups which had the means to face the risks of such long-distance migration. Emigrants were not the poorest peasants but small tenants who had a little something to sell or pawn (house, livestock, implements, land), but also the craftsmen, small proprietors, the small business and commercial men. This was especially true of the early phase when the very high costs of travel acted as a rigorous social selection process, winnowing out all but the most suitable and most determined. Acute observers of the Calabrian scene noted this too in the early years of the great boom in movement to the USA. A Calabrian scholar who published an *Essay on the Economy* in 1905 distinguished a first phase in the emigration, from 1870 to 1881, in which 'among the possible causes of the phenomenon, those with a psychological content predominated over the purely economic motives'. 'In this period those persons left who had a certain financial security, because I cannot believe, given the risk and uncertainty of the rewards, that they would liquidate everything they had to hurl themselves into the unknown.'[59] Official statistics confirm this guess. The demographic census of 1881 had a category called 'absent from the kingdom'. For the entire Crotonese the census recorded 9 persons compared to 3,168 for the Cosenza district and 15,065 for Calabria. The same writer, G. Scalise, noted too how the composition of early emigration was by no means wholly rural.

[55] A. Branca, 'Relazione sulla seconda circoscrizione', pp. 121–2.
[56] F. S. Nitti, *Inchiesta sulle condizioni*, p. 175.
[57] *Ibid.*, p. 170.
[58] *Ibid.*, p. 158.
[59] G. Scalise, *L'emigrazione dalla Calabria. Saggio di economia sociale* (Naples, 1905), p. 29.

After the countrymen . . . come in decreasing orders of magnitude the artisans, the masons, the manual labourers, the stone-cutters and the domestics. There is a certain number of commercial travellers and small businessmen, especially in the period 1881 to 1901 . . . It seems ironical that under the category 'indigent' there were only 11 persons in the entire 26 years. As significant and relatively strong is the exodus of persons calling themselves members of the free professions, particularly so if one recalls that the greater part of such persons will travel in the higher classes and hence escape the statistics. In the period 1891 to 1901, in six years, the number of professional people, including doctors, who left Calabria, amounted to 1,621.[60]

The labourers of the *latifondo*, then, found themselves facing insuperable obstacles to emigration because they stood below the economic limit for which emigration was a realistic aspiration. Their utter wretchedness was the main obstacle to escape through emigration. This is clear from all the evidence. From the beginning of the phenomenon, that is, during the 35 years to 1905, the rate of emigration from the *comune* of Isola di Capo Rizzuto was zero. Only in the period of maximum movement to the USA from the Italian south, when some 300,000 persons left the area, 50,000 alone from Calabria, is it possible to observe a flow of labourers leaving the Crotonese.[61] Yet in this case we are looking at something more like a consequence of emigration itself, of a tendency for the phenomenon to spread across whole areas, something inherent in such migratory movements,[62] than an active push to escape their wretchedness. Even then, the 1910 Nitti enquiry observed,

In the zone of the true *latifondo* it is hard to find genuine emigration. Emigration takes place, in fact, more broadly and more regularly, where small land-owning exists. The first emigrants sell some land and go; then they send back money for others to follow or even the *pezzettino* (the ticket) itself.[63]

Having a certain sum of cash was also a requisite of the countries to which the emigrants headed. Many emigrants arriving with literally nothing were sent home, lest they become a burden on the meagre public charities during their search for work.[64]

[60] Ibid., pp. 16–17.
[61] V. Bruno, *La diffusione territoriale*, pp. 172–80.
[62] Ibid., pp. 223–8.
[63] F. S. Nitti, *Inchiesta sulle condizioni*, p. 41.
[64] Società Geografica Italiana, *Indagini sull'emigrazione italiana all'estero, 1880–9* (Rome, 1890), pp. 30–1.

The resources of an individual firmly fixed in a traditional society are by no means just economic. There are a series of social institutions of great power which protect the individual and never leave him to face life's vicissitudes in utter isolation, as we have seen in our examination of peasant society in the Cosentino. Family, kinship, friends, the neighbourhood, even marriage itself represented supports, which, if bent in the right way, could offer more than just a ticket for the trip to the United States. Even if the individual himself had too little on his own, he could always get a loan. The individual actor in the little drama of emigration represented in his person the whole social order. His capital came to him through using the numerous 'obligations' which circulated in all primary personal relationships. The first emigrants were thus relatively well-off peasants, artisans and small traders, of whom we have spoken. Even in later phases they remained a notable element in the flood, but the most relevant novelty in the second phase was that solidarity among kin, friend and village had extended the chances of emigration to new, less wealthy segments of the peasant population, that is, to the friends, kinsmen and fellow villagers of the first group of emigrants. The presence of a solid fabric of primary relationships explains why villages show a higher rate of emigration than towns or cities. As Scalise speculated,

> The proportion of emigrants from the provincial or district capitals and of communities with more than 10,000 inhabitants, in the quinquennium 1897–1901, was found to be much lower than in smaller centres. The villages have neither works nor factories which can hold their workers to the job so that the lower rates of emigration in the cities, I think . . . derive from the fact that there when workers have no money for their passage they find nobody willing to lend it to them without real guarantee, whereas those of the countryside . . . find through the greater intimacy in which they dwell in restricted ambiences, persons who will lend them money on their word alone.[65]

In many villages of the Cosentino this intimacy became institutionalised and led to the formation of leagues or cooperatives which lent money to peasants at very low or no rates of interest at all. Nitti collected many examples:

---

[65] G. Scalise, *L'emigrazione*, pp. 20–1.

'I could not go to America because I didn't have the money. Before, there was no league; now there's the league and it will lend it to you.'

'At first there was no money; so to find money to go to America was hard ... Now it's easy to find money ... Those who emigrate pay punctually with their savings the loan they got to go.'[66]

Exploitation of traditional institutions proved particularly evident in the case of matrimony: 'Some get married without consummating the marriage and on their return join their wives in wedlock, for it was their dowries which met the expenses of the journey.'[67]

The situation of the Crotonese was utterly different. The labourers of that zone lacked the necessary primary relations. Family, friendship, kinship, neighbourhood, village solidarity were for them abstractions. Let us begin with the family. The typical domestic unit of the labouring class in the Crotonese might be described as a 'disintegrated nuclear family'. It lacked a well-defined principle of internal cohesion and regulation of relations. It was 'held together' neither by the paternal authoritarianism of the Plain of Gioia Tauro nor by its multi-functionality as an economic and political as well as a socio-educative organism, as in the peasant society of the Cosentino. It was just an elementary biological unit and always threatening to break apart because it lacked internal cohesion.

One cannot forget the remarkably high rates of death among persons of productive ages which we noticed above. Stories of life among the peasants of the Crotonese always contained an account of the calamitous loss of some close relative: a father, a son, a brother. The population of the zone lived in constant terror of being overwhelmed by death, and not because of a vague 'insecurity of life' which sprang from the backwardness of their agricultural technology or from the values of some yet vaguer 'peasant society'. These people were frightened, because those nearest to them did die and often appallingly. Their very misery made relationships themselves weaker. Hence parents were the only people able to look after children. If they died, the calamity was total and frequently irredeemable. The nuclear family

---

[66] F. S. Nitti, *Inchiesta sulle condizioni*, pp. 162–3.
[67] *Ibid.*, p. 160.

crumbled and the orphans became 'nobody's people', swelling the army of vagabonds, servants and wanderers. The principles of lineal descent, so important to the barons of the *latifondo* and the peasants of the Cosentino, scarcely played a role in the proletarian families of the Crotonese. As Brasacchio wrote, 'Poverty undermines the cohesion of the family. Both the old and young gradually get away from it. The young, especially, pervaded by a spirit of independence, disappear quickly and sometimes cut themselves off completely. The old remain isolated and only weak links tie them to their children and grandchildren.'[68] The weakness of family relations was not compensated for by a robust tissue of 'horizontal' relationships of friendship or kin. Relative indifference seems to have been normal among cousins, nephews, grandchildren and so on. Nor among the social actions of the *bracciante* was there much trace of 'emotional friendship' nor of 'instrumental friendship' which we saw in the 'society of permanent transition' on the Plain of Gioia Tauro.

Marriage as an economic and social institution, involving economic exchange and alliances among potentially hostile groups, did not exist in the Crotonese. Whereas in the Cosentino peasant society satisfied its economic needs through, and built the entire edifice of social integration upon, the institution of marriage with its division of labour between the sexes and with the reciprocal obligations of relatives, in the Crotonese there was no principle of any kind in the complex regulation of such relationships. The survival of the individual depended on his participation in the market for labour. Matrimony was in no sense a 'total social fact' but a formality which tended to be carried out as rapidly and simply as possible. There was no protocol governing the ritual exchange of gifts. As Brasacchio noted, 'often at about twenty the young people formed a family nucleus and lived completely apart from their relatives'.[69]

Emigration by a member of such a family was not easy. No member could count on the support of any other. This fact, combined with the misery of the material conditions of life, made

[68] G. Brasacchio, *Nuovi orizzonti*, p. 214.
[69] *Ibid.*, p. 128.

flight from the soil an unrealistic enterprise. To these two characteristic features of the labouring class in the Crotonese which blocked emigration and encouraged class struggle, two others must now be added: the weak entrepreneurial individualism and the intense sociality of the Crotonese, both of which were tied in turn to the position of the labourer within the autocratic universe of the *latifondo*. The status of a labourer on the estate was that of a producer and not that of entrepreneur. Emigration was itself a manifestation of the spirit of enterprise. I am thinking here of an essentially pre-industrial type of enterprise, which consisted less in the search for, and introduction of, innovation in the productive process than in an attempt to combine traditional elements in an advantageous way. The great transatlantic migration of the years between 1880 and 1915 was an attempt to preserve the independence of spirit and that form of autonomy and self-sufficiency which characterised the world of peasants. Emigration and class struggle, then, really represented two forms of social rebellion which often involved very different protagonists: individual peasants with the whole weight of the world of the family-enterprise behind them the former; the agrarian proletariat on the edge of starvation firmly incapsulated within a system of social classes the latter.

The *bracciante* of the Crotonese lacked initiative and was a poor entrepreneur. His socialisation and mode of life were shaped by the themes of dependence and subordination arising from the autocratic organisation of production. Somebody else directed his work. He and his family were part of a vertical apparatus of coercion and control which expressed the autocracy of the great proprietors. Norms and standards absorbed from childhood in such an environment had nothing to do with responsibility for the management of the family-enterprise but with ideas of a more abstract kind, of obedience and of rebelliousness against the hierarchy. The values transmitted were at once both more conservative and more revolutionary than those of peasant society in the Cosentino. The rural proletariat of the Crotonese had a double visage. 'Because he often earns his wages in an extremely precarious job, the consequent continuous subjugation to the proprietors and large tenants have made the peasant docile, obedient and patient. But in his soul many are the contradictions...'[70] Violent rebellion was always just around the corner. At times he seemed to be 'a sober reasoner, endowed with good sense, who accepted the justice of things and respect for his neighbours.' At others, he was transformed into 'a loquacious quarrelsome troublemaker who does not hesitate to stoop to every manifestation of arrogance... His religious spirit oscillates between the purest expressions of faith and the most lurid blasphemies.' He was at one and the same time 'moderate and incendiary, mild and blood-thirsty, docile and stubborn, modest and braggart.'[71]

The labourer of the Crotonese had no experience as an entrepreneur. His separation from the means of production was virtually complete. He had little knowledge of agricultural techniques and had no hope of becoming an efficient organiser of production. This utter lack of professional skill typical of the labourer in the *latifondo* became a key issue in the dispute between the 'technicians' and the 'politicians' during the land reform which abolished the *latifondo*. The 'technicians' opposed the idea of turning the Crotonese into an area of small peasant proprietorships, which was, of course, attractive to the members of the De Gasperi government. After all, the land-owning small peasant was supposed to be the bastion of conservative (and Christian Democratic) good sense. For Rossi-Doria, Pantanelli and the other experts, the *bracciante* of the zone was not ready to become a small peasant proprietor, not least because he lacked the necessary technical skills.

> The old tiller of the soil was accustomed to looking after the cattle of the proprietor or simply to working the earth. He had no experience of organising cultivation according to rational methods. To impose on him suddenly the need to confront new combinations, change crop rotations, to introduce new systems of cultivation, was asking too much of him... On the contrary, the organisation of new properties, certainly with reduced dimensions compared to the old *latifondo* but nevertheless still quite extensive... would permit the regrouping of numbers of peasants in production cooperatives.[72]

If to these cultural and economic characteristics we now add the

[70] *Ibid.*, p. 126.
[71] *Ibid.*, p. 127.
[72] J. Meyriat, *La Calabria*, p. 166.

element I have called the elevated level of 'sociality' which distinguished their mode of life, dwelling, working and communicating, we shall be able to grasp subjectively how impossible emigration and how comprehensible class struggle was to them. I use the word 'sociality' not 'social cohesion' in order to emphasise the purely mechanical quality of social life, that is the fact that the Crotonese labourer found himself living in, indeed could not succeed in staying alive except in, the closest connection with persons in precisely his condition. This reality had nothing to do with any active solidarity, reciprocal help or the like. It was just a fact. This type of society was immediate; it was a physical reality of proximity and common task, as unlike the integrated *Gemeinschaft* of the Cosentino peasantry with its complex systems of mediation and reciprocity as it was unlike the 'society of permanent transition' with its instrumental friendships and artificial kinship.

In a sense there was more 'society' in the *bracciante* of the Crotonese than in the much more mixed figures of the Plain of Gioia Tauro or in the peasants in the Cosentine mountains. The family ties were weak; habitation was very centralised, places of work very collective. The labourers lived 'massed' in rural cities of eight to ten times the size of the *casale* of the Cosentino. They worked in squads. They were raised and taught by the street, by the class, by quarter or neighbourhood, by the estate itself as a place of work, in general by the world beyond the family. Their social order was the result of a common fate and not the result of the operations of a myriad of semi-sovereign social entities at the basis of society. In their great capacity to form masses, there was simply 'the necessity to live together with people who have everything in common'.[73] Hence their rebellion against the social order followed the lines of their particular type of sociality and their particular status. It expressed itself in an intense collective counter-attack on the proprietors not in the expression of individual enterprise such as emigration.[74]

---

[73] G. Brasacchio, *Nuovi orizzonti*, p. 129.
[74] This 'preference' of landless labour for class struggle instead of emigration would appear to have had wide influence on the course of the flood of migratory labour. The southern-Italian region with the highest proportion of 'pure' proletarian rural labour was Apulia, and it showed the lowest rates of

The crisis

An explanation of the crisis of the latifondist system must begin with a preliminary set of observations. Fascism reinforced the *latifondo* in two ways: (a) it reinforced the autocracy of the owner and accentuated the disequilibrium within the labour market; (b) Mussolini's drive toward economic autarchy, 'the battle for grain', pushed the *latifondo* towards greater cereal production. Both phenomena accentuated and sharpened the anger and resistance at the base of the system, of the labouring class, which exploded in violence at the beginning of the 1940s.

The rise of fascism multiplied the efficacy and extent of the autocratic power of the owners. Such power had shown a notable solidity, but before the 1920s had never been so securely supported by the power of the state. Under the new regime the *latifondisti* felt themselves secure as never before. For the first time in their history they felt secure enough to consider one or two cautious modifications of their economic activities and a few timid changes in the structure of the enterprise. Mechanisation of the *latifondo* made a few steps forward. By the end of the 1930s the statistical annual of Italian agriculture recorded that the use of agricultural machinery in the province of Catanzaro per hectare cultivated was now notably higher than the regional and southern averages.

It was in this period too that the great estate began to grow again territorially. The barons began to buy up the remaining bits of independent peasant property and those capitalist enterprises

emigration. Many authors noticed the connection and emphasised it. In the final report of the Faina enquiry of 1910, for example, there is the following observation:

> To the peasant of the first years of the century there were three ways to react: resign oneself to a life of misery, rebel, or emigrate. He preferred to emigrate. The rural workers of the Basilicata gave the first example, followed by those of Calabria, followed again at a short distance by those of the Abruzzi and the Campania. The Apulians did not move . . . In Apulia, the rural masses remained at home. Always very numerous, they had recourse to the force of association, something favoured by their agglomeration in cities and by the class struggle. In the other regions, by contrast, the peasant chose, by emigrating, to set himself a very well-defined, determined and clearly individualist goal. (Cited in A. Serpieri, *La struttura sociale dell'agricoltura*, p. 176.)

which had failed to survive the regime's new autarchic programmes and their consequent exclusion from world markets. Within this picture of crab-like extension of latifondist production must be set the establishment for the first time of a consistent nucleus of heavy industrial production. The *latifondisti* supported the government's decision to establish on a substantial scale a chemical plant of the Montecatini group and immediately afterwards another initiative of the multi-national enterprise Pertusola.

In a way the *latifondisti* were moving towards the model of Prussian development, the alliance of great estates and heavy industry. This alliance rested on two mutually interesting concessions. Montecatini was supposed to supply the great estates with their fertilisers at favourable prices, while the proprietors were, if not to encourage, at least to put no obstacles in the way of the flood of unskilled workers needed by the new plant. The proprietors controlled the labour market so completely that they felt safe in allowing a part of the seasonal migratory labour force to be diverted to the factories. A small industrial working class began to emerge drawn from the Ionian coastal zones of the province of Reggio Calabria. Local labourers were excluded from this process and until the 1950s for all practical purposes there were two labour markets in the Crotonese, mutually exclusive.

The reasons for this separation must be sought in part in what we have already seen. The *braccianti* of the *latifondo*, although they were strictly a labour force to be hired on the spot for any purpose, were not hired for work in the factory because the proprietors prevented it. They put obstacles in the way of any weakening of the essential circuit of local, resident labour. In addition the physical condition of the local labour force was so poor that they were not capable of undertaking the heavy work demanded in the Montecatini plant. The number of deaths, mutilations and poisonings which marked the early years of the plant terrified the local population and made them less than eager to seek work there. By comparison the *latifondo* was preferable. Seasonal workers were more disposed to industrial employment because of fundamental shifts in the status of seasonal work. Less and less was the migrant a young peasant securely located in a close network of family associations, which meant that migration was only a temporary phenomenon. Already by the 1920s evidence began to accumulate of peasant societies crumbling and beginning to expel members. The crisis of migratory labour was worsened by the closing of the United States through two new immigration laws of 1921 and 1924 and, in a wider perspective, by the declining demand for unskilled labour which the world recession brought about. On the seasonal labour market there were now impoverished peasants thrown off their lands by the crises in non-cereal production and they sought work not as a short-term expedient but as a long-term solution. Frequently they took families with them as they moved.

Seasonal migration began to deposit population. This change contributed to the demographic boom in the Crotonese in the late 1920s and 1930s. In those years the rate of increase stood at 2 per cent per annum with occasional peaks of 3 or 4 per cent, and for Crotone itself of 5 to 6 per cent. The Crotonese grew 3 times faster than the regional average and 4 times the national, 5 times the southern-Italian averages.[75]

After the first flush, when the new workers temporarily filled the void in the supply of labour, the old disequilibrium returned, more acute than ever. The proprietors now found themselves in an even more advantageous position and could yet again lower wages for the *braccianti*. Autocracy and disequilibrium on the labour market seemed to dominate the social order as never before in the past. To this security internally, there was added the greater security towards the outside world, especially on the national market for grain. Tariff protection assured the *latifondisti* secure outlets more remunerative than in the past, so that the estates themselves gained in value. The *latifondo* settled itself for more than twenty years round the pole of cereal cultivation. And it was just here in the bonding of the *latifondo* to cereal production at the very moment in which rapid population growth had begun to alter the social structure that the roots of the final agony of the system can be seen.

The latifondist system became ever more rigid. Its margins of movement narrowed. The Crotonese *latifondo* of the fascist era had lost that flexibility which enabled it to switch suddenly from

---

[75] The figures here are drawn from the same sources as those cited in note 54.

cereal crops to sheep-herding and which had always allowed it to keep its labour force under control. Its sudden conversions had broken and annulled both attempts to organise rebellion and to press for higher wages. The formation of an increasingly numerous population on the ground, stable in its settlement, raised the social costs of the old-style conversions. Simple reduction of the demand for labour of the old style, even using the engines of repression available on the estate, could no longer be contemplated. The *latifondo* had its hands tied while population grew steadily. In the short run it favoured the autocracy of the barons but in the long run it could only destabilise their power.

The crisis of the *latifondo* began with the mobilisation for war. Suddenly and unexpectedly, labour became scarce as men were conscripted. After 1939, agricultural wages went through the roof and the *latifondisti* could no longer resort to the traditional method of coping with high wages by converting their lands to pasture. Social cost alone was not the only reason. Now the state forbad them to reduce grain production. From 1938, grain had been increasingly regulated. Compulsory storage had been introduced and other norms held the *latifondo* on the track of maximum cereal production. Substituting male with female and child labour was not easy, given the characteristics of the local population. A policy of 'savage mechanisation' was simply beyond the financial and technical horizons of the barons of the Crotonese, even if the climate with its uncertainties had been more favourable for large-scale capital investment.

For the first time the *latifondisti* faced the one thing that they had always hoped to avoid. They depended on their *braccianti*. The ironies multiplied. The system functioned only if the patron controlled the labour force completely. Now the person of the labourer reversed the process of alienation by interposing a human being between the owner and the object of his desire, the quantity of labour for sale by each cipher in the system. The ultimate dependence of proprietor on labour became revealed in its transparent structures. As long as the market operated by its automatic processes, the fiction had been preserved that labour and capital were equally independent 'factors of production'. In the instant that the market began to tip in favour of the labourers, the system began to creak.

The final stage of class conflict began in 1943 and lasted until the beginning of the 1950s. In July 1943 Mussolini fell from power. The crisis of the regime rapidly became the crisis of the *latifondo*, a connection which, I believe, has been underestimated. The fall of fascism struck the political prop of baronial power and knocked it from beneath the system. The events of 1943, to change the metaphor, 'lifted the lid' of the system and let the pent-up forces out. After all, support of the state had been the most specific, definable prerequisite of the system. The *latifondo* had, by governing and policing privately its immense holding, exercised state powers within the Crotonese and neighbouring regions. The state had tolerated and actively abetted this partial usurpation of function. When, at last, the revolt of the landless labourers began in 1943, it attacked the state and took on at once forms of political organisation. The labourers formed leagues, cooperatives and self-governing associations with which to fight the power of the state. Their aims were vast and rather ill-defined and went well beyond what after 1946 became the official objective of the movement, individual conquest and division of the land.[76] The peasants attacked the *latifondo* as such. The revolt differed from all previous risings. It was political and it lasted for a long time. Once it broke out, it took six years to subside. The *latifondo* was not the sort of structure which could sustain a resistance over that period of years.

Political action combined with scarcity of labour. The popular struggle grew more violent, its aims and language more incendiary. Like a legendary monster in its agony, the *latifondo* lashed out with its reptilian tail. In 1945 it expelled thousands of small tenants and sacked hordes of labourers in one last paroxysm, and turned back to pasture. The collapse of fascism had brought down the pillars of fascist legislation and at least the *latifondisti* were now legally free to try their last coup. Tenants had lost their legal protections in the debacle of the regime and found themselves expropriated. Prices of cattle and animal products had rocketed during the period, and the landlords seized the moment. As Rossi-Doria put it, writing in 1947,

---

[76] P. Arlacchi, 'Alcune riflessioni sulle lotte contadine nel Mezzogiorno', *La parola socialista*, nos. 2–3, 1975.

The price of grain had remained fixed in 1944 and 1945 at 900 to 1,000 lire... by 1946 it had risen to 2,300 to 2,700. It looks as if it will reach 4,500 this year. The grain-price index compared to pre-war levels went up by 7 times in the first two years, 18 times last year and very likely will go up by 36 times this year. At the same time the indices of livestock prices and animal products, products which represent the alternative activity of this area of extensive production, went up by 40 times in 1945, by 55 times in 1946 and stand today at 65 times pre-war levels. The comparison of the two indices is very important. It is easy to see how the temptation to convert from grain to pasture must make itself felt... The outstanding obstacles to revoking contracts are easily brushed aside. The effects, too, are easily imaginable. The figures are eloquent. In 1938 the area under cereal culture in the whole of the Mezzogiorno was 2,271,180 hectares, of which Sicily made up 776,579. This year those two figures have fallen to 1,832,182 and to 502,410; 450,000 hectares have been taken out of production, 275,000 in Sicily alone. That represents in round figures 25 per cent of the surface under cultivation today, but for Sicily as much as 55 per cent.

These numbers make me tremble. They embody the tragedy which the latifondist zones of the Mezzogiorno are acting out today. They contain the explanation of the bitter struggle which the peasants of these zones are fighting today.[77]

In the Crotonese the final thrashing about of the *latifondo* was bound to be even more violent than in other parts of the Mezzogiorno or even in Sicily. In their last desperate attempts to save their positions, the owners cut back ruthlessly on the demand for local labour. They eliminated both the heavy and light hoeing. Soil was turned over and weeded as little as possible and then only by the least competitive labourers from the labour market, especially old men. The result was an unemployment so desperate that it inflamed rather than weakened the resistance of the *braccianti*. By 1946 the ranks of the unemployed were swollen by veterans released from the forces and prisoners of war returning home. The struggle reached its peak of violence in the autumn and winter of 1946 and 1947.

The description of the course of the great battle for the soil may be left to the historians. As a sociologist I have been trying to build a model of the *latifondo* as a static system of social and economic relations. I have tried to explain how it worked structurally. In concluding this chapter, I must point out that, if

[77] M. Rossi-Doria, 'L'agricoltura del Mezzogiorno', *Il Ponte*, no. 7, 1947.

the analysis I have presented is right, the provisional order of the late 1940s which put an end to the system was a recognition that a certain sort of utopia had come to an end, the utopia of the *latifondisti*. The barons of the Crotonese had tried to give birth to a society based on market forces and social classes in a situation of extreme social and cultural disintegration.

Conclusions

No author, I suppose, likes to draw conclusions from a piece of research which has occupied him for a long time, and I am no exception in this respect. Instead, I have decided to add a kind of postscript to the research rather than to compose a conclusion in the classical sense. In the remaining few pages I shall try to answer a question which must have occurred to some readers who have stayed with me this far: what happened to the three types of society analysed in this book during the course of the great post-war transformation of Italian society and of the Mezzogiorno? The answer arises in part out of the next stage of my research and may be summarised briefly.

1. Post-war Italian development has consisted in great measure in breaking up the autonomy of the traditional socio-economic systems of the Italian south. There have been two main agents of change: long-distance *domestic* migration and state intervention on a grand scale in the economy of the Mezzogiorno. Both of these phenomena were without precedent in Italian history. Both have had during the twenty years from the early 1950s to the early 1970s a revolutionary impact and have transformed economy and society. Migration within Italy and state expenditure in the south have been the motors of the 'great transformation' which has literally altered the face of the countryside and brought to an end an entire civilisation by substituting for it another.

Domestic long-distance migration has consisted in the insertion into industrial society of some four million young Italians from the south, persons who came from different areas, cultures, traditions, mentalities to those among whom they found new jobs. This imposing circulation of men, manners and ideas has turned out to be the most powerful unifying element in the whole history of Italy. Mass internal migration has finally 'made us into Italians'. From the economic point of view, southern-Italian migration created a national labour market in a country which had never had one. Both north and south had until recently known two types of market for labour: the local and the international. The great trans-oceanic migration from the Italian south and from many northern areas had provided an Italian supply of unskilled or semi-skilled labour for an international demand but had left untouched those local markets, based on natural factors such as climate and geography. A modern, national, *competitive* market for labour came into being in Italy only after the Second World War through the displacement of millions and millions of people from south to north. This upheaval represented the most profound transformation in the entire history of Italy, indeed, the only sort of revolution of which it has been capable.

In the very moment in which the southerners went north, large-scale state intervention in the economy of the south began. This, too, turned out to be revolutionary in its impact on pre-existing equilibria. I do not share the view widely held on the Italian intellectual left that state intervention has been a conservative force, simply a vehicle for political corruption and clientelism by the Christian Democrats. Such an evaluation projects the experience of the later 1970s into the earlier period; the 1950s and 1960s were, in fact, very different.

In order to appreciate the novelty of the fact that the state suddenly began to transfer resources from the north to the south, you have to bear in mind a much larger historical span. Up to the end of the Second World War the unitary state which emerged from the upheavals of the *Risorgimento* had governed the Italian south according to a semi-colonial formula. Central authority gave little or nothing in exchange for the natural and financial resources which it drew from the Mezzogiorno. Its tasks were reduced to the minimum. It levied taxes and maintained public order, frequently, as we have seen in the case of the society of permanent transition of Gioia Tauro or the world of the great *latifondo* in the Crotonese, by delegating powers to local elites. It organised, by the systematic intervention of prefects and state employees, the 'fixing' of elections and the manufacture of political consensus for the governing parties. The 'southern question' could easily appear – and, in fact, was often seen by observers – as little different from a case of colonial exploitation.

In spite of all that, the position of the ex-Kingdom of the Two Sicilies with its capital of Naples cannot be simply compared to a colonial relationship somewhere in the Third World. There was a basic difference which manifested itself only during the post-war 'great transformation'. Southern under-development was within the same state structure. Hence, as soon as the institutional situation allowed it, even in Italy, the state began to carry out one of its most important functions in Western democracies, the redistribution of collective resources. For all its well-known limits and mystifications, the Italian state began to produce redistributive effects from the beginning of the 1950s with the agrarian reform laws and the foundation of the Cassa per il Mezzogiorno, the vast state-run investment fund for the south.

From the point of view of the reigning order in the south, the effects of state intervention and large-scale domestic migration consisted in a rapid 'thawing' of traditional fundamental socio-economic systems. For the first time, real circuits of communication and exchange became possible, linking isolated mountainous regions with their coastal neighbours. One began to see genuine geographic and occupational mobility within the region, whose proportions were great enough to stand comparison with the waves of people going north or abroad. In some regions, like Calabria, the economic, cultural and territorial revolution of the 1950s and 1960s changed forms of settlement, structures of houses, techniques and ways of living which had survived for centuries.

2. Although public expenditure and migration had created structural interdependence among socio-economic universes formerly independent and had given birth to ties of regional and national extent, they had effects which were neither uniform nor homogeneous in the various ambients of the Mezzogiorno. The two motors of the 'great transformation' had to take account of

the nature of the pre-existing institutions, especially in Calabria. The form assumed by the post-war metamorphosis in each regional or sub-regional environment must be seen as the result of various permutations and combinations among 'forces of change' and 'factors of traditional resistance'.

For the purposes of our analysis, it is important to underline the element constituted by the conservation of the internal differences in the Mezzogiorno and Calabria. These differences survived in spite of the processes of regional integration which took place along the axes linking the mountainous settlements and the coastal plains and in spite of the turbulences created by the regional labour market. They persisted even under the impact of the establishment of new political institutions, such as an autonomous regional government endowed with considerable powers.

This conservation of the internal diversity of southern Italy, if on new bases, found expression in three different models of change in the traditional social systems. The peasant society like that of the Cosentino was almost completely dissolved by the great exodus of migrant workers. Nor was this migration like the grand trans-oceanic movements we have seen. The protagonists were no longer social 'deviants' not integrated into the structure of the family farm nor the young peasant to whom the task of reconstructing the economic and social system had been entrusted and who for that reason had undertaken a temporary migration overseas. Toward the end of the 1950s the exodus from peasant villages began to reveal that the principal actors were the family-farm units themselves. During the course of the 1960s, as the current directed toward the northern-Italian industrial triangle of Genoa–Turin–Milan began to prevail over those directed to other countries, the whole process began to assume the physiognomy, quite unmistakable, of a global disintegration of an entire social system and of a kind of 'anticipatory socialisation' in the early stages of another. Family-enterprise and reciprocity lost their priority and centrality in the strategy of socio-economic relations. Internal urbanisation swelled rapidly, so that within twenty years the population in the provincial capital, the city of Cosenza, doubled.

The rapid demographic expansion of Cosenza city was in large part a consequence of the expansion of the tertiary sectors of employment, itself a consequence of the massive intervention of the state. If the post-war migratory flight provided the blow which shattered traditional peasant society, state intervention offered the basis on which a new sort of society began to reassemble itself. The model of change in post-war Cosentino might be summarised as a transition from a 'pure' peasant society to a 'compact tertiary' socio-economic order. The foundation and growth of huge directing centres of the great public agencies, the 'Opera Sila', the savings institutions and investment agencies etc., joined the spread and multiplication of an impressive complex of territorial infrastructures and advanced tertiary institutions. The Cosentino, the area least developed historically as a mercantile centre, suddenly became the pilot area for regional development, site of the new experimental university and the home of a relatively solidly integrated social structure based on a new white-collar middle class whose roots lay in the peasant village.

The disintegration of the latifondist system was even more radical than that of the peasant community. Latifondist society and economy disappeared utterly within a few years and left scarcely a trace. The process did not end in a new, stable and definite system of relations. From the beginning of 1943, as we saw in Chapter 3, a cycle of struggles, occupations of the land and repression began which ended by liquidating the system and destroying its principle of operation, that is, the autocracy. With the beginning of the 1950s the area saw a wave of emigration which ran for years. Some of it was caused directly by the shock of the struggles in the preceding decade, but much was a result of the tremendous shifts in ownership and status occasioned by the collapse of the old agrarian order and the sudden emergence of an entirely new structure of ownership, in effect a complete renovation of the whole productive apparatus and its personnel.

Emigration and intervention by the state shattered the remaining framework of the autocratic bureaucracy of the Crotonese and its *latifondo*. A new native class of little entrepreneurs rushed into the social and economic vacuum. Little agricultural enterprises, small businesses and small tourist enterprises sprang up everywhere like mushrooms. All social, political and economic relations became and remain fluid. Polycentrism and the socioeconomic diversity, unlike the solidity of the Crotonese, left the area essentially anarchic. Horizontal conflict spread, and increasing doses of deviance began to strike the social order. There were signs of anomie and in due course the inevitable emergence of mafia behaviour.

The post-war evolution of the society of permanent transition in the Plain of Gioia Tauro differed drastically from the two preceding types. No general replacement of the social structure took place. Instead, a gradual crisis issued in a complete transformation of the form and function of the power of the mafia. When the Second World War ended, this area began a slow but certain period of decadence. National and international trade were reactivated but under less favourable conditions. The classical products of the Plain of Gioia Tauro, the olive, orange, lemon, faced the competition of newer producing regions in Spain, North Africa and Greece, which offered better quality at lower prices.

The two great motors of change, emigration and state intervention, operated here less radically and in quite different ways than in the Cosentino or the Crotonese. The difference is most marked in the type of emigration. In the Plain emigration continued along customary lines. Semi-qualified and qualified male workers left the area for short stays abroad and returned. Numbers were much smaller than in the Cosentino or the former latifondist areas which in these years were being literally emptied by the exodus of entire blocks of population. State intervention, above all in agriculture, had the effect of sustaining rather than overthrowing the traditional systems of production.

Another contrast was in the investment in infrastructure. Elsewhere in Calabria investment in roads, housing and sewage had demanded the evolution of an apparatus new to the peasant world, an apparatus of new sorts of enterprises and the erection of new *ad hoc* markets for modern products. In Gioia Tauro such an apparatus already existed. Hence, the very construction of new elements of modern infrastructure, rather than overturning traditional modes of production, acted to conserve and stabilise traditional ones. Gioia Tauro already had the necessary economic diversification to absorb the new impulses.

Conclusions

The specific development of this society lay in the counterpoint between the maintenance of the traditional morphology and the progressive decay of its economic structures. During the 1950s and 1960s, the society of permanent transition began to 'rot' slowly, inflaming its traits of instability, friction, and conflict, that anarchic character which had already distinguished it from other southern social orders.

The behaviour and power of the mafia, however, only followed the course of the crisis up to a certain point. The crucial change in the mafia in the years after 1945 was the gradual but definite detachment of mafia power from its society of origin. The old mechanism of social integration by the mafia gradually snapped during the 1950s and 1960s. In the 1970s we saw a spectacular escalation of the new entrepreneurial mafia in all the principal sectors of economic development.

Arcavacata   PINO ARLACCHI
20 May 1982

Index

Abruzzo, region of, 12, 62
Aggression, as socially sanctioned, 98
Agrarian systems, 2, 5; in the Italian south, 14–23, 24–5, 54, 70–1, 128, 130–4
Agriculture: capitalist, 12, 72–3, 83, 84, 130, 132, 133, 142, 143, 144–5, 146–7, 148–9, 150, 160; censuses of, 147; export and, 84; feudal, 120, 130–4, 136, 144–5, 166; labour market and, 162–3 (Table 32), 166–7; 'Mediterranean Garden' and, 77, 138; types in Calabria, 71 (fig. 3), 77; types of, 5, 10, 11 (Table 1), 12, 14–16, 24–5, 83, 129 (Tables 26 & 27), 135–6
Alvaro, Corrado, 29, 43, 50, 51, 81, 82
Anglo-American Military Government, 117
Anthropology, 1, 4; and marriage, 45; and 'total social facts', 45, 48, 57
Apulia, region of, 14, 123, 125; olive crop in, 93 (Table 18), 94, 95 (Table 19), 169
'Area-Types', 3; communities in, 10 (n.3), 67 (n.1), 123 (n.1.); as models, 4–5, 7–8, 123, 132, 199, 202; use of soil in, 11
Argentina, 8
Artisans, 89; in Gioia Tauro, 82, 84, 100, 102
Aspromonte Mountains, 74, 79
Australia, 8
Avellino, 10, 62

Bagnara, 85
Banfield, E.C., 48
Barracco Family, 127, 171, 172; Alfonso, 127
Basilicata, region of, 45, 61, 62
Berlingieri Family, 127; Don Giulio, 127, 153
Bloch, Marc, 132, 167
Bourgeoisie, absence in Crotonese, 154, 176; in commerce of Gioia Tauro, 78, 82, 84–5, 89; as landowners, 16, 21, 41, 72, 159
Braccianti (landless labourers), 6, 7, 55, 118, 123, 155, 157, 159–60, 168, 170, 171, 172, 174, 176, 179, 188, 189, 190, 193, 194, 195, 197
Brasacchio, G., 172, 179, 188
Brigandage, 17; and peasant society, 40, 57, 98

Calabria, 2, 3, 4, 5, 9, 10, 12, 14, 24–5, 28, 86–7, 153, 154, 159, 168, 169, 176, 179, 185; brigandage in, 40; cereal production, 138 (Table 28); commercial class in, 81–2; emigration from, 60–1, 175 (Table 34), 184, 185, 201; family in, 43, 50; land-holdings in, 15 (Table 3), 74 (Table 14), 126 (Table 25), 153, 159 (Table 14), 126 (Table 25), 153, 159 (Table 14), 126 (Table 25), 153, 159; mortality rates in, 181, 182; olive production 92 (Table 17), 93 (Table 18), 94, 95 (Table 19; population of, 67, 68 (Table 13), 69 (fig. 2), 70; poverty in, 176, 177, 179; supply of labour in, 163 (Table 32), 164 (Table 33), 166–7; types of

206

Index

agriculture in, 24–5, 28, 71 (fig. 3), 72, 73–4, 77–8, 94, 138, 139, 202
Camorra (Neapolitan underworld), 62
Canada, 8
Capitalism, 16–17, 20–1, 157; and agriculture, 130, 132, 133, 141, 142, 143, 144–5, 146–7, 148–9, 151, 157, 160, 171; and the labour market, 162–5; and peasant society, 50–1, 150; and 'primary accumulation of capital', 41, 144, 160, 166
Caporali (private police on *latifondo*), 155–6, 157, 160; and labour recruitment, 169–70, 172–3
Caputo, L.A., 60
Carabinieri, 155
Cassa per il Mezzogiorno (Southern Italian State Development Agency), 201
Catanzaro, Province of, 4, 98, 168, 169, 192; disease in, 179, 181; seasonal migration in, 168–9
Catholic Church, 40
Cereal Culture, 131, 138 (Table 28), 140 (Table 30), 157–8, 164; expansion of, 167–8, 192, 197; tariffs and, 141–2, 167, 194
Chinautla Indians, 108
Christian Democratic Party, 190, 200
Ciro, *commune* of, 88
Citrus fruit, as products, 77, 78, 97
Cittanova, *commune* of, 88
'Civil society', 99, 104
Class conflict, as type of social action, 40–1, 42, 89, 98, 171, 173, 174–5, 176, 189, 191, 196, 197
Clientelismo, 16, 19, 20, 22, 54, 171, 172, 200; and friendship, 109; and mafia, 117, 118
Colonialism, 200, 201
Commesso (agent in trade), 81
Comparaggio (co-parenthood), 51, 107; and social integration, 105, 110
Conca Cosentina, see Cosentino
Contracts in tenancy, *appoderate*, 12, 14, 23–4, 35, 76, 130; in the Crotonese, 135, 161; in marriage, 45–6; share-cropping, 128, 129 (Tables 26, 27), 143
Cooperative movement, 40; in Calabria, 90 (Table 16); weakness in Gioia Tauro, 89

Cosentino, 3, 6, 9–10, 11, 12, 176; communities studied in, 10 (n.3); emigration from, 59–60, 63–4, 175 (Table 34), 184, 186, 202, 204; family in, 22–3, 25, 27–8, 32–4, 36, 38, 39 (Table 12), 99, 100 (Table 24), 101, 102, 103, 106, 186; friendship in, 108; population in, 10, 67 (Table 13), 68, 69 (fig. 2), 70; as type of peasant society, 5, 6–7, 14, 23–4, 26, 27–8, 29, 30, 32, 33, 36, 37, 38, 42, 46, 48–9, 50–1, 54, 56–7, 63–4, 83, 89, 101, 107, 120, 123, 130, 175, 188, 191, 202, 203
Cosenza, city of, 5, 10, 14, 202–3; province of, 4, 39, 60, 84, 109; vale of, 9, 12, 23, 26, 29–30, 32, 34, 35, 39, 42, 45, 55
Crati river, 9, 55, 56
Crotone, *commune* of, 153, 167, 177, 179
Crotonese (Marchesato of Crotone), 3, 4, 6–7, 11, 40, 123, 124–5, 152, 167, 181; 'barons' in, 40, 127, 153–4, 155, 159, 171–2, 196; *braccianti* in, 155, 157, 162–3 (Table 32), 164 (Table 33), 165–6, 170, 172, 176, 187–91, 193, 195; cereal production in, 135, 136, 138 (Table 28), 139 (Table 29), 194–5; disease in, 179, 180 (fig. 5), 181, 182; emigration from, 173, 174, 175 (Table 34), 176, 184, 185, 187, 204; family in, 187–8; great estates in, 88, 123, 124–7, 134, 143, 152–3, 203; immigration into, 166–7, 169–70, 171, 194; industrialization in, 193; life expectancy in, 182, 183 (fig. 6), 187; poverty in, 176, 177, 178, 179, 183; settlement pattern, 147 (Table 31), 164–5; social control in, 150, 152, 154, 155, 156, 158, 160, 174, 176, 187–9
Cutro, *commune* of, 127, 167, 175, 179, 182

De Gasperi, Alcide, 190
Deviance, 43–5, 46, 118, 150, 204; and emigration, 62–3, 202
Dickinson, R.E., 163, 164, 165 (fig. 4)
Disease, types of, 179, 180 (fig. 5)
Division of labour, 22, 23, 25, 48, 83, 91, 135, 156

Economic development: 'Prussian model of', 193; and

Index

Economic development – *cont.*
  underdevelopment, 91, 149, 201
Economic rationality, 50–1, 52; and the *latifondo*, 128, 132–3, 136, 137, 139, 140–1; and markets in Gioia Tauro, 79–80
Economy: customary relationships in, 16, 17, 20, 40, 51–2, 167; monetization of, 16, 17, 105, 141; national markets in, 5, 14–15, 36, 40, 46, 55, 87–8, 200
Elections, 201; and mafia, 117
Elites: circulation of, 98; local and the state, 200–1; and the mafia, 112, 117
Emigration: from the Crotonese, 174, 175 (Table 34), 176, 183, 184–5, 188–9, 190, 203; from Gioia Tauro, 87, 204; reciprocity and, 58–9, 64, 186–7; as regulator of peasant society, 39, 46, 57–65, 66–7, 173, 174–5 (Table 34), 176, 191, 194; from the Sila, 166–7; social origins and, 59–60, 87, 183–4, 185, 186, 189; temporary character of, 59–60, 63–4
Employment: in peasant agriculture, 24–5, 99 (Table 22); in tertiary sector, 203; and underemployment of rural labour, 163–5 (fig. 4), 166, 169, 170, 197; women and, 25–7
Engels, Friedrich, 176
England, 17, 18, 160, 161, 176

Faida (the blood feud), 105, 107, 121
Family, father's authority in, 22–3, 25, 27, 29, 102, 104; nuclear, 6–7, 22, 103, 107, 187; as repressive agent, 22, 27, 28, 30, 43, 98, 150; size of, 32–3 (Table 9), 34, 36, 38, 39 (Table 12), 64, 99 (Tables 21 & 22), 100 (Tables 23 & 24), 101
Family-enterprise (peasant holding), 5, 6, 10, 23–9, 30–1, 32, 34, 36, 43, 47, 48, 99–101, 147, 148–50; commercial, 81, 99; destruction of, 23, 38, 56–7, 103–5, 202; Marxist analysis and, 41
Family solidarity, 27, 28, 43, 103, 186; absence in Crotonese, 187–8, 191; in Gioia Tauro, 102, 106, 110
Farms, types of 12, 31, 34
Fascism, 192; as prop of *latifondo*, 196
Ferrara, plain of, 125

Feudalism, 16, 17, 20; in Calabria, 166; and the *latifondo*, 120, 130–4, 138, 144, 157–8, 171; relations of production under, 134–5; seigneurial relations under, 171, 172
Figline Vegliaturo, *commune* of, 175
First World War, 64
Foerster, R.F., 61, 62
Foggia, province of, 168
Food, consumption levels of, 177, 178 (Table 35); as object of exchange, 49–50
Franchetti, Leopoldo, 18, 18 (n. 12), 19 (n. 13), 135
Friendship, instrumental, 108, 109, 110; as social institution, 107–8, 176, 188

Gabellotti (Sicilian tenant farmers), 158–9, 160; contrast with Marx's *Pächter*, 160
Gaetani family, 127
Galantuomo (southern Italian landowner), 17, 18, 21
Gallucio, Giuseppina, 127
Gemeinschaft/Gesellschaft, 2, 6, 59, 91, 106, 191
Genoa, 82, 202
Germany, 8
Gioia Tauro, *commune* of, 74, 85, 86
Gioia Tauro, plain of, 3, 4, 5–6, 11, 14, 27, 67, 78, 79, 80; agriculture in, 70–2, 73–4, 92–8, 138, 204; artisans in, 82, 84, 89, 100, 102; commercial bourgeoisie in, 81–2, 84–5, 119; communities studied in, 67 (n.1); *comparaggio* in, 107; family in, 99–105, 106–7; friendship in, 108–9; mafia in, 98, 105, 111–17, 118, 120–1, 155; markets in, 78–80, 87–8, 96; olive production, 92–7; population, growth of, 67, 68 (Table 13), 69 (fig. 2), 70, 73, 86; size of land-holdings in, 74–5 (Table 14), 76 (Table 15), 77; social integration in, 104–5, 110–11, 116–17, 120–1, 187, 188, 191, 206; social mobility, 88–9, 101, 110, 118; traditional values in, 106–7, 118, 123
Gissing, George, 9, 124, 177, 179
Gramsci, Antonio, 16, 18; and 'the agrarian block', 18, 88–9, 128; and 'the great social disintegration', 16–17

Index

'Great Depression' (1873–96), 164
Greece, 204

Hess, H., 115
Hobbes, Thomas: and society, 50; and Gioia Tauro, 105, 114
Honour: and mafia, 111–12, 114, 118, 121; as socially sanctioned, 105, 106, 118–20

Illegitimacy in peasant society, 43, 44, 150
Industrial worker, as social type, 150–1, 176
Industrialization: in the Crotone, 193; in Italy, 199–200
Industriante (Calabrian estate manager), 158, 159, 160–1, 162
Infant mortality, 33, 180 (fig. 5), 181, 182
Ionian coast, 2, 4, 77, 124, 193
Ionian Sea, 9, 153
Isola di Capo Rizzuto, *commune* of, 127, 171, 175, 182, 185
Italy: age structure in, 182; national market in, 5, 14–15, 38, 55; northern region, 178 (Table 35), 200; olive production of, 93 (Table 18), 95 (Table 19); poverty in, 177, 178 (Table 35); southern region, 4, 10, 12, 54–5, 114–23, 177, 178, 185, 200; types of agriculture, 70–1, 72, 90–1, 124, 125, 128, 131, 133, 138; unification of, 5, 14, 15, 16, 17, 20, 38, 40, 55, 86, 154, 200

Jacini, S., 183
Joachim of Fiore, Abbot, 153

Kautsky, Karl, 44, 46–7, 141, 145, 146, 149, 150
Kingdom of the Two Sicilies, 201
Kinship, 2; networks of, 7, 106–7, 150, 172, 173, 176, 187, 188, 202; reciprocity and, 21 (n. 16), 43, 48–9, 58–9, 105, 110, 186, 187
Kula, W., 132, 134

Labour: as commodity, 171, 172; rural market for, 7, 21, 83–4, 85, 142, 143, 148, 150, 151–2, 156, 158, 162, 163 (Table 32), 164 (Table 33), 165, 166, 167, 168, 194; salaried, 83, 128, 129 (Tables 26 & 27), 144, 146, 157; urban market for, 149, 150, 151, 193, 200
Ladinos Indians, 108
Lake Arvo, 153
Land-holding: in the Crotonese, 124–28, 132, 137, 152–3; in Gioia Tauro, 74–5 (Table 14); parcellisation of, 127–8, 145, 147; by size, 12–13, 31 (Tables 6–8), 33, 34, 75 (Table 14), 76 (Table 15), 77, 124–5, 126 (Table 26), 127, 140 (Table 30); by type, 15 (Table 3)
Landless labourers, 6, 7, 43–4, 153, 156, 167–8, 196; not allowed to marry, 44, 47; size of families, 100 (Table 23)
Landlords, 12, 14, 20–1; bourgeois 'barons' as, 16–18, 40, 127; English, 17–18, 160–1; as entrepreneurs, 14, 135, 137; and social prestige, 119, 142, 144
Latifondo (great estate), 2, 6, 7, 40, 72, 120, 123, 128, 179, 192; abolition of, 190, 194, 196, 203; autocracy as prop of, 152, 153–4, 155, 156, 157–8, 169, 174, 189. 192, 194, 195, 196, 203; 'barons' as owners of, 16–18, 40, 127, 144, 152, 153–4, 155, 159, 167, 171–2, 192–3; class struggle on, 98, 171, 173, 174–5, 176, 195, 196, 197; emigration from, 174, 175 (Table 34), 185, 195; growth of, 88, 147–8, 168, 169, 197; and the labour market, 124, 128, 130, 143, 147, 148, 151, 152, 156, 157, 158, 162, 164–5, 166, 167, 168, 169, 170–1, 172–3, 174–5, 193, 194–5, 197; mortality rates on, 180 (fig. 5), 181; origins of, 20–1; poverty on, 176–7, 179, 181, 185; private police on, 155–7; size of, 124–6 (Table 25), 127, 152–3; as type of enterprise, 128, 130–1, 132, 133, 134, 135, 136, 137, 139, 140–1, 143, 147, 148, 151–2, 156–7, 158, 159–60, 161, 171, 173, 174, 176, 194–5, 197–8; wages on, 169, 170, 171, 172, 176–7, 194
Lazio, region of, 125
Leninism, as analytic instrument, 41
List, Friedrich, 35
Local government, 18–19
Lucifero Family, 127

Mafia: as *comportamento* (behaviour), 98, 105, 111–17, 118; and honour, 118–19, 121; and politics, 117, 118; its social function, 6, 116–20, 121, 155, 205; as sociological 'type', 118, 160; and the state, 116–17; in the USA, 63; wealth, limits of, 119; in western Sicily, 117
Malaria, 86, 170, 176, 177, 179, 181
Markets: in Gioia Tauro, 91–2, 121; and the *latifondo*, 131–3, 136, 141; logic of, 105, 120, 149; national, for labour, 200; types of, 78–80
Marriage: in the Cosentino, 42, 44, 45, 46, 49, 53, 188; in the Crotonese, 188; and emigration, 58–9; in the Plain of Gioia Tauro, 81
Marx, Karl, 48, 149; and capitalist farming, 160
Marxism, as analytic instrument, 41
Matera, 45
Mauss, Marcel, 50
'Mediterranean Garden', as type of agriculture, 77–8, 138
Mediterranean society, as type, 1
Melissa, *commune* of, 167, 180, 181, 182; life expectancy in, 183 (fig. 6); mortality rates in, 180 (fig. 5)
Merchants: native, 79–80; outsiders, 78, 119
Mercurio-Amoruso, M.S., 182
Meridionalisti (students of the Italian south), 18, 190
Messina, Straits of, 85
Methodology, models and, 7–8, 36, 91, 103, 118, 132
Mezzogiorno (the Italian south), 8, 14, 15, 16, 17, 18, 22, 23, 26, 70, 83, 88–9, 125, 144, 201–2; cereal production, 138 (Table 28), 197; emigration from, 175 (Table 34); olive production, 93 (Table 18), 95 (Table 19); population structure of, 182; supply of labour in, 163 (Table 32), 164 (Table 33); traditional, 4, 5, 8, 16–17, 18, 20, 37, 55, 123, 128, 200; 'transformation' of, 72, 159, 166–7, 199, 200, 201, 202; uniformity of, 1–2, 201
Migration, of labour, 84, 85, 162, 166, 167, 168–9, 170, 172, 173, 193, 199–200, 201
Milan, 82, 125, 202

Milone, F., 73
Modernisation, as concept, 1–2, 91, 174
Molise, province of, 12, 125
Montecatini Chemicals, 193
Monte Nero, 153
Moore, Barrington, 162
Mussolini, Benito, 192, 196

Naples, 144, 201
Napoleon Bonaparte, 19
New York, 62
Nicastro, 88
Nitti, Francesco Saverio, 60–1, 172, 184, 185
North America, 39, 57
Novara, province of, 169

Occupational mobility, 83
Olive oil as crop, 72, 78, 92 (Table 17), 93 (Table 18); instability of, 91, 92–3, 94, 95 (Table 19), 97; market for, 96; yields on, 73–4, 77, 97
Omertà (traditional code of silence), 19
'Opera Sila' (state development agency), 203

Palmi, 85, 88
Paola, 88
Paternalism, 20, 171; as social control, 102–3, 187
Peasant enterprises, types of, 15, 25–7, 37 (Table 11), 135–6, 147, 189
Peasant farms, by size, 32–6, 75 (Table 14), 76 (Table 15)
Peasant proprietors, 12, 15, 128, 129 (Table 26), 146, 169; in Crotonese, 135, 139, 144, 190, 192; emigration and increase of, 64–5; in Gioia Tauro, 76, 88; *kulaks* as, 41
Peasant society: in the Cosentino, 5, 11–12, 23–9, 32, 33–5, 40–1, 43–6, 48–9, 52–3, 56–7, 98, 120, 123, 175, 202–3; in France, 48; and market forces, 16–17, 21, 33, 38, 46, 56, 121, 150, 167, 194, 199–200; as 'pure' type, 5, 10, 12, 48, 54, 98, 102, 120, 123, 150, 203; settlement patterns in, 26, 77, 147, (Table 31); and sexual relations, 28–9, 43–4, 56; types of, 2, 5, 8, 10, 14–16, 26–7, 29, 36, 47–9, 52–3, 120–1, 135–7, 150, 171–2
Pertusola Co., 193

Piane Crati, *commune* of, 175
Piedmont, Kingdom of, 14, 18
Piedmont, region of, 125
Piromalli, 'Don Mommo', 118
Po Valley, 124, 138
Polanyi, Karl, 18, 149
Polish peasantry, 27–8
Population: age structure of, 182; of Cosentino, 10, 64; density of, 10, 67, 164; fertility and, 180 (fig. 5), 181; of Gioia Tauro, 67–8, 73, 86; growth of, 17, 38, 67, 68 (Table 13), 69; mortality and, 180 (fig. 5), 181, 182, 188
Poverty: 'culture of', 118; on *latifondo*, 176, 177, 178 (Table 35), 179, 183, 185, 188
Prefectoral system, 19, 201
Priests, relations with peasants, 40
Protein consumption, 177, 178 (Table 35)

Quesnay, François, 140

Rebellion: emigration as form of, 188–9, 190; violence and, 190, 191, 196
Reciprocity: as basis of emigration, 58–9, 64; 'negative' type of, 21 (n.16), 54–7; as principle of exchange, 47–54
Reggio Calabria, province of, 4, 89, 92, 94, 109, 193
Reina, Ruben, 108
Relations of production: under capitalism, 145, 152, 171; under feudalism, 134–5, 152, 172; on the *latifondo*, 128, 130, 132, 152, 156, 157, 171–2
Rent: agricultural, 12, 31, 128, 135; Marx on, 160
Repaci, L., 172
Repression: through *clientelismo*, 20, 22, 54; through mafia, 6; as relationship of production, 156, 157; and social integration, 16–17, 29–30, 54–6, 152; through the state, 17, 19, 54
Risorgimento (movement for Italian unity), 200
Rispetto (relationship between peasant husband and wife), 28–9, 56
Ritenna, la (principle of exchange), *see* reciprocity

Rohlfs, G., 98
Rosarno, San Fernando di, *commune* of, 86
Rossi-Doria, Manlio, 10, 15, (n.8), 70, 72, 131, 138, 143, 190, 196
'Rural city' (type of peasant settlement), 26, 191
Rural proletariat, 44, 83–4, 124, 128, 130, 148, 149, 151, 158, 159; casual labour and, 165–7, 168, 169, 172–3, 193; misery of, 176–7, 179, 183
Russo, Giovanni, 172

Sahlins, M.D., 51, 55, 104
Salerno, 14
San Giovanni in Fiore, *commune* of, 153
Sardinia, 125
Savelli, *commune* of, 88
Scalise, G., 184, 186
Scandale, *commune* of, 153
Schumpeter, J., 144
Scotland, 8
Second World War, 1, 7, 29, 36, 37, 81, 117, 181, 200
Sereni, E., 137
Sexual relations, in peasant society, 28–9, 43–4, 56
Sicily, 2, 12, 84, 123, 125, 158–9, 197; and mafia, 115–16, 117
Sila mountains, 9, 152–3, 157; emigration from, 166–7
Sindaco (mayor), 18, 19
Slavery, American black, 162
Social class, 7, 37 (Table 11), 40–1, 150; in Marxist analysis, 41–2, 143, 144, 151, 171, 173, 174
Social integration, 110–11, 148, 150, 202; absence in Gioia Tauro, 104–5, 114; horizontal types of, 150, 155, 176, 188, 204; mafia and, 6, 98, 105, 111, 114–15, 116, 120–1, 187; reciprocity and, 2, 5, 43, 47–57; vertical types of, 22, 30, 40; weak in Crotonese, 188–9, 191
Social mobility, 6, 36, 38, 150; American mafia and, 63; in Gioia Tauro, 83, 84–6, 88–9, 97, 98, 101, 110, 118
Social structure: in the Cosentino, 30, 36, 40, 41–2; in the Crotonese, 130, 141, 143, 151–2, 160, 176; in Gioia

Social structure – *cont.*
  Tauro, 83, 85, 89, 106, 117, 118; in the
    Mezzogiorno, 18, 21, 37 (Table 11), 89
Society: modern, types of, 1–2, 4, 91–2,
    120, 181, 202–3; of 'permanent
    transition', 5–6, 7, 57, 91–2, 104, 105,
    107, 111, 112, 116, 120, 121, 204, 205;
    traditional types of, 1–2, 4, 16–17, 20,
    29, 36, 37, 50–4, 91, 105, 111, 120,
    133, 167, 186
Sociology: and ideal types, 118, 132;
    tools of, 91, 103
Sonnino, Sidney, 18, (& n. 12), 19
    (n. 13)
South America, 57
Spain, 204
State: and *clientelismo*, 20–1, 200–1; and
    decline of family, 103–5; and
    intervention in the *Mezzogiorno*, 199,
    200–1, 203, 204; and the *latifondo*,
    154, 155, 196; and the mafia, 111,
    113, 114, 116–17; Piedmontese type
    of, 17–18; and repression, 17, 18, 57
Status, in Weberian sense, 142, 144
Stone, Lawrence, 104
Strati, Saverio, 83
Strongoli, *commune* of, 88, 167
Switzerland, 8

Tariffs, 141–2, 167, 194
Taurianova, *commune* of, 74
Tenancy: Marx on, 160; types of, 12, 14,
    18, 23–4, 31, 128, 135, 161
Tentori, T., 45
Terratico (peasant employed on great
    estate), 15

Thomas, W.L., 27
Trade unions: and the *latifondo*, 171,
    173; and mafia, 117
Trasumanza (annual cattle drive to the
    mountains), 77–8, 132, 153, 157
Trupia, P., 53
Turin, 202

United States of America: closed to
    immigrants (1921 & 1924), 194;
    Italian emigrants in, 61, 62, 63, 175,
    184, 185
Urbanisation, 149
Usi civici (common lands), 16, 17, 19,
    20, 40, 55, 57, 166–7; division of in
    Gioia Tauro, 88

Vico, Giovani Battista, 6
Violence: in Gioia Tauro, 105, 112–13,
    118; on the *latifondo*, 154, 155; and
    social integration, 6, 54, 55, 103,
    116–17, 152, 189–90

Wealth: attitude towards, 98, 99;
    relation to 'honour', 118–19
Weber, Max, 104, 116, 142, 143
White-collar class, 203
Wolf, Eric, 47
Women: in the Cosentino, 25–7, 42;
    emigration and, 60; employment of,
    26 (Table 5), 27, 84, 85; in Gioia
    Tauro, 27, 84, 85, 102; *rispetto*
    (respect) and, 28–9

Znaniecki, Florian, 27
Zurlo Brothers, 153